Oscar Browning

DATE DUE

www.elibron.com

Elibron Classics series.

© 2005 Adamant Media Corporation.

ISBN 1-4021-7318-0 (paperback)
ISBN 1-4021-2044-3 (hardcover)

This Elibron Classics Replica Edition is an unabridged facsimile
of the edition published in 1895 by Methuen & Co.,
London.

THE AGE OF THE CONDOTTIERI

THE AGE OF THE CONDOTTIERI

A SHORT HISTORY

OF

MEDIÆVAL ITALY FROM 1409-1530

BY

OSCAR BROWNING

AUTHOR OF "GUELPHS AND GHIBELLINES"

METHUEN & CO.
36 ESSEX STREET, W.C.
LONDON
1895

CONTENTS

THE AGE OF
THE CONDOTTIERI

CHAPTER I

RETROSPECT AND PROSPECT

In the first section of this history, entitled "Guelphs and Ghibellines," the fortunes of the peninsula were traced from the death of the Emperor Frederick II. in 1250 down to the Council of Pisa in 1409. In the present section it is proposed to carry on the narrative down to the fall of Florence in 1530. Having arrived at the middle point of our long journey, it will be convenient to cast an eye both forwards and backwards and to consider briefly the fortunes of the five principal states of Italy, Milan, Florence, Venice, Rome and Naples, during these three momentous centuries. We will shortly recapitulate the steps by which they gradually attained the rank of states, and follow their destinies to the point where they are just about to merge into a common Italy.

Milan was the first of the Italian towns to undergo the transformation from a commune to a country. In the previous book we witnessed the rise of the power of the Visconti, and have seen how that power was eventually concentrated in the hands of one of its members, Gian Galeazzo. We have read how he destroyed his uncle by treachery, how he overthrew one after the other the little tyrants of the Italian towns, and how at length he was invested by the Emperor with the Duchy of Milan. In this new position he extended his power over Genoa, Bologna and Tuscany till at last Florence alone resisted his encroachments, and he was stretching out his hand to grasp the crown of Italy. Death surprised him suddenly on September 3, 1402, and broke the thread of his designs. His government had its brighter side. He created a new state to meet the exigencies of the times. He was obliged to make it his chief object to levy taxes to maintain his wars, but justice was well administered, and prosperity increased. His centralized and autocratic government was effective for the objects it had in view. He surrounded himself with men of letters. He built the Cathedral of Milan and the Certosa of Pavia. He was the first of modern princes. Anarchy followed upon his death.

Filippo Maria, his son, who reigned till 1447, is a most unlovely character. He knew no other arts of government but those of treachery and cunning. A coward, shut up in his Castle of Milan, he engaged in all the quarrels of the age, and he always contrived to press the disasters of his enemies to his own advantage. He defeated the Florentines at Zagonara in 1424; often conquered by the Venetians he as often renewed the war; in the contest between Anjou and Arragon for the throne of Naples he weakened each party in turn. He gained his victories by the help of mercenary generals, the greatest of whom was Francesco Sforza. In 1441 he gave his only child Bianca in marriage to Sforza, and on his death Sforza was able to succeed him.

Sforza was a man after the heart of the fifteenth century, a great captain, an acute politician, a mixture of the fox and the lion, ready to shed blood if necessary; otherwise a friend of impartial justice. He founded a dynasty; he conquered a kingdom which he left powerful and well-governed; he constructed public works; he held one of the most brilliant courts in Italy. He died March 8, 1461, celebrated by men of letters as just, great, and magnanimous. He had succeeded in all his designs, but the state which he had founded had no internal strength. It had been moulded by his hands alone, and could be moulded anew by the hands of another.

Galeazzo Maria Sforza, the son of Francesco, was dissolute and cruel. He was accused of having poisoned his mother, he buried some of his subjects alive, he squandered his treasures in useless festivities. He was at last murdered on December 26, 1476, in the Church of Santo Stefano by three conspirators who had prayed to the Saint that the blow might not fail to effect its object. His brother Ludovico, called Il Moro or the Moor from his swarthy complexion, ambitious, timid and restless, seized the dominions of his nephew Galeazzo, and played an important part in that enslavement of Italy which we shall have to describe at a later period.

The history of Florence is a strange contrast to that of Milan. Throughout all the changes and vicissitudes of its fortunes it kept steadily in view the preservation of liberty and the maintenance of democratic government. In 1293 the Ordinances of Justice struck a heavy blow at feudalism. The nobles were excluded from office, the city was governed by an oligarchy of merchants. The *arti maggiori*, the more important merchant guilds, had overcome the *grandi*, the nobles; their activity and enterprise extended the borders and founded the greatness of the republic. In a period of peace and prosperity the *arti minori*, the smaller guilds, were able to assert their power; but a too violent and unrestrained democracy paved the way for the predominance of the Medici. But the Medici did not, like the Visconti, gain their power by the arts of tyranny. They did not torture their enemies alive, or give them to be devoured by dogs. They pursued a consistent policy for more than a hundred years, and arrived at the summit of power by courtesy and firmness. In 1378, in the rising of the Ciompi, Salvestro de' Medici took the side of the lesser guilds and when the greater guilds and the Albizzi returned to power Averardo de' Medici remained quietly immersed in money-making. His son Giovanni was the real founder of the fortunes of the house. The Medici always took the popular side; they rose by securing a constant majority in the elections, and as their power increased it seemed as if the republic was only assuming a more popular form. The great Cosimo succeeded his father Giovanni in 1429 at the age of 40. Enriched with commerce he used his wealth to increase his influence, but he was careful to preserve the habits of a private citizen. Driven into exile by the Albizzi he returned to Venice where he was received as a prince. The following year he was recalled to Florence by the popular party, and then threw off the mask. He cast down all the powerful rivals who might stand in his way, and raised his own creatures of humble birth to influence in the State. For himself he never stepped out of the rank of a private citizen, and held no office in state. He governed by means of a *balia,* a kind of caucus, composed of citizens devoted to his interests who elected the principal magistrates for a period of five years. He remained in outward appearance a quiet and peaceable banker, devoted to his trade. He spent but little money on himself but was profuse towards the Republic. He built churches, libraries, and palaces; he founded the Platonic Academy, he surrounded himself with men of letters and placed Florence at the head of European culture. He established intimate relations with foreign powers. Pope Nicolas V., Francesco Sforza of Milan were his devoted friends, Macchiavelli and Guicciardini all united in his praise. For thirty-one years he maintained his power in this fickle and capricious town, and deserved the name which he acquired of the Father of his Country.

Lorenzo, the grandson of Cosimo, was a man of very different character. He was a bad man of business and left his bank to be managed by others. He spent such large sums of money on himself that he deserved the appellation of the Magnificent. He reduced himself to poverty by his extravagance, he alienated his fellow-citizens by his lust, he recruited his private finances from the public treasury, and was shameless in the promotion of his private favourites. The means taken to overthrow him served only to consolidate his power. The conspiracy of the Pazzi came to a head in 1478. It was generally believed to have been arranged in the Vatican by the pope himself, Sixtus IV. On April 26 the two brothers were attacked in the Cathedral of Florence at the moment of the elevation of the host. Giuliano was killed, Lorenzo escaped. The populace rose in tumult and put the conspirators to death. Lorenzo found himself powerful enough to weaken his enemies for ever, and seized the opportunity to change the form of government. Instead of the balia a council of sixty was appointed in 1480. It was co-optative and was indeed a balia with larger powers. The republic of Florence henceforth existed merely in form.

Lorenzo de' Medici was a tyrant, but a more attractive and winning tyrant cannot be imagined. The city was never more rich or more prosperous. Lorenzo was not only the protector of literary men, but a distinguished man of letters himself. Without an army to support him, without any legal or constitutional position he not only governed Florence and Tuscany, but held the balance of power in Italy. His enemy Sixtus IV. was dead and his successor Innocent VIII. was his friend. The enmity which raged between Ludovico Il Moro and Ferdinand of Arragon enabled Lorenzo to keep both of them in check. But his power had no elements of stability; it was likely to fall with its author. Lorenzo had sacrificed the interests of his people to the interests of his family, and his family could only maintain their power by establishing a virtual sovereignty.

Venice exhibits a type of government different to those either of Florence or Milan. Florence beginning with the rule of an autocracy became gradually more and more democratical and submitted at last to the despotism of an individual; Venice by degrees consolidated the government of a close and jealous oligarchy. Venice from its foundation was untouched by any admixture of German elements. She knew no emperor and no feudal aristocracy. Her distant commerce, her vice-ducal governments were from the first favourable to the growth of a rich merchant class, while the common people were kept well employed at sea. It is unnecessary to recapitulate at any length the changes of constitution which have been already described in full. It has been shown how the power of the Doge was gradually limited on one side and that of the people on the other; how the *Maggior Consiglio*, or Greater Council became the dominant power in the State; how it was confined at last to certain favoured families; how the resistance of the great nobles was suppressed and the oligarchy confirmed by the Council of Ten. Pisa and Genoa were the natural rivals of Venice in the field of maritime trade but Pisa was destroyed at Meloria in 1284 and the Genoese were finally defeated at Chioggia in 1380. From this epoch a new period began. Venice hitherto engaged in extending the limits of commerce and civilization further and further to the East was now pressed by enemies on both sides. On the West she had to contend with the despot of the Lombard plain; on the East with the growing domination of the Turk. In defending herself from abroad she did not always employ the most exalted means. Beginning with the conquest of Padua and the destruction of the family of the Carrara she gradually established an empire on the mainland, the *terra firma* of her historians. The fifteenth century which was an epoch of decadence for the rest of Italy, opened a season of glory for the republic of the lagoons. She was the bulwark of Christianity against the advancing Moslem. Step by step she disputed the ground against the invader, and developed in this unequal and hopeless struggle the highest qualities of heroism and devotion. For the first and the last time in history a city attained to the rank of one of the great powers of Europe.

The strength of Venice might have sufficed for these

efforts if it had not been exhausted by other struggles. In 1426 under the Doge Foscari began the war with the Visconti which lasted till 1447. It was carried on with the greatest energy. Carmagnola and Carrara were beheaded between the two columns on the Piazzetta of St. Mark. But the triumph of Venice was short-lived and the capture of Constantinople in 1453 dealt her a mortal blow. The Turks advanced under Mahomet II., Negropont, Caffa, Scutari were lost in turn. Venice had to maintain the fight single-handed. Towards the end of the century we find the republic occupied by internal interests, involved in the intrigues of Italian politics, no longer caring to be the guardian of the peninsula against the invader, or of Christianity against the Infidel. The discovery of America, the doubling of the Cape of Good Hope, deprived her of her ancient commerce. She was no longer the link of union between the East and the West. Her territory was still considerable on the West where it was bounded by the Adda. She possessed Ravenna, Cervia, Faenza, Imola and Roveredo. She held dependencies on the Adriatic coast of Naples. The loss of external power brought with it, as it often does, the canker of internal corruption. The state was governed by a city; the city was governed by a small party among the citizens. Extravagance and luxury increased with gigantic strides; egoism took the place of self-devotion. Such was the position of Venice when it had to face Europe, arrayed against it in the league of Cambray.

The condition of Rome was very different from that of the rest of Italy. The pontiffs of the fourteenth and fifteenth centuries were employed not so much in attempting to acquire an empire over the consciences of men, or a general influence over the sovereigns of Europe, as in forming and consolidating their own temporal power. During the residence of the Popes at Avignon, which is known as the Babylonish Captivity, that power was reduced to very small dimensions. Rome was a free state and the Orsini, the Colonna, and the governors of Vico were independent sovereigns. Cardinal Albornoz, as the regent of Innocent VI., succeeded in building up a new dominion with the help of the petty tyrants of the cities of Central Italy, and popes Urban V. and Gregory XI. followed the same course. The schism which divided the church prevented the establishment of order. This confusion of authorities was put an end to by the Council of Constance which in 1417 deposed the three existing popes and elected Oddo Colonna, who took the name of Martin V. From his election a new period began, the popes became more than ever absorbed in purely temporal interests, and the papal court reached a depth of abasement unequalled by that of any court in Italy. Martin V. was the best pope of his age. He entered Rome in 1420 and found it a nest of beggars and brigands. Before his death in 1431 he had reduced the City and the Campagna to something like order and security, and deserved the title which he obtained of *Temporum Suorum Felicitas*. But this success was obtained ·by means which were not without their disgrace. He shamelessly favoured the family of the Colonna, and he supported in turn each of the claimants to the crown of Naples. He was brought back to Rome by Joanna II. but he transferred his support to her enemy Louis of Anjou and afterwards to his conqueror Alfonso of Arragon.

The successor of Martin V., Eugenius IV., had a stormy

reign. Driven out of Rome in 1434, he took refuge in Florence and sent Vitelleschi, Archbishop of Florence and patriarch of Alexandria, to execute his vengeance. By measures of the greatest cruelty the city was reduced to obedience, and Eugenius lived in it peaceably for three years before his death in 1447. His successor Nicholas V., forms a striking contrast. He was entirely devoted to literature; he employed the revenues of the papacy in the collection of ancient manuscripts, and made Rome a great centre for literary men with the finest library in the world. He laboured to make Rome superior to Florence in beauty as well as learning, and he commenced those great works of building which were continued by Julius II. and Leo X. Nicholas died in 1455 and was succeeded by Calixtus III., a Spaniard of the family of Borja or Borgia, the creature of Alfonso of Arragon. He reigned only three years, but the first of the Borgias gave a foretaste of the miseries which that name was afterwards to inflict. He filled the city with Spaniards, and thought of nothing but amassing money and enriching his nephews, one of whom was the notorious Alexander VI. Æneas Silvius Piccolomini who became pope under the name of Pius II. was a worthy successor to Nicholas. He was one of the most striking characters of the age and was devoted to erudition. He employed the authority of the papal throne to stimulate a crusade against the Turks, and wrote a letter to convert the Sultan Mahomet II. He died at Ancona in 1414, his eyes fixed towards the East, longing to commence the enterprise for which he had laboured so long, and believing that it would be effected by his successors. Paul II. whose papacy lasted seven years was an enemy of learning, but was not destitute of merit. He repressed brig-

andage with a severe hand, was a stern maintainer of
discipline and reformed the practices of the Roman Court.
The next three popes, Sixtus IV., Innocent VIII. and
Alexander VI. occupy the saddest period in the papal
history. The first was a violent tyrant without scruples
and without shame. His nephews, the Riario, exhibited an
abandonment of dissoluteness which could afterwards
scarcely be improved upon by Cæsar Borgia. Sixtus is
believed to have formed the conspiracy of the Pazzi in
order to obtain the money of the Medici. In politics he
was a faithless traitor. He took the side first of the Venetians against the Neapolitans and then of the Neapolitans
against the Venetians. It is said that he died at the
news of the siege of Bagnolo in 1484.

> Nulla vis sævum potuit exstinguere Sextum,
>   Audito tantum nomine pacis obit.

> No war could quell Pope Sextus' cruel pride,
>   The name of peace was whispered .. and he died.

After his death the papal see was sold to the highest
bidder. This was the Cardinal Cibo, who chose the name
of Innocent VIII. By taking the side of Anjou against
Arragon, he threw all Italy into confusion, and peace was
with difficulty secured. In Rome all offences could be
compensated for by fines which went to swell the possessions of his son Francesco. Innocent VIII., was the
first pope who openly acknowledged his children. He
married his son to the daughter of Lorenzo de' Medici,
and made her brother Cardinal at the age of 14. His
sons and nephews openly led the most scandalous lives.

Franceschetto Cibo lost 14,000 florins one night gambling with the Cardinal Riario. False bulls were sold and indulgences to secure pardon to assassins. Every night the dead bodies found in the streets were thrown into the Tiber. When Innocent VIII. died in 1492 it seemed impossible that the world would see a more abandoned pontiff, but a worse pope arose in the person of Alexander VI.

The history of Naples during this period is a monotonous narrative of confusion and disaster. The glory of the Southern Kingdom ends with the deaths of Manfred and Conradin. The rule of the Angevin dynasty was fatal to the prosperity of the country. The kingdom reached the extremity of anarchy under Joanna I., who married four husbands in succession. Her cousin Ladislaus had subdued the barons, conquered his internal enemies, obtained authority over Rome, and was marching northwards with a large army aspiring to become King of Italy when he died of poison at Perugia in 1414. His sister Joanna II. was a viler and more worthless repetition of her predecessor of the same name. Martin V. by whom she had been crowned in 1419 incited in the following year Louis III of Anjou to contend against her worthless favourites. She in turn proclaimed Alfonso of Arragon as her successor, whom she afterwards deserted for René of Lorraine. After long and ruinous wars peace was secured by the entrance of Alfonso into Naples on June 2, 1442, and the establishment of the dynasty of Arragon. Alfonso died in 1458 and left his hereditary dominions Spain, Sicily and Sardinia to his brother, Naples, the fruit of conquest, to his natural son Ferdinand who is generally known as Ferrante. The Pope did not allow him to enjoy his kingdom without dispute. Pope Calixtus claimed Naples as a papal fee.

The Angevin Barons rose in arms; René of Lorraine disembarked on the Western coast. Ferrante spent six years in establishing his power; he maintained it by cunning and astute diplomacy. He was able to contend against external enemies but he could not resist the onslaught of Charles VIII. Ferrante as an old man saw the significance of the storm and urged the powers of Italy to unite against the common danger. He died in 1494 with this prophetic entreaty on his lips.

The long drama which we have described was a prelude to the coming disaster. The condition of the smaller states of Italy, Ferrara, Faenza, Rimini and Urbino was as deplorable as that of the larger. We find the same strange contrast between a high degree of literary culture and enthusiasm and the deepest political degradation. It has been said that Italy at this time was not worse than the rest of Europe, that Louis XI. was a monster of cruelty and deceit, and that Ferdinand of Arragon was notorious for duplicity and cunning. It might be answered that these sovereigns were at least striving towards a great end. Each of them wrought after his own manner the unity of his country, whereas the crimes of Italy led only to her disunion and insignificance. But Italy could not have been all bad. Had the corruption of her rulers spread throughout the people, her case would have been hopeless, her future impossible. Venice and Turin still preserved some remains of morality and virtue, and there is no reason to suppose that the great mass of the people had deserted the better ways of their fathers. If power was concentrated in few hands so also was the crime and the extravagance which accompanied power.

We have now traced the course of the five principal

Italian states down to the time when they are about to be absorbed under the pressure of a common tyranny. We make a halt at the pontificate of Alexander VI., and the expedition of Charles VIII. The greater part of this book will be consecrated to the narration in detail of the events which we have here attempted to convey in a bird's-eye view.

CHAPTER II

JOANNA OF NAPLES—MUZIO SFORZA—BRACCIO DA MONTONE AND CARMAGNOLA

THE period of Italian history which extends from the Council of Pisa to the march of the Emperor Sigismund upon Rome in 1436 is one of great confusion. It is a time of chaos and anarchy, during which no striking individuality, no predominant power make it easy for us to group the events in due subordination. But the same epoch was one of the most flourishing periods of Italian Art. To the first quarter of the fifteenth century belong the early sculptures of Donatello, the doors of the baptistry of Florence, cast by Lorenzo Ghiberti, which Michael Angelo declared worthy to be the gates of Paradise, the first frescoes of Masaccio and the Church of Santa Maria Novella. During it Filippo Brunelleschi was appointed to construct the marvellous dome of our Lady of the Flower. On May 3, 1410. Pope Alexander died and Baldassare Cossa was elected his successor under the name of John XXIII. His quarrel with Ladislaus of Naples still continued, but in 1412 a treaty of peace was arranged between them by the good offices of the Florentines. Peace was still better assured by the death of Ladislaus in 1414. Italy was well rid of this unquiet spirit.

Ladislaus before his death had given his consent to the summoning of a general council at Constance. The place was happily chosen as being neither Italian nor German and yet near enough to both countries to be of easy access. Ladislaus had been moved to this course by the new Emperor Sigismund. Sigismund was King of Bohemia, the younger brother of Wenzel, or Wenceslaus, King of Germany, and a scion of the famous line of Henry of Luxemburg. After a short war with Venice and negotiations with Milan and the Pope, a general Council was convoked at Constance for November 1, 1414. At the Council, the Italians were found to be present in by far the largest numbers so that a salutary rule was made that votes should be taken not by individuals but by nations. There was the same difficulty as before in persuading the rival popes to abdicate their functions. John XXIII. promised to resign, but ran away in disguise to Schaffhausen. He was caught and imprisoned in 1415. Gregory XII. recognized the authority of the Council and surrendered the tiara. Benedict XII. held out obstinately at Perpignan and was solicited to retire by Sigismund in person. At last even his own Spaniards fell away from him and he was deposed in July, 1417. The papal throne was now vacant and before the election of a new pope there was an opportunity of reforming the Church in head and members. The opportunity was lost and the bonds of obedience were drawn tighter than ever. The teaching of Wicliffe was condemned; John Huss who had come to Constance under a safe conduct was tried, found guilty and burnt, his ashes being thrown into the Rhine. Jerome of Prague met with no better fate, but the fire of reforming zeal kindled at their stakes burnt long and brightly in the country of their birth. Ottone or Oddo Colonna was elected Pope with the name of Martin V. His first act was to dissolve the Council. It had carried no reforms, but it brought into a clear light the dissensions which existed in the Church; and the persecution of reformers only prepared the way in Germany for the work of Luther and Melanchthon.

King Ladislaus was succeeded on the throne of Naples by Joanna II., at that time 46 years old. In vice and shamelessness she was a worthy successor of her earlier namesake. She had been married to William, Duke of Carinthia, son of Duke Leopold III. of Austria, but she was now a widow and under the control of Pandolfello Alopo, her Grand Chamberlain. Attendolo Sforza, the famous *condottiere* Captain, was the Commander of her troops, and she shortly afterwards married Jacques de Bourbon, the Count de la Marche, who Alopo believed would be entirely in his power. It is useless to waste time over the domestic revolutions of this debased court. Sforza was put into prison, Jacques, contrary to the terms of his marriage contract contrived to be crowned king. He then proceeded to ill-treat his wife and to deprive her of independent power. He threw her into prison, but the people arose and liberated her. She chose a new favourite by name Giovanni Carraciuolo, and Sforza was set free to command her armies.

We now meet with a second *condottiere* as leader of mercenary troops, Braccio da Montone, first a companion in arms, and afterwards a rival of Sforza. Profiting by the confusion of Italy he had managed to acquire for himself a state of which Perugia was the centre, and he had extended his conquests down the valley of the Tiber

as far as Rome. The Neapolitans could not allow the
Capital of Italy to fall into his hands, and they could the
more easily prevent it as they already had the powerful
fortress of St. Angelo in their hands. Sforza was dis-
patched to the rescue. On his arrival Montone retired,
and Sforza entered the city in triumph on August
27, 1417.

The condition of Italy was indeed deplorable when
Pope Martin V. set out to return southward to his new
dominions. Elected in November 1417 he remained for
several months in Constance. On April 22, 1418, he
finally closed the Council, summoning a new one to meet
at Pavia to continue the work of renovating the church.
Crossing Savoy he entered Lombardy and celebrated mass
in the Cathedral of Milan. He remained at Mantua from
November 1418 till February 1419, and passing by Ferrara and the Romagna, without touching Bologna, which
with a number of smaller towns had declared her independence, he arrived at Florence, then flourishing under
the rule of the Guelph aristocracy. As Rome and Beneven-
tum were in the hands of the Neapolitans he thought it better
to remain in the capital of Tuscany, and in fact he stayed
there for a year and a half. He took up his abode in
quarters specially prepared for him in the Convent of
Santa Novella, the Church of which he consecrated in
October 1420. He obtained from the duke of Bavaria
the release of Baldassare Cossa from his long imprisonment. The aged pontiff came to Florence to throw himself
at the feet of Martin to do him obeisance and to recognize
him as the true father of the Christian world. He was
invested with the purple of a Cardinal, but died soon
afterwards in November, 1419, and was buried in the

Church of San Giovanni so dear to the poet Dante. The history of Rome and Naples during the next few years is a tissue of the most complicated intrigues. Joanna adopted as her son, and named as her successor in the Kingdom, Alfonzo V. of Arragon, one of the most prominent princes of that age, a model of all knightly accomplishments. A quarrel had broken out between Sforza and Carraciuolo, the Queen's favourite, which had the most disastrous consequences. Joanna was at first well disposed towards the Pope. He recognized her as Queen and gave his authority for her coronation. Sforza had been sent by her against Braccio da Montone to conquer the states of the Church which were still in his possession. But Sforza was severely defeated in June 1419 between Viterbo and Montefiascone. In the following January Sforza came to visit the Pope at Florence, but the boys sang under their windows:

> "Papa Martino—non vale un quattrino
> É Braccio valente che vince ogni gente."

"Pope Martin is not worth a farthing, it is the hero Braccio who conquers everyone."

At the end of February Braccio himself came to Florence accompanied by four hundred horse and forty foot. His lofty and imposing stature caused general admiration. The Florentines reconciled him with the Pope who confirmed him in the possession of the towns he occupied, Perugia, Orvieto, Narni, Rieti and Assisi.

A complete change now took place. Sforza and the Pope having become friends, deserted the cause of Joanna and supported a rival claimant to the throne of Naples in the person of Louis III. of Anjou. Let us consider

who he was. In June 1386 Joanna I., pressed by the
Hungarian party, had adopted as her son and successor
Louis I., of the second house of Anjou, son of John II.
King of France, and descended from the earlier house of
Anjou through the female line. Louis I. had borne the
title of King of Naples from 1382 to 1384. His son Louis
II. bore the same title from 1384 to 1417. He had
died three years after Ladislaus and left his claims to his
son Louis III., who now won the favour of Pope Martin
V. and the *condottiere* Sforza. From this time Naples is
again torn in sunder by the quarrels of Louis and Alfonzo and the struggles of the Angevin and Arragonese
parties for the possession of the throne. It is a curious
example of the complications of interest in this troubled
time that Louis actually asked Alfonzo, who was his
cousin on his mother's side, to lend him a fleet in order
that he might disembark his troops at Naples, and seemed
surprised when the request was refused. He received,
however, a promise that he should not be hindered from
equipping a fleet in Genoa, where he armed five large
ships and nine galleys. Louis arrived with his fleet in
the Gulf of Naples in the middle of August. At the
beginning of September the galleys of Arragon appeared,
under the command of Raimondo Polirione. Joanna gave
the Castello Nuovo into his possession which he accepted
in the name of his master Alfonzo. The King of Arragon was at this time besieging Bonifazio in Corsica, and
seemed in no hurry to join his adopted mother. Driven
from Bonifazio by the Genoese, he went to Sardinia and
to Sicily, and did not reach Naples till the end of June
1421. Joanna had in the meantime summoned Braccio
to her assistance, who entered the capital at the beginning

of that month. Naples was divided into two camps, one the Angevins under Louis and Sforza, the other the Hungarian or Arragonese or Durazzian, under Alfonzo and Braccio. In November 1421 the Pope with the assistance of the Florentines succeeded in concluding a kind of peace. Both claimants were to leave the kingdom, Alfonzo was to retain the title of Duke of Calabria, Joanna was to retain the Kingdom of Naples and after her death the question of inheritance was to be settled by the Pope.

The peace really came to nothing, Louis went to Rome where he remained for a long time feeding on vain hopes. Pope Martin had been there since the previous autumn. He found the city at peace, but poor and desolate. He did what he could to raise it and deserves to some extent the title which his biographers have given him of Father of his Country. After this, confusion in Naples became worse confounded. Queen Joanna became jealous of Alfonzo. Sforza and Braccio who were the real rulers of the Kingdom, had a conference and became friends, remembering the fair days of their youth when they learned the art of war together under Alberico da Barbiano. By the help of Braccio, Sforza was reconciled with Joanna and the great Seneschal. Braccio kept his title of Constable of the Kingdom and Governor of the Abruzzi. In the spring of 1423 the relations between Joanna and Alfonzo became more strained. The Queen invoked the assistance of Sforza, and Alfonzo summoned Braccio to his aid. Sforza obtained a victory over the Catalans and Alfonzo was shut up in the Castello Nuovo. In June, Alfonzo, by the help of a Catalan fleet, recovered his ascendancy. Louis was now in high favour with Joanna. She created him Duke of Calabria, adopted him as her son and declared him heir to the throne. In October 1427 Alfonzo was compelled to return to Spain. He left his son Peter in his place with only a small army.

During the last six months of the year 1423 Braccio had been engaged in the siege of the great city of Aquila. Sforza was determined to drive him from his enterprise, and with this end attempted to pass the river Pescara so as to take him in the rear. It was Monday January 3, 1424, a day marked as unlucky by the Astrologers. The passage by the usual ford was disputed by soldiers of Braccio, and Sforza was compelled to cross at the very mouth of the river. First crossed five horsemen, then Sforza's son Francesco, then Michelotto d'Attendolo, then Sforza himself and a few men at arms. The first who crossed engaged with the soldiers of Braccio, Francesco distinguishing himself by a valour beyond his years. Sforza called upon the rest of his company to ford the river, and when they would not obey because a breeze was blowing from the sea and roughening the water, he entered the river again to show that there was no danger. As he held out his hand to support a sinking page, his horse 'Scalzanacha' stumbled and fell. The horse recovered itself, but Sforza fell into the water and never rose again. Thus perished one of the first and one of the greatest of the Condottieri. He was of more than the common height, neither thin nor fat, large-limbed, strong and robust, sound in mind and body. His appearance was terrible and severe, his eyes were set deep into his head, he had a hooked nose, and a face bronzed by the sun. He was a man of few words and could scarcely read or write, but he was wise and prudent in counsel, full of courage and spirit in times of danger, full of affection for his family, his country and his servants. Such is the character drawn of him by Minuti his companion in arms.

The soldiers of Sforza determined to avenge the death of their chief. Like the black Brunswickers they placed themselves in mourning, darkening their helmets and decking their chargers with black housings. The battle was fought under the walls of Aquila on June 2, 1424. It lasted eight hours, and no prisoners were made on either side. Braccio was defeated and fell wounded in the head. He was carried into the city and died there, refusing all food and the aid of doctors. He was in character far inferior to Sforza. He knew neither pity nor religion, nor had he any affection except for his comrades in arms. A Chronicler says of him, " In his army he was loyal and valiant, but he was impious and heretical in his life; he believed neither in God nor the Saints, he despised the offices and services of the Church, never heard mass and was most cruel." By the desire of the Pope his body was carried to Rome and buried in unconsecrated ground. The principality which he had formed was broken up.

Filippo Maria Visconti, the second son of Gian Galeazzo, succeeded his brother Gian Maria in 1412. He was naturally of weak health and whether at table, in bed, or on the chase, surrounded himself with doctors. In his early youth he delighted in the arts of war, but with advancing years he became stout and sickly, and had to content himself with hunting. He was a master of dissimulation. At the same time he was no despiser of literature, and studied the poems of Petrarch and Dante and the histories of Livy. He could not bear to be alone, and sometimes summoned his guards to watch round his bed, as he often passed sleepless nights. He was reputed religious and charitable, but he was very superstitious and believed in augurs and astrologers. He undertook no military enterprise without consulting the stars, and it is said that the signs of heaven foretold his death three years before it happened. His power depended upon his army, and the efficiency of his army depended upon the excellence of the Condottieri leaders whom he was able to attract to his service. The chief among these were Francesco da Carmagnola, Niccolo, Piccinino, Francesco Sforza and Angelo della Pergola. Francesco Bussone was born at Carmagnola in Piedmont about the year 1390 and according to the usage of those days took the name of his native town. He became by degrees not only the head of Visconti's army but the prime minister of his dominions. By the help of this general and by a combination of courage and duplicity Filippo Maria gradually recovered most of the possessions which his father had held in North Italy. One of Carmagnola's first enterprises was to capture the Castle of Trezzo, whose ruins now rise majestically from the green waters of the rushing Adda, which was then held by the family of Colleoni, Bartolomeo the last and the best of the Condottieri, being then a boy of sixteen. The castle surrendered in the early days of 1417. In 1424 Visconti became master of Genoa by treachery, and in the following year he made an attack upon the Italian provinces of Switzerland. Up to the year 1422 he had made no attempt to recover the former possessions of his house in Tuscany, and the Florentines had no reason to doubt his honour or his good-will. But war between these powers broke out in consequence of a dispute about the little town of Forlì in the Romagna.

Giorgio degli Ordelaffi died in January 1422, leaving a son Tebaldo nine years old. His mother was Lucrezia, daughter of Ludovico Alidosi, lord of Imola. He desired to make himself guardian of his grandson, but the people of Forlì, jealous of the supremacy of Imola, determined to give themselves to the Church. Filippo Maria seized the opportunity of meddling in the business on pretence of supporting the wife of the deceased duke. The people called two Milanese condottieri to their aid. Great was the agitation in Florence. Giovanni de' Medici tried to prevent the Republic from taking part in a quarrel from which they could gain nothing, but the war-party eventually prevailed and a Florentine army was sent to the assistance of the Duchess. In a few months the Florentines suffered no less than six defeats. Between September 1423 and October 1425 they were beaten at Ponte a Ronco, Zagonara, at Val di Lamona, at Rapallo, at Anghiari, and at La Faggiuola. In their trouble they turned to Venice for assistance and their prayer for vengeance against the Duke was reinforced from an unexpected quarter. Francesco Carmagnola had been living for some time in a kind of exile at Treviso. In August 1425 he discovered that Filippo Maria had formed a plot to poison him. He flew to Venice, spoke against the Visconti, and entered upon negotiations with Amadeo, Duke of Savoy. The Doge of Venice at this time was one of the most distinguished of the line, Francesco Foscari. His predecessor, Tommaso Mocenigo, who had died on April 4, 1423, at the age of eighty, had warned the republic against him as a restless and unquiet spirit. The ambassadors of Filippo Maria and of the Florentines were both at the Court of the Rialto at the close of 1425. To the Duke the Venetians offered their mediation between himself and the Florentines, but a month later they accepted the alliance with Florence, the Doge urging them to declare war to avenge the injuries they had suffered, and to tread under foot the common enemy of all, and to give lasting rest to the whole of Italy. By the terms of the alliance which was solemnly published on January 27, 1426, it was arranged that Venice was to have the conduct of the war, that the conquests made in Lombardy were to go to Venice, and those in Tuscany to Florence and also those in the Marches so far as they did not interfere with the supremacy of the Church. Carmagnola was made commander in chief.

The first operations of Carmagnola were directed against Brescia, which fell into his hands in March 1425. In July the Duke of Savoy joined the league on the condition that the city of Milan if conquered was to pass to him. But the task of the allies was by no means an easy one. The war with the Turks was still proceeding, and Negropont was threatened. Genoa prepared a large fleet to help her suzerain the Duke of Milan, Germany and Hungary were hostile, Filippo Maria sold Forlì and Imola to the pope to provide himself with money. The only thing which helped the allies was the misunderstanding which prevailed amongst the mercenary generals of the Duke. At last on December 30, 1426, before a single important battle had been lost or won peace was made at Ferrara by the intervention of Pope Martin V. Brescia with all its dependencies was to remain in the hands of the Venetians.

When the news of the peace reached Milan there was an outburst of patriotic fury. We are accustomed to regard the government of these Italian princes as purely personal, and to view them as making peace and war solely for their own interest and advantage. Here we see the people and the nobles coming forward in a time of peril to rally round their sovereign. The Emperor Sigismund also put pressure upon the Duke to break the treaty which he had just ratified and refused to confirm the Venetians in the possession of Brescia. By the exertions of the Milanese nobility and the influence of the Emperor the war was renewed. But the result was only to give a more complete victory to Carmagnola. At the battle of Maclodio, fought on October 12, 1427, the Duke was entirely defeated and a very large number of prisoners was taken, amongst whom was Carlo Malatesta whom Filippo Maria had placed at the head of his army in order to appease the quarrels between his condottieri generals. A scene followed the battle which throws a curious light on the manners of the time. The Duke's troops consisted almost entirely of mercenaries. They had no ill-feeling towards the soldiers against whom they had fought, nor the prisoners which they had taken. The consequence was that all the prisoners on both sides were liberated during the night or in course of the next day. This was a common but not an universal practice. One reason for it was undoubtedly the desire amongst the professional soldiers that the state of war should continue, and that they should not on the conclusion of a lasting peace be sacrificed to the vengeance of the people. After this battle Amadeo VIII., Duke of Savoy, with the characteristic fickleness of his house, made peace with Filippo Maria at Turin on December 2, whereas he had sent him letters of defiance on August 27. Thus Savoy and Milan were united under the protection of the Emperor against Venice and Florence. The Duke of Milan was to marry Maria, the daughter of the Duke of Savoy, and to receive the town of Vercelli as her dowry. The second wife of Filippo Maria was the unfortunate Beatrice di Tenda, the widow of Facino Cane. The Duke had married her from motives of policy, but at first loved her dearly and gave her the City of Monza. He afterwards tired of her and she was executed in August 1418 on a false charge of adultery, protesting her innocence. He married Maria of Savoy on October 6, 1428.

Before this, peace had been signed at Ferrara on April 19 between the combatants again by mediation of the Pope. The conditions were that Brescia together with the conquests made in the district of Cremona were to go to Venice, that Bergamo should be surrendered to the same government; that the possessions of Carmagnola in the Milanese should be restored to him but without the right of alienation, and that the Duke of Milan was to form no new alliances in Romagna or in Tuscany.

The peace did not last long. Francesco Sforza, who had after a breach again entered the service of the Visconti, recommended a renewal of the struggle. The Florentines had declared war against Paolo Giunigi, the lord of Lucca. Filippo Maria was bound by the treaty of Ferrara not to interfere in the affairs of Tuscany. He contrived, however, by means of Sforza and Piccinino actually to give assistance to Lucca and to harass the allies of Florence.

He amused the Venetians and Florentines with negotiations, and sent continual messages to the Emperor Sigismund urging him to march upon Italy, promising that when
he came he would declare himself against the two Republics. Both parties were suing for the support of Francesco Sforza. The Duke succeeded in securing him by
offering him the hand of his illegitimate daughter Bianca
Maria, born in 1425, and now therefore only five years old.
The death of the Pope Martin V. and the succession of
a Venetian, Gabriel Condolmier, under the title of Eugenius
IV., made no difference in the course of events. War
broke out openly in the Spring of 1431.

A few days after the commencement of the war on
March 16 the Venetians were defeated at Soncino, and
on June 22 their fleet under Niccolò Trevisani was utterly routed by the fleet of the Visconti under Eustachio
Pacino. It was engaged in the siege of Cremona on the
side of the river Po, while Carmagnola invested the city
by land. Carmagnola gave no assistance to the Venetian
fleet, but whether this was due to deliberate treachery,
or to his being deceived by false information, cannot be
ascertained. At any rate his conduct on this occasion
formed one of the principal grounds of his impeachment.
Carmagnola also failed to support an attack made upon
Cremona on October 18, when the Venetians had occupied
the castle of S. Luca and one corner of the city walls.
The Cremonese certainly thought that they owed their
salvation to his negligence. At the beginning of the following year the Venetians began to be still more suspicious
of their general. Messengers sent by Visconti were continually coming to his camp, and on February 22, 1432,
the Venetian Senate was compelled to tell him not to trust

any ambassadors of the Visconti who only meant to deceive. It was known that Carmagnola desired a principality for himself, and the Venetian government probably believed that Visconti's messengers were talking to him of other matters than peace.

At length on March 29 the Council of Ten met to deliberate on the fate of the Commander-in-chief. Some were in favour of arresting him openly, others of employing artifice. The latter prevailed. A special messenger, Giovanni d'Imperio, was sent to Carmagnola who was then at Brescia, with orders to invite him to come to Venice to consult upon the spring campaign which was just about to open. If he refused, the governors of Brescia were to seize him and imprison him in the Castle. Carmagnola accepted the invitation at once. At Padua he was treated with distinguished honour, probably with the view of lulling his suspicions and preventing his escape. He arrived at Venice on April 7. He was received by the Doge with apparent affection, but his suite was not allowed to follow him. On entering the Doge's palace he was conducted to a prison and said with a sigh, "I clearly perceive that I am dead." On April 11 his chancellor was examined under torture. Carmagnola himself was not exposed to the rack because one of his arms had been severely wounded, but fire was applied to his feet. The trial was interrupted during the holy season of Easter, but afterwards the judges applied themselves to the inquiry day and night. At length on May 5 the matter was referred to the Council of Ten. His guilt was soon agreed upon, and the only question was as to his punishment. A minority were in favour of confining him in a strong castle, but the majority voted that on that very day at the accustomed hour, and in the usual manner he should be led, with a gag in his mouth and his hands tied behind his back, to the space between the two columns in the square of St. Mark and there beheaded. His wife who lived at Treviso was to have a pension, and provision was also made for his daughters. The execution was carried out on March 5, 1432, after sunset. Materials do not exist for determining the guilt or innocence of Carmagnola, we know, however, that the judgment of the Council of Ten was not given without careful inquiry and long deliberation. If they had wished to assassinate him they could easily have done so. It is probable that they had proofs of his treachery. The desire of every prudent condottiere of those days must have been to carve out a little government for himself as a retirement for his old age, and the pursuit of this end was not always consistent with chivalrous loyalty to any master whom at the time he happened to be serving. These professional warriors of no country and of no principles, served only for pay and could always be bought by a higher bidder. The impeachment of Colleoni is a pendant to the execution of Carmagnola.

After this tragedy peace was not long in following and a new treaty, the third, was concluded at Ferrara on April 7, 1432. It was framed on the basis of the *statu quo*. The Duke of Milan engaged to surrender his conquests and not to meddle any more in the affairs of Tuscany or the Romagna.

CHAPTER III

THE EMPEROR SIGISMUND—POPE EUGENIUS IV.—THE RISE
OF THE MEDICI—ALFONZO OF ARRAGON

In 1432 the Emperor Sigismund undertook his journey
to Rome. Pope Martin V, a Colonna as we know, had
died on February 20 and the rival party of the Orsini
prevailed in the next election. As we stated in the last
chapter the choice of the Cardinals fell on Gabriel Condolmier, a Venetian, sister's son to Gregory XII. He was
forty-seven years of age, vigorous and young for his time
of life. Experience showed that his nature was weaker
and more inflammable than his friends had expected. His
first public act was to recognize the Council of Basel:
his first step in the government of Rome was to persecute
the hated stock of the Colonna, and to destroy their
castles and fortresses. The chief objects of the Council
of Basel were the reform of the Church in head and
members, the quieting of the trouble of the Hussites in
Bohemia, and the union of the Greek and Latin Churches.
The Greek Emperor, hard pressed by the Turks, was ready
to consent to this union, but his consent was of little
value. The Emperor and the Pope regarded the Council
with very different feelings—the Emperor was anxious for
a settlement of the trouble in Bohemia, and for a union
of Christendom against the heathen. The Pope was

afraid of the inauguration of a reform which could only begin with himself, yet he went so far as to send Cardinal Cesarini to Basel to open the sittings of the Council in his name, and to preside in his place. The Council was of short duration. The Pope, afraid of the influence of Germany and of the court of France, summoned the Council to meet at Bologna. The Council refused to obey, declared itself superior to the Pope, and summoned him before them in turn. Sigismund took the side of the Council against the Pope.

The Emperor did not appear in Italy with that pomp which some of his predecessors and ancestors had exhibited. He was accompanied only by a hundred Hungarian horsemen. He found Italy, as we have described it above, in a state of war, and as he had been principally invited by Filippo Maria he naturally took the side of Milan against the republics of Venice and Florence. Sigismund entered Milan on November 22, 1432, and was crowned with the iron crown of Lombardy three days afterwards in the Church of Sant' Ambrogio. The ceremony was performed by Bartolomeo Capra, Archbishop of Milan, while Niccolò Piccinino, the condottieri general, representing the Duke of Milan his master, offered to the new sovereign the golden ball as the symbol of universal sovereignty. Sigismund stayed for some time in Milan, as the Pope was not willing to expedite his journey to Rome. In February he moved on to Piacenza, Parma and Lucca, and reached Siena in July 1432, where he remained for nine months which were consumed in negotiations with the Pope. The situation was not without its humourous side. Sigismund desired the Imperial crown, but he would not receive it unless the Pope recognized

3

the Council of Basel and recalled the decree which had dissolved it. The Pope was anxious to crown the Emperor, but he was afraid of being deposed himself by the Council, and therefore refused to crown Sigismund unless he consented to the Council being held in an Italian town. An arrangement was at length agreed to in April by which Eugenius was to be recognized as the undoubted pope of Christendom.

Sigismund made his solemn entry into Rome on May 21, 1432, the festival of the Ascension. He was crowned on May 31 by the Pope in St. Peter's, but without the splendour of attendant vassals which had so often graced that ceremony. He remained some time in Rome, lodging at the palace of the Lateran, whilst the Pope dwelt at the Vatican. The Emperor confirmed the ancient privileges of the Church, beginning with those granted by Constantine; the Pope renewed in Sigismund the empire of Charles the Great. When Sigismund left Rome in August he was very friendly with the Pope, but he had lost his interest in the Council, also he was disposed to take the part of Venice rather than that of Milan. He returned to Basel in the guise of a modest traveller on October 11, 1433.

The Emperor had scarcely left Rome before a terrible storm burst upon the Pope. It did not proceed directly from the Council but from Filippo Maria Visconti, who doubtless felt encouraged in the attack by the hostility of the Council to his Holiness. Niccolò Fortebraccio, a condottiere leader and nephew of Braccio da Montone, who had never laid down the sword, and was now in the pay of the Duke of Milan, pressed on through the Sabine mountains, overran the Campagna, captured the Ponte Molle, and presented himself at the Porta del Popolo on August

25, 1433, only eleven days after the departure of Sigismund. He demanded the title of Standard-bearer of the Church, took Tivoli on October 7 and kept it till the month of June in the following year. He was supported by the Colonna family, whom the Pope had declared the public enemies of the Church. Eugenius had no one to help him but Giovanni Vitelleschi, a strange product of these days, a Cardinal and a patriarch, but a bloodthirsty and cruel soldier. Another danger fell upon the Pope from the North. Francesco Sforza attached to the fortunes of Filippo Maria by the promise of his daughter's hand, treacherously seized a number of towns in the March of Ancona, and said that he was empowered to do so by the Council. Eugenius saw no way out of his difficulties but to recognize the authority of the Council, which he did on December 15, 1433. Sforza was reconciled to the Pope in March 1434, was recognized as Marquis of the March of Ancona, and was appointed Standard-bearer of the Church. Fortebraccio refusing to submit, was attacked by Sforza, but he found an unexpected ally in another condottiere leader, Niccolò Piccinino. With his assistance he pressed Rome so hard that Eugenius had no resource but to fly. The citizens were in rebellion and the old republic was proclaimed. A pirate named Vitellio of Ischia engaged to receive the Pope on board his ship at Ostia. At midday on the fourth of June the Pope, disguised as a friar, with a single monk as his attendant rode on a mule to the Tiber bank. A sailor carried the Pope on his back and laid him down in the boat. The fugitive was recognized and the whole town ran to the riverside. Another boat was launched in pursuit but stuck fast in the mud. Stones, lances and

arrows were discharged at the flying bark. The rowers
laboured stoutly while the pope lay in the stern covered
by a large shield. Below the church of St. Paul outside
the walls a large boat filled with armed men came out
to intercept them. The skipper of the Pope's bark
determined to charge it or run it down, but the boat
was old and rotten and the assailants avoided the shock.
Danger was now passed, and they reached the ship of
Vitellio in the roads of Ostia. On June 12, 1434,
Eugenius landed at Pisa and reached Florence on June
23. He was the last Pope who was violently driven out
of Rome until Pius IX. in the middle of the present
century.

The Pope found Florence in a state of considerable
confusion. We have now reached the period when the
Family of the Medici began to play an important part in
the history of their country. The origin of this family
is not exactly known. It is supposed that they came
from the Mugello, a district in the Apennines between
the Arno and the Emilian Road. It is certain that for
a considerable time they held only a subordinate place
in Florence. They had the character of being good,
steady, careful merchants, of popular sympathies, opposed
to the reigning oligarchy of the Albizzi but not prominent
or powerful enough to excite hatred or invite destruction.
We heard of the name of Salvestro de' Medici at the time
of the conspiracy of the Ciompi. The real founder of the
greatness of the house was Giovanni, the son of Averardo,
who was born in 1360 and died on February 20, 1429.
He took advantage of the Council of Constance and the
increased facilities of communication in Europe to extend
his relations with various countries. Florence, we have

already seen, was the most flourishing commercial town in Europe. The staple product was wool, but Florence also imported roughly made woollen clothes from other countries, dyed and refined them by a process which was long preserved as a jealous secret, and exported them again to the countries from which they had already come. The artisans who pursued this trade formed the *arte* or guild of the *Calimala*. Besides this they were the bankers of Europe, and the name Tuscan or Lombard was used as a sort of euphemism for banker or usurer which had a disagreeable sound. The business relations of Florence were carried on principally with London and Bruges, also with Avignon and Genoa, and to a considerable degree with Venice.

Giovanni at his death left two sons, Cosimo and Lorenzo, one born in 1389 and the other in 1395. The relations of his house with the two last popes, John XXIII. and Martin V., had been of a most friendly character, and his son Cosimo had represented the interests of his house both with one and the other. Cosimo had accompanied John XXIII. to the Council of Constance, and the Medici constructed the tomb in the Church of San Giovanni in which the ashes of Baldassare Cossa now repose. It was not likely that the oligarchical party of the Albizzi could view with indifference so formidable a rival. The heads of this party after the death of Maso degli Albizzi in 1417 were his sons Rinaldo, Niccolò da Uzzano and Palla Strozzi. The Albizzi first appear in the history of Florence in the middle of the thirteenth century. They came originally from Arezzo. About the year 1370 they were attacked by a rival family, the Ricci, and they were the first to use the means which the constitution gave them, the *Ammonire*, the *balia* and the powers of the *parte guelfa*, to establish their new supremacy upon a firm basis. In 1379 they were exiled but returned in 1382 more powerful than ever. They became the dictators of the city and although their rule was not unstained by the cruelty of the age, there can be no doubt that the period of their government was one of great splendour and prosperity to the state. Maso degli Albizzi died, as we have said, in the year 1417 at the age of 74. His son Rinaldo was then eight years old. But the governing and moderating spirit of the party was Niccolò da Uzzano. He was by far the most powerful man in Florence. Palla Strozzi was rather a man of letters than a politician. He was a man of the highest character, and his modesty was equal to his powers. He was one of the richest men in Florence, richer than Giovanni de' Medici, and he spent his wealth in the furtherance of learning. Peace was preserved at Florence by the equilibrium of these opposing forces. The Republic had never been more flourishing or more prosperous. But a touch might destroy the charm. The shock came in the attempt to conquer Lucca, a town whose varied fortunes must often occupy the attention of the historian of mediæval Italy, and which still maintained a provoking independence, under the family of the Guignigi. The attempts to reduce Lucca ended in failure and disgrace. Fillipo di Ser Brunelleschi, who was at that time building the marvellous dome of the Cathedral at Florence, offered by diverting the course of the Serchio to surround Lucca with a lake which should throw down the walls. But the lake turned out to be no better than a frog-pool and Brunelleschi lost reputation as a man of science. Rinaldo degli Albizzi lost his prestige as a statesman. He tried to recover his position by an attack on Cosimo de' Medici, and as Niccolò da Uzzano had died during the siege of Lucca, there was no one to hold him in check. Giovanni was summoned from his villa to Florence and was imprisoned in the Public Palace. At first he feared for his life, but he was able to use his money with good effect. He was condemned to be banished for four years to Padua, his brother Lorenzo was sent to Venice, and the rest of the Medici family to Rome, Naples and Ancona.

Cosimo was received in his expatriation rather as an ambassador than as an exile, and his life at Padua and Venice was not less brilliant than it had been at Florence. The Medici left Florence on the evening of October 3, 1433. This therefore was the condition of things when Pope Eugenius arrived at the city in June 1434. But a revolution was at hand. The signory which came into office on September 1, 1434 was favourable to the Medici. Rinaldo attempted to prevent the return of his enemy by force. He and his friends assembled in arms to the number of 600. The signory summoned the people to their assistance and they thronged into Florence in crowds. The Pope who was inclined to favour Cosimo, tried to reconcile the two parties by means of Giovanni Vitelleschi, bishop of Recanati; but in vain. The Medici were recalled, Rinaldo degli Albizzi was driven into exile and never saw his country again. The supremacy of the Medici in Florence dates from this time. Cosimo became Gonfaloniere di Guistizia for the months of January and February 1435. The government of the Albizzi had lasted forty years, which was undoubtedly one of the most brilliant epochs in Florentine history. During it Florence

withstood with glory and success the converging attacks of
foreign foes, and she was more rich in consolidated wealth
and power than she was when it began.

We must now turn our attention to the affairs of Naples. King Louis of the second house of Anjou, who
had been recognized by the Pope, died without heirs at
Consenza in November 1434 and on February 11, 1435,
the first house of Anjou-Naples came to an end in the
person of Joanna II. By her will she had declared as
her heir René, Count of Provence and Duke of Anjou.
He was the possessor of a number of titles but of little
real power. He was Duke of Bar, Duke of Lorraine,
King of Naples and titular King of Arragon. His daughter
was the wife of Henry VI. of England, the ill-fated
Margaret of Anjou. Four days after the death of the
Queen the Neapolitans appointed a Council of Regency
and raised the banner of René. The Queen had left at
her death in gold and jewels the immense sum of five
hundred golden ducats. With this treasure an able and
energetic king could have secured the welfare of the State.
But when the Neapolitan ambassadors arrived in Provence to invite René to come to Naples they found him
a prisoner in the hands of the Duke of Burgundy. His
wife Isabella and his second son Louis, who were not in
prison, were able to accept the offers of the Neapolitan
mission and they reached their capital with a small fleet
on October 18, 1435.

The validity of Joanna's will was contested by Alfonzo,
who hurried from Sicily to defend his kingdom, while
the Pope declared that on the failure of the heirs of
Charles of Anjou the crown of Naples reverted to him
as a papal fief. The Duke of Milan took the side of

René against Alfonzo, and sent a Genoese fleet to defend
Gaeta against the attacks of Alfonzo. The Arragonese
fleet was defeated in August, 1436, off the island of Ponza,
and Alfonzo with his brother John, King of Navarre, and
the chief of his barons were taken prisoners. They were
conducted first to Genoa and then to Milan where Alfonzo by his ability and charms completely won over the
capricious Filippo Maria. He persuaded him that it was
to his real interest to prefer the advancement of Arragon
to that of France, and he left him a devoted friend. This
sudden and romantic change created a great impression
in Europe. The Pope was in despair. Genoa in dis-
quiet at the fickleness of Filippo Maria renounced his
allegiance to the Visconti. Alfonzo returned to Naples
to conduct the war against Isabella of Lorraine. The
Pope assisted René as the lesser of two evils, but his
general Vitelleschi, who had before this reduced Rome to
the Pope's obedience, could effect but little and returned
to his master at Ferrara.

René himself obtained his liberty in 1438. The cause
of his imprisonment is so characteristic of the manners
of the time that it is worth while to relate it, although it
is only remotely connected with the history of Italy.
Charles II., Duke of Lorraine, had died in 1431, and having
no male heirs, had left his duchy to his daughter Isabella
and her husband René of Anjou. The will was contested
by the Duke's nephew, Anthony Count of Vaudemont.
René, whose right was also acknowledged by the Emperor
Sigismund, began the war with spirit, but on July 2, 1431,
was taken prisoner by Philip II., Duke of Burgundy, who
supported the cause of Anthony. He was liberated on
poarle in April, 1432, but not wishing to break his faith

as a knight, or to sacrifice the hostages which were being retained for him, he returned of his own free will to prison in May 1433, and remained there for three years, not being able to obtain his liberty without paying a large sum of money. He now arrived at Naples on May 19 bringing with him his eldest son John, and on Ascension Day, May 22, he rode through the city in triumph. From this time a struggle of varying fortunes continued between the two rivals, René being generally established at Naples and Alfonzo at Gaeta. René proposed to settle the quarrel by single combat, an offer which Alfonzo scornfully rejected. At length in 1444 some of Alfonzo's troops were enabled to enter the city by an old and disused aqueduct. Francesco Sforza, who had declared for the side of René, could give no efficient help. The unfortunate Angevins took refuge on board a Genoese galley and sailed for Northern Italy and France. The Pope, seeing that René was hopelessly defeated, made peace with Alfonzo in June, 1443, who reigned from that time undisputed King of Naples.

In the meantime the exiles from Florence, as the only hope of returning to their homes, stirred up Filippo Maria to attack their city. The principal general on the side of the Visconti was Niccolò Piccinino. He was quite worthy to rank with the great condottiere leaders of his time, but he failed to found a dynasty and was treated with gross ingratitude by his master. His adversary was Francesco Sforza, in every way a worthy antagonist. Piccinino was a pupil of Braccio da Montone, Sforza of his father, so that the Condottieri were divided into two Schools, the Sforzeschi and the Bracceschi, each with its own traditions and names of warfare. The struggle began

in the Territory of Lucca, but was continued in the
Romagna. It would be idle to attempt a detailed account
of the conflicts of these equally noted generals. On one
occasion Piccinino, after a defeat, was carried in a sack
through the field of battle to appear unexpectedly in another place. The war was decided by the battle of Anghiari
fought on June 29, 1440, in which Piccinino was defeated
and half his army taken prisoners. In the following
year, as we have already heard, Filippo Maria reduced
to extremities, was forced to give to Sforza the hand of
his daughter Bianca Maria and to mark him out as heir
to the Duchy of Milan. Piccinino complained bitterly
that his rival had been preferred before him. The peace
of Casciano closed the war between the two republics
and the Duke. Venice obtained Bergamo, Brescia
Peschiera and the Riva di Trento. Sforza received
Cremona as dower with his wife. The independence of
Genoa was recognized and Florence acquired the Casentino, the upper valley of the Arno immortalized in the
verse of Dante, containing the magic names of Campal-
dino, Poppi, Romena, and Bibbiena, which had hitherto
been subject to the Count Guido da Polenta as an Imperial fief.

During this period Pope Eugenius had been at war
with the Council of Basel, and was gradually getting the
best of the contest. The Council had entered too hastily
on the path of reform. It had aimed blow after blow at
the power of the papacy, and had roused up powerful
advocates in its defence. Torquemada now supported the
papal infallibility of which Thomas Aquinas had been the
champion in earlier days. One of the most important
subjects before the Council was the union of the Greek

and Latin Churches and the choice of the city in which the Council of reconciliation should be held gave rise to heated controversy. The Pope was willing that it should be summoned at Constantinople, but the Council refused to place their heads in the mouth of the Turks. They wished the Greek fathers to come to Basel, but the Patriarch of Constantinople replied that the personal presence of the Pope was essential, and he could not be expected to go to a place which had been the scene of rebellion against him. At last the two parties changed the scene of the intended conference, one choosing Avignon and the other Florence or Udine. At the beginning of these negotiations it had been arranged that if the Council were held in the East the Eastern Church should bear the expense, if in the West the expense should fall upon the Pope. When it was practically settled that the Council should be held somewhere in Italy, the Pope equipped four galleys in Venice and sent them to Constantinople, where they met a similar fleet coming from Avignon. The Greek Emperor, John Palæologus, together with the fathers who were to attend the Council, embarked on the Pope's Galleys and on September 17, 1437, the Pope issued a bull convening the Council at Ferrara; an order which was not recognized by the fathers at Basel.

The first meeting of the Council of Ferrara was held on January 8, 1438. It was very scantily attended and none but Italians were present. On January 27 the Pope entered the city with a splendid retinue. On February 8 the swift-sailing imperial galley which bore the Emperor of the Eastern world entered the harbour of San Nicolò del Lido. The Doge Francesco Foscari went immediately to pay a visit to the Emperor on board his galley, and on the following day, which was a Sunday, he received him on board the Bucentoro, accompanied by Venetian senators and nobles. The Byzantine Emperor made his entry into Venice to the strains of music and amongst the cheers of the populace. On the last day of February Palæologus left Venice and on April 9 the representatives of both Churches were united at Ferrara under the Presidency of Eugenius IV. The Greek and Latin theologians discussed the points of difference between the two Churches without any practical result, the most important question being the retention of the word "Filioque" in the Nicene creed which implied the double procession of the Holy Spirit from the Father and the Son, a doctrine not accepted by the Greek Church. The Council of Basel was by no means in a humour to submit. On January 23, four days before the arrival of Eugenius at Ferrara, it had declared the Pope suspended from his pontifical authority in answer to his decree of the previous February which excommunicated the Fathers of the Council. In March it declared the Council of Ferrara schismatical; in May it asserted that General Councils received their authority directly from Christ, and in June it actually deposed Eugenius. In October it appointed electors for a new Pope, amongst whom was Æneas Silvius Piccolomini, afterwards Pope under the name of Pius II. In November it confirmed the election of Amadeus of Savoy, the Hermit of Ripaille; in February 1440 it ordered the Christian world to pay him obedience as the true pontiff. Thus the Schism was complete. Alfonzo of Arragon and Charles King of France took the side of the Council against the Pope. Germany had the opportunity of anticipating the Reformation by a hundred years.

Just at this time, on December 9, 1437, the Emperor Sigismund died, and was succeeded by his stepson Albert of Austria. The Pope's Council could not remain long at Ferrara. The plague broke out in the town and Piccinino was threatening the neighbourhood with his mercenary troops. So in January 1439 Eugenius removed the Council to Florence. Here the process of reconciliation went on with great rapidity. The Greek theologians eventually declared themselves satisfied as to the points in dispute between the two Churches. They admitted that the Holy Spirit did in a certain sense proceed from both Persons of the Trinity, that leavened as well as unleavened bread might be used in the Holy Eucharist, and that Purgatory really existed. They agreed that the Pope, the Bishop of Rome, should be considered as the first head of Christendom, that the Bishop of Constantinople or new Rome should be the second, of Alexandria the third, of Antioch the fourth, of Jerusalem the fifth. On June 9 the Greek Patriarch died, declaring his adhesion to the Roman Church. To celebrate and confirm this union a solemn service was held on July 6, 1439, in the Cathedral of Our Lady of the Flower. The Emperor and the Pope were present, together with the Fathers of both Churches. The Greeks were placed on the Epistle, the Latins on the Gospel side. The Gospel was sung in both languages and during the mass was read the Bull of Union, drawn up in Greek and Latin as subscribed by the members of the Council. No Christian can recall the memory of this momentous function held under the dome of Brunelleschi, which half a century later resounded to the preaching of Savonarola, without deep emotion. Eugenius might well feel that the disunion of Christendom had been permanently healed and that the Church of Christ would henceforth form one fold under one shepherd, and be able to meet with a united front the assaults of Islam and of infidelity. But national feeling proved then too strong, as it has proved since, to admit of the establishment of a single Church which should embrace all nations. To the Act of Union one signature was wanting, that of Mark of Ephesus, and the Greek Church has professed to follow that single voice.

We have said above that Amadeus of Savoy had been elected as pope and recognized by the Council of Basel. He was the eighth Count of Savoy, son of the Red Count and grandson of the Green. He succeeded in 1391, bought the Country of Genevois of which Annecy was capital in 1401, was made first Duke of Savoy by the Emperor Sigismund at Chambéry in 1417, and inherited Piedmont in the following year. On the death of his wife in 1434 he abdicated his throne and retired to the delightful monastery of Ripaille on the Lake of Geneva. There he founded the order of St. Maurice and lived with six companions as the richest and mightiest of all the hermits of Christendom. The Council thought him a desirable choice because he was reported to be very rich, was connected with very powerful families and held one foot in France and one in Italy. He accepted the tiara with some hesitation in January, 1440, and took the name of Felix V. He had, however, no power and was not recognized by any important persons except Alfonzo of Arragon. Germany remained neutral in the schism. He resigned the papacy on April 7, 1449, and died on January 7, 1451.

Albert King of Hungary, Bohemia and Germany died on October 27, 1439. He was succeeded as King of Germany by his uncle, who three years later became the Emperor Frederick III., and reigned for more than fifty years. Pope Eugenius, having made peace with King Alfonzo in 1443, found it possible to return to Rome. The same populace which had driven him out with stones and arrows now streamed across the Ponte Molle to welcome him back. After an exile of nine years he found the Eternal city indeed a contrast to Florence, one the most civilized city in Europe, the other a desolate wilderness. He summoned a Council to the Lateran and thundered from that palace against the Council of Basel and his rival Felix. His last days were embittered with war. In 1446 a war broke out between the republics of Venice, Bologna, Florence and Genoa on the one side, and the King Alfonzo, the Pope, the Duke of Milan, and the Lords of Rimini on the other. Francesco Sforza led the army of the Republics. The Duke was entirely defeated and the forces of Venice pressed nearly to the gates of Milan. This success of the Venetians produced a strange revolution in the state of affairs. Sforza hoped at some time to be Duke of Milan, and he did not care to see his future duchy diminished by Venetian conquests. Also Cosimo de' Medici thought it better for the interests of Florence to preserve an equilibrium between all the states than to allow the predominance of one. By his mediation negotiations were opened between Francesco Sforza and his father-in-law, and they were hastened by the impatience of the Venetians, who suspecting the treachery of Sforza, attacked some towns belonging to him in Lombardy. Sforza deserted the republican league and became Commander-in-chief of the Duke's forces. But his assistance came too late. Sforza was just about to help his father-in-law when he heard of his death on August 13, 1447. Pope Eugenius IV. had died in the previous February, and had been succeeded by Giovanni Parentucelli, called of Sarzana, but really born at Pisa in 1398. He was Archbishop of Bologna and Cardinal of Santa Susanna, and took the title of Nicolas V. The last act of Eugenius had been to sign a Concordat with Germany. The Emperor Frederick III., for a present of 100,000 florins and the promise of being crowned at Rome, surrendered the cause of the Council of Basel and did homage to the Pope. Thus the cause of the Reformation in Germany was lost, and the German Church sank step by step into its former condition of subservience.

CHAPTER IV

AFTER the death of the Duke Filippo Maria, Milan was
in a condition of the greatest confusion and embarrassment. There was no son or near relation to claim the
fief by right of inheritance. It is said that the Duke
the day before his death had made a will, in which he
declared Alfonzo of Naples as his successor, but it is a
great question whether this will was genuine, and if it were,
it is doubtful whether the Duke had a right to dispose
of an imperial fief by testament. Two other pretenders
to the coronet were Francesco Sforza, who had married
the Duke's daughter Bianca Maria, and was the best
defence against the hostility of Venice, and the Duke
of Savoy, who was the brother of the widowed Duchess.
Francesco Sforza was, as we know, the son of Attendolo
Sforza, the great condottiere general. It is said that the
founder of the family attached himself by an accident to
the career which brought him so much distinction. He
was a woodman working in the forests of Cotignola.
Some mercenary troops passing by asked him to join them.
He said that his answer should depend upon whether his
axe when he threw it remained sticking in the tree or
fell to the ground. It remained suspended, and he followed the voice of destiny.

Two days before the death of the Duke, Nicola Guarna wrote to Sforza urging him to come to the city, " Consider what the state of things is, and how you will be off if our Lord dies and you are not here." On the day of the Duke's death he wrote again. On the following, Antonio Guidoboni informing him of what had occurred, and urging him to come, said, " As soon as you are here half the game is won." The moment the Duke's death was known, the Arragonese party filled the fortresses with Neapolitan troops, and the chief mercenary generals took the oath of allegiance to King Alfonzo. The people of Milan were of a different opinion; they wished for none of the three alternatives. They were tired of princely government and longed for the establishment of their ancient freedom. They rose in insurrection and declared that with the extinction of the Visconti dynasty the sovereignty reverted to the Town itself. The government remained in the hands of the Great Council of eight hundred, out of whom were elected a small council of twenty-four, four from each of the six wards of the city. These were to stand at the head of the new constitution, the Golden Ambrosian Republic, as Conservators and Defenders of Liberty, "Capitanei et Defensores Libertatis illustris et excelsæ communitatis Mediotani." The condottieri in search of their own interest left the King of Naples and swore allegiance to the Republic. The Neapolitan soldiers in the forts were bought off for the sum of 17,000 florins. The freedom of the city was secured.

But the Venetians were in no mood to make peace with the new power. The Empire of the Duke was hopelessly broken up. Venice had good hope that the whole of it would fall into her hands. In Lodi the Guelph

party drove out the Ghibellines and surrendered the city to
Venice. Piacenza did the same. Pavia, Parma, and Tortona
declared their independence. Asti was occupied by the Duke
of Orleans, who laid claim to the whole of the Milanese
in the right of his mother Valentina Visconti, the sister
of Filippo Maria. Cremona was in the hands of Sforza,
as part of his wife's dower. Brescia had been for some
time in the power of the Venetians, the only towns which
remained in their allegiance were Como, Alessandria and
Novara. The danger of entire dissolution roused the
people of Milan to redoubled efforts. Sforza was promised
the possession of Brescia and Verona if he could win
them back from the Venetians. The new Republic
made a great mistake in taking Sforza into their pay,
as he could have no other purpose than to recover the
dominion of his father-in-law for himself. It would
have been better to have made terms with Venice,
however hard. The two sons of Niccolò Piccinino left
the service of Venice and attached themselves to Sforza,
and the Milanese by the advice of Sforza took into
their pay the great condottiere leader, Bartolomeo Colleoni.
Strengthened by these reinforcements Sforza first turned
his attention to Piacenza and Pavia. Pavia was at this
time as much torn by parties as Milan itself. The
people wished for freedom, but the castle was occupied
by Matteo Bolognini and also by Agnese del Manio, the
mother of Bianca Maria who was the wife of Sforza.
By her intervention Pavia delivered itself to Sforza
under the condition that it should not be made subject
to Milan. The Milanese were naturally much distressed
at this sign of self-seeking on the part of their general, but they were too weak to resent it. The Este

were pressing them on one side, the Correggi on the other, the Doge of Venice was threatening Tortona, the Duke of Savoy had designs on Novara and Alessandria, the Marquis of Montferrat was bestirring himself, and Dresnay, the lieutenant of the Duke of Orleans, was attempting to extend his power from Asti. The Duke of Savoy at this time was Lewis the elder, who succeeded to the Dukedom when his father Amadeus VIII., now Pope Felix V., retired to the hermitage of Ripaille. Lewis is described by his contemporaries as being a strong man, handsome and affable, fluent of speech but indolent in action, inconstant and variable as were so many of his line. He often sought his father's advice, but was believed to be guided rather by the influence of his wife Anne, Princess of Cyprus. Men complained that he impoverished his own country to enrich the house of Lusignan. On November 15 Francesco Sforza took Piacenza by storm: the town was given up to the most horrible excesses of the soldiery. The fate of Tortona was remarkable. It surrendered itself secretly to Sforza shortly after he had got possession of Pavia, but the people of Milan ordered Bartolomeo Colleoni, who had just defeated Dresnay in the territory of Alessandria, to drive out Sforza's representatives and to occupy the town for themselves. Sforza on his part took no notice of this insult.

The two republics again attempted to order peace, and their representatives met at Bergamo for that purpose in January, 1448. But the peace had to be ratified by the Great Council at Milan, and the party of Sforza was thoroughly opposed to it. By his intrigues the project was given up, and in May, 1448, the war broke out with new vigour. The resources of the young republic began to fail; it had no money to pay its mercenaries; one after another they dropped off, the most important loss being that of Bartolomeo Colleoni, who joined the service of Venice. Sforza continued to serve the Ambrosian Republic, knowing that he could afford to wait for the accomplishment of his ends. In the early summer of 1448 the war was pursued with energy in the valley of the Adda, and the Venetians suffered severe defeats in the summer and the autumn. Their fleet was destroyed at Casalmaggiore on the Po, but the most important feat of arms was the siege of Caravaggio which began at the end of July and lasted for six weeks. It concluded with the battle of Caravaggio on September 15, in which the Venetians were most severely defeated. The Venetians trusted to recover themselves rather by diplomacy than by force. They knew that the Milanese were jealous of the power of their general, and they thought that they would be able to estrange him from their service. On October 18, 1448, a treaty was signed at Rivoltella, a small village close to Peschiera, between the Venetians and Sforza, by which Venice bound herself to assist Francesco in the conquest of Milan with 4000 cavalry, 2000 infantry and 13,000 ducats a month. If Sforza was victorious, the Adda was to form the boundary between the two countries. It is probable that the Venetians did not really desire that Sforza should conquer Milan, but they reckoned that the Milanese from fear of having him as their master would make peace with them on favourable terms.

The generals of Milan were Francesco Piccinino, the son of the famous Niccolò, and Carlo Gonzaga, who was afterwards Duke of Mantua. The Ambrosian republic in despair turned for assistance to the chief potentates of Europe, to the Emperor Frederick III., to King Alfonzo, to Charles VII. of France, to the Dauphin, afterwards Louis XI., to Philip the Good, of Burgundy, to Lewis of Savoy. There exists in the archives of Geneva a volume of eighty letters which passed between Pope Felix V. and his son with regard to the league of Milan. Sforza crossed the Adda and gained numerous successes. Milan was torn asunder by Guelphs and Ghibellines. Gonzaga tried to conciliate the popular party in order to gain the Dukedom for himself. Upon this the Ghibelline nobles turned their eyes to Sforza and thought of offering him the Dukedom upon certain conditions. The result of this was that they were driven from the town and many of them took refuge in Sforza's camp. The popular party abused the power that they had won, and the consequence was that the two Piccinini went over to Sforza. It is wearisome and unnecessary to follow the details of the conflict. In September, 1449, the Venetians made peace on their own account with Milan, as the popular party in Milan saw in this the only means of procuring their independence. The Venetians offered to admit Sforza as a party to the arrangement on favourable terms, but he refused as the terms did not comprise the freedom of Milan. Sforza was determined to reduce the city by famine. He could effect this by blocking the passages over the Adda so that the Milanese could receive no assistance from the Venetians. The two bridges over the Adda were at Trezzo and at Brivio. The first was guarded by a castle with a bridge and was in the power of Sforza, the second was not difficult to blockade. Month after month the distress in Milan grew greater. An attempt made by Bartolomeo

Colleoni to relieve the blockade by passing to the lake of Como by the Val Sassina, although it was one of the greatest feats of that general, did not effect its purpose. At the end of February Milan was in the extremity of despair. The first breath of spring was scarcely felt, several months must elapse before the harvest, and what was the harvest of that sunburnt plain, scorched by the flames of war and trampled down by innumerable battles? Crowds of hungry men, followed by their wives and children, fled from the city to find nourishment in the fields. Sforza forbade that they should have any assistance. The people became irritated against the Venetians. The heads of the Republic met in the church of Santa Maria della Scala, but the populace of the Porta Nuova rose in tumult. The government tried in vain to suppress it. The Venetian ambassador, Leonardo Venier, was massacred, the magistrates fled, and the people summoned the principal citizens to meet in the same church of La Scala. Gaspare di Vimercate exposed the impossibility of procuring freedom, and the danger of submitting to any other lord but Sforza. His name was at once accepted. Some days were spent in settling the conditions and the instrument was finally signed on March 3, 1450.

Sforza made his triumphal entry into the conquered city on March 25. He came to Milan from Monza. Outside the Porta Ticinese he was met by the chief men of the city, by Bianca his wife, Galeazzo Maria his eldest son and his brother Alessandro. A triumphal car and a canopy of white silk embroidered with gold had been prepared for him but he refused these gauds as "the superstition of kings and great princes." He entered the city and proceeded to the cathedral, there he was clothed in white silk according to the ancient custom of the Dukes, he took his seat with his wife by his side and listened to a discourse by Castiglione, the author of the Cortegiano. He was confirmed as Duke by the voice of the people, received the oath of allegiance from the representatives of the wards, and took into his hands the sceptre, the sword, the banner, the keys of the gates, and the seal of the Visconti dukes. He then created his son Galeazzo Count of Pavia. For some time he was not recognized by the King of France, who claimed the duchy of Milan for the Duke of Orleans, nor by Frederick III. of Germany, who regarded the duchy as escheated to the imperial crown. He was, however, recognized by the ambassadors of all the Italian States except Venice and Naples. The Pope, Florence, Genoa, Siena, Ancona and many others sent their envoys to congratulate him. It is a characteristic fact that just at this time the Council of Ten at Venice discussed for the second time the propriety of accepting an offer to poison the newly-crowned Duke.

Recent researches have made us acquainted with the constitution of the government of Milan at this time, which was not as arbitrary as might be thought at first sight. A council of twelve members, called the secret ducal council, assisted the Duke in the government. This owed its origin, at least in part, to the similar institution in the Ambrosian Republic. There was a special council of three members for affairs of justice, and another to superintend the revenues. These were carefully ordered and were composed of taxes on merchandize and cattle, of dues payable at the gates, of a tax on grinding corn, and of a money contribution called *carrigio*. The army was divided into two parts, the ducal army of Lombardy and the field army for external wars.

We have said above that the accession of the new Duke of Milan was recognized by Pope Nicolas V. He was a great contrast to his predecessor, his youth was spent in studying and copying ancient manuscripts, and he used the power of the Papacy to give a strong impulse to his favourite pursuits. His reign is the beginning of a new era, the dawn of the Renaissance. He cared nothing for war, he employed artists to build, chisel, and paint for him. A hundred men of learning translated for him the treasures of antiquity and were well rewarded for their exertions. In 1450 he celebrated the general peace of Italy by a jubilee attended by an enormous crowd of pilgrims who brought countless offerings to the Holy See. Such a concourse had not been seen since the great jubilee of 1300, under Pope Boniface VIII., which we find so often recorded in the verse of Dante.

The great object of Sforza at his accession was to confirm his power; the Venetians were his bitter enemies. The Republic of the Adriatic formed a league with Alfonzo, Lewis of Savoy, William of Montferrat, and the Republic of Siena. Florence and Milan were close allies. Cosimo de Medici sent Agnolo Acciajuoli on an embassy to Charles VII., who was able to announce from Tours in December, 1451, that the King was willing to conclude an alliance with Milan and Florence. Above all Sforza desired the recognition of the Emperor. Frederick III. had been promised the Imperial crown by Eugenius IV., who had also purchased from him for 100,000 gulden the recognition of the Pope by Germany. It was arranged that the Emperor was to marry Eleanora of Portugal, the niece of Alfonzo of Naples. The marriage and the coronation were arranged by Æneas Silvius Piccolomini, one of the greatest men of the age, afterwards Pope under the name of Pius II. Frederick refused to pass by Milan to receive the iron crown of Lombardy for fear that he might be compelled to recognize the usurper Sforza. He passed by way of Ferrara to Florence, and was betrothed to his bride at Siena on February 24, 1452, an event which is commemorated by a cross still existing outside the walls of Siena, and by one of Pinturrichio's frescoes in the Piccolomini Library. He entered Rome in triumph, was crowned there in March, and went on to Naples for the solemnity of his marriage. He was the last Emperor who was crowned in Rome. He returned by way of Venice, but left without honour or respect.

We have now reached the furthest verge of the middle ages. They are passing away, and the modern world is arising in their place. Frederick was the father of Maximilian and the great-grandfather of Charles V.

The Emperor had given his countenance to the cause of Venice against Milan, but he had never joined the league between Venice and Alfonzo on the one side, and Milan and Mantua on the other. The King of France had two courses before him, he could either press his own claim on the Duchy of Milan, or he could support the right of his ward, René of Anjou, to the throne of Naples. As we have before indicated, he preferred the latter course, and in 1453 René was sent with an army to assist Sforza. He did, however, very little good, and soon returned to his own Provence.

Just at this time an immense effect was produced by the taking of Constantinople by the Turks. We know that in our own day this city is considered by most impartial statesmen to be a place of too great importance to be in the hands of any first-rate European State. It was of still greater importance then. The conquest of New Rome, once the chief seat of Imperial majesty, and the second capital of Christendom by a militant band of heathen roused Europe to the duty of uniting against the common foe. The call was felt most strongly by Venice, which had always stood in the vanguard of the struggle. The Pope also summoned to Rome the representatives of the Italian powers to treat of peace in his presence. The result of these feelings was the peace of Lodi, signed on April 9, 1454. The Adda and the Oglio were to form the boundary between Venice and Milan. The peace of Lodi is an important epoch in the history of Italy. It was initiated, not by the petty lords of independent cities, but by two great states, the ancient Republic of St. Mark, and the Duchy of Milan, under the energetic rule of a victorious soldier. The Italian states, whether willingly or not, all took part in it. Florence accepted the peace on May 14, and it received the adherence of Siena, Lucca, Perugia, the lord of Piombino, Bologna, Borso Marquis of Este, Duke of Modena and Reggio, Lewis of Mantua, the Ordelaffi of Forli, the heads of the family of Malatesta, the Manfredi of Faenza and Imola, Ancona, Carlo Gonzaga of Mantua, the Malaspina of the Lunigiana and other lesser lords. The Correggeschi of Parma submitted to Sforza: the Marquis of Montferrat and his brother accepted the peace; Lewis of Savoy gave his adhesion in August, 1454; and Borso d'Este restored to the Duke of Milan the territory which his brother Lionel had occupied in the Parmesan.

Italy was now at peace, and the five great powers kept

each other in equilibrium. In the North, Venice was a counterbalance to Milan; in the South, Naples formed a counterpoise to Rome; in the centre, Florence, the chief depository of the wealth of the Peninsula, and the main source of its culture, held the scales between the north and the south. It is convenient to date the revival of learning in Italy from the peace of Lodi or of Fra Simonetta as it is sometimes called. It was followed by a league for 25 years between the Pope, Alfonzo, Naples, Florence, Venice and Milan. It was the fear of the Turks, the taking of Pera from the Genoese, the threatening of the coasts of the Mediterranean by Turkish cruisers which brought about the first league of the Italian powers. Pope Nicolas lived just long enough to see it completed; he died on March 24, 1455. He was a scholar Pope, who defended the Papacy, not by armies and intrigue, but by placing it at the head of modern culture. On his death-bed he addressed to his Cardinals an apology for his life and reign. He claimed to have healed the schism of the church, to have recovered its estates and protected them by fortresses, to have enriched the papal treasury with books, manuscripts, and countless works of art; and to have done all this not by simony or niggardliness, but by the legitimate revenues of a peaceful reign. This boast was true enough, and these arguments might defend the Papacy against the attacks of the councils of Basel or of Constance. But the other side of the picture is that Nicolas was the first of the worldly popes, the fore-runner of Leo X. What would St. Francis of Assisi or St. Catherine of Siena have thought in hearing, as the bitterest lament, that the Muses and Apollo wept tears of sorrow over his tomb?

He was succeeded by Calixtus IV., an old man of 77,

of great learning and honourable character. He was a
Spaniard of Xativa in the province of Valencia, he was
in the confidence of Alfonzo of Arragon, and he first
connected with the papal tiara the detested name of Borgia. His short reign was unimportant, the Pope on his
sick-bed was surrounded by monks and nephews. His
only passions were the crusade against the Turks and the
advancement of his family. Calixtus sent emissaries into
all lands; nuncios and friars were despatched into every
country. The treasures of Nicolas were squandered,
jewels sold, books robbed of their costly binding to fit out
a fleet of sixteen triremes, which only succeeded in plundering a few islands in the Archipelago. Far more
important was the defeat which the conqueror of Byzantium suffered at the hands of John Hunyadi before the
walls of Belgrade on August 9, 1456. The conditions of
Europe were not favourable for a great united effort.
France dreaded an invasion from England, England was
preparing to attack France, Germany refused to move.
Alfonzo was more angry against Genoa and Milan than
against the Turks. It needed something more than the
power of a feeble old man, however good and however
much respected, to weld the warring jealousies of Europe
into a phalanx of attack against the infidel.

The affairs of Genoa now become of importance for
Italian history. Genoa, which had for a long time been
subject to Milan, recovered its liberty in 1438. There
was an old naval rivalry between the Genoese and the
Catalans which made the Genoese the persistent enemies
of Alfonzo of Arragon. The two principal families in
Genoa were the Adorni and Campo Fregosi, of great power,
but of plebeian origin. The old nobility found themselves

excluded from offices and power. In 1441 Gian Antonio del Fiesco placed himself at the head of the ancient families of the Doria and Spinola, allied himself with the Duke of Milan and the King of Naples, and attacked the power of Tommaso Campo Fregoso who was then Doge. At the close of 1442 the Doge was suddenly deposed and the government committed to a *balia* of eight men, of whom Rafaelle Adorno was one. Almost immediately afterwards he was elected Doge, but with limited power. Peace was now concluded with Alfonzo of Naples and quiet continued for a short time. In 1447 Rafaelle Adorno was forced to give way to his cousin Bernabò. He was in his turn driven out, and was succeeded by more than one of the family of Campo Fregoso. In fact, out of the thirty-one Doges who reigned between 1339 and 1527 seven are Adorni and fourteen Campo Fregosi; from 1446 no other names but these are seen upon the roll. In 1453 Piero Fregoso was unable as Doge to defend the colony of Pera, and the other Genoese settlements on the Black Sea, as well as the island of Corsica had to be surrendered to the Bank of St. George, a trading company invested with powers of government similar to the old East India Company of England. Alfonzo was embittered against Genoa from the favour which it had always shown to France and especially towards René of Anjou, and he gave his support to the family of the Adorni. Piero Campo Fregoso saw no other hope of safety than to seek help from France. In 1458 Charles VII., King of France, was solemnly declared Lord of Genoa, and he sent as his representative John of Calabria, son of René of Anjou, the titular King of Naples. Alfonzo continued the war with great vigour against this new enemy but died on June

27, 1458. After his death the throne of Naples was again disputed. Arragon and Sicily went to his brother Ferdinando, Naples he left to his natural son Ferdinand, who was generally known as Don Ferrante. Alfonzo had endeavoured to secure the peaceable succession of Ferrante by marrying a son and daughter of Ferrante to a son and daughter of Francesco Sforza. Calixtus III., notwithstanding the benefits he had received from King Alfonzo, refused to recognize his natural son as his heir. He rather supported the claims of John of Calabria, of the house of Anjou, but it is probable that his real object was to secure the throne of Naples for one of his nephews. If the Pope had conceived any idea of the infamy with which the advancement of his sister's sons would stain the name of Borgia he would have suffered them to remain in the obscurity of Valencia. The race of the Borgias in mediæval Rome has been compared with that of the Claudii in the ancient city. They were by nature strong of body, full of passion, ambitious, unprincipled, appropriately represented by the bull which they bore on their arms. Two of them, young immature men, he made cardinals, adopted them and gave them his own name. A third, Don Pedro Luis, his uncle's favourite, was designed for a throne, either that of Naples, Cyprus or Byzantium. The Vatican was overrun by Spaniards. The Spanish language took the place of the Italian, the faction of the Borgias (the Spanish orthography is Borja) went by the name of the Catalans.

Don Pedro Luis Borja was the most powerful and the most brilliant man in Rome. When he saw the Pope's death approaching he fled from the vengeance of the Romans and retired to Civita Vecchia where he died of fever. His uncle Calixtus III, expired on the day succeeding his flight, August 6, 1458.

The successor of Calixtus III. in the papacy was a remarkable man, early known in the world, Æneas Silvius Piccolomini, sprung from a noble family of the city of Siena, who now took the name of Pius II. In the conclave, Cardinal Bessarion had said that he would not vote for Piccolomini because he had a disease in his feet, and that the Church, threatened by the Turks, had need of a very active Head. The event shows how much he was mistaken. The new Pope had first made himself known as a poet and a man of letters. In 1430 he became secretary to Cardinal Capranica, and accompanied him to the Council of Basel. He travelled all over Europe and was one of the first cultivated Europeans to become acquainted with the condition of Germany. His life is full of romance. Once in a storm off the coast of Scotland, he made a vow that if he were saved he would walk barefoot to the nearest chapel of pilgrimage, and he suffered all his life from gout in consequence of the performance of his vow. He was created poet-laureate in Frankfort by the Emperor Frederick III. He was afterwards secretary to Frederick's chancellor, Caspar Schlick. In 1445 he left the Emperor for the Pope, took orders and was made a Bishop by Nicolas V. He did not finally leave Germany till 1455, when he was sent to convey the homage of the Emperor to Pope Calixtus. He was made a Cardinal in the following year. He had lived a life as varied and as full of interest as a condottiere; he had attained high rank but had not been able to amass a fortune. At the conclave it was difficult to obtain a majority, Estouteville, Archbishop of Rouen, was the favourite candidate, but there

5

were objections to having a French Pope. At last Roderigo Borgia arose and said "I vote for the Cardinal of
Siena;" the rest followed his example, and Piccolomini
heard of his election with tears. His very election was
a sign of revolution. For the first time a travelled, cultivated, astute man of the world was seen upon the papal
throne. He took the name of Pius as a natural accom-
paniment to that of Æneas. He would say of himself,
"Sum pius Æneas fama super æthera notus." The Emperor
was delighted with the choice. Pius II. was fifty-three years
of age when he assumed the tiara, small and weak, bald-
headed, looking pale and aged, a martyr to the gout.
Men who expected to find in him a literary Pope, a
second Nicolas V., were disappointed, the one object of
his efforts was the recovery of Constantinople from the
Turks. He summoned the princes of Christendom to
meet at Mantua for the discussion of this common object. He said that God had made him Pope to liberate
the Church from this affliction. He was sensible enough
to recognize Ferrante as King of Naples.

We must return to the affairs of Genoa which we left
in the hands of the French. In the spring of 1461.
Paolo Campo Fregoso, Archbishop of Genoa, and
Prospero Adorno, forgetting their quarrel for the moment,
entered the city and drove the French back into the
castle. After some vicissitudes Adorno was elected Doge,
and the Genoese asked Sforza to assist them in driving
out the French. The battle took place on July 17, 1461,
the day of Sant' Alessio. The French were entirely
defeated, and it was ordered that the victory should be
commemorated by an annual festival. After the battle
the animosities between the two rival families again broke

out, and Ludovico Campo Fregoso was made Doge. In 1461 Charles VII. of France died and was succeeded by Louis XI. He had always been a friend of Sforza, and he now made him a present of Savona together with his rights over Milan. At the beginning of 1463 Paolo Campo Fregoso, the Archbishop, became Doge of Genoa and was recognized by Pius II. His rule was so tyrannical as to be unbearable, and his first thought was to take vengeance on those who had at any time opposed him. Sforza sent Gaspare Vimercate to press his claims to the city, and in April, 1464, Sforza was acknowledged as Lord of Genoa.

The Congress of Mantua led to but little result. The Pope delivered a great oration on September 26, 1459. He showed that if the Turks conquered Hungary there would be no obstacle to their progress. Passing through Carniola and Triest they might descend upon Italy with the same ease with which they might disembark at Brindisi. He proclaimed a crusade on January 14, 1460, and so closed the Congress. Notwithstanding the zeal of the Pontiff, the plan for a crusade appeared to languish. There was a great want of money, this was unexpectedly supplied by the discovery of some alum mines at Tolfa in the neighbourhood of Città Vecchia by Giovanni De-Castro, a friend of the Piccolomini family. He wrote to the Pope, "I announce to you victory over the Turks." These mines continued to be profitably worked till 1814. when artificially made alum took the place of the natural mineral. In 1463 the Pope told the astonished world that he would lead the crusade himself. In the Bull of October 22, 1463, he says, "We will not fight with the sword because our feeble hand can scarcely raise itself to bless the people; we will fight not with the sword but with prayer, we will stand on high on the poop of the ship, or on a high hill near the battle to bless our friends and to curse our enemies." The Pope, although he knew that he was dying, determined to travel to Ancona, where the crusading fleet was to rendezvous. He left Rome on June 18, 1464, the prelates and the people took leave of him at the Ponte Molle, and he continued his journey with a few companions. He reached Ancona on July 11. He found in the town some thirty thousand French and Spanish adventurers who, when they discovered that the Pope had no intention of paying their expenses, retired to their homes. There were only two papal galleys in the harbour. On August 12 the Doge Christoforo Moro arrived with twelve galleys. From the window of his palace the Pope gazed at the Venetian fleet as it entered the port, and fixed the day of Assumption, August 15, for receiving the Doge. But on that day he died. When the cardinals had finished the sacred rites he called them round his bed, and said: "My hour is come, God calls me." He spoke of the crusade which he had twice attempted, and asked pardon for his many shortcomings. His last words were addressed to the Cardinal of Pavia, whom he begged to pray for his soul. The forty thousand ducats found in the Pope's chest were given to Matthias, King of Hungary. Everyone felt that after the Pope's death the crusade was at an end. On August 16 the Doge left Ancona, and returned to Venice on August 23.

Francesco Sforza was now nearing his end. We have already alluded to the marriage of his daughter Ippolita Maria with Alfonzo of Calabria, son of Ferrante, King of Naples. Frederick, the brother of Alfonzo, came to Milan in the summer of 1465 to receive the bride, but when the marriage train had reached Siena it was stopped by order of the Duke. This was caused by the death of Giacomo Piccinino, who had been treacherously thrown into prison by Ferrante. The circumstances which attended this would be incredible if they were not supported by irrefragable evidence. Piccinino had come to Milan from his capital Sulmona in the summer of 1464 at the request of Sforza. The Duke received him with every demonstration of affection and gave him the hand of his daughter Drusiana. Piccinino then left for Sulmona, intending to go to Naples, if he could do so with safety. He sent one of his friends, Brocardo Persico, to sound the intentions of Ferrante, and his reports were most reassuring. Piccinino therefore went to Naples, but there is no doubt that his death, which was warmly desired by Ferrante because he was an adherent of the Angevin party, had already been conceded by Sforza as a price of the alliance with Naples. As a mark of friendship Sforza had given to Piccinino Pietro Pusterla, one of his own "orators" or official speakers, and there is no doubt that this man was thoroughly informed of Sforza's most secret intentions and had no other design than that of conducting Piccinino to death. Suddenly the mask was removed. On St John's day, June 24, when both Naples and Milan were gay with festivity, Piccinino came to the Castello Nuovo to take leave of Ferrante as he desired to return to Sulmona to meet his wife Drusiana. He was received with affection but was suddenly seized and imprisoned, together with his son Francesco and others. Ferrante justified his conduct in a circular letter full of empty phrases addressed to the potentates of Italy. Dru-

siana, who had not reached Sulmona, returned to her uncle
Alessandro in Pesaro, the *Bracceschi* soldiery of Piccinino,
insulted and oppressed, took refuge with Domenico Malatesta, and the territories of Piccinino yielded themselves
spontaneously to Ferrante. The pope and the King of
France accused Sforza of having consented to the imprisonment of Piccinino; Sforza wrote a long letter of
sorrow and expostulation to Naples, and to gain more
credit for his innocence he stopped the marriage train
of Ippolita at Siena, and sent his son Tristan to demand
the liberation of the prisoner. On July 7 a battle took
place between the Arragonese and the Angevin fleets in
the Bay of Naples. Ferrante was victorious. It was
said that Piccinino, anxious to see what was going on, had
climbed upon a table in his cell and had fallen down
and broken his leg. Certainly he died a few days afterwards, in all probability strangled by order of Ferrante.
Tristan wrote from Naples to urge that Piccinino being
dead could not be brought to life again, and that Ippolita's marriage had better be concluded. The Pope, the
Florentines and Ferrante joined in the entreaty, and Ippolita entered Naples on September 14, 1465. The letters
found by Buser in the National Library at Paris and
published by him in 1879 leave no doubt that Sforza
was privy to this disgraceful act of treachery.

Sforza's last enterprise was to assist his friend Louis XI.
in the war against his vassals which ended with the peace
of Conflans. For this purpose he sent his eldest son Galeazzo Maria to command his troops, and the young prince
was permitted to don the *Fleur de lis* of France as an
addition to his arms. Francesco died after two days' illness on March 8, 1466, at the age of sixty-five.

CHAPTER V

THE affairs of Florence now claim our attention. After the return of Cosimo de' Medici in 1434, his great object was to confirm his relations both at home and abroad, and to establish them in the fullest security. He found a favourable field ready for him in Florence, as his party had prepared the way for him. The heads of the hostile factions had been banished, and many of their supporters had been executed. It was easy for Cosimo to claim the credit that during his term of office he had exiled no one and done no one any harm. This was not so much from any inherent gentleness of character or from any especial dislike of violence or bloodshed, but from calculating cunning. He knew how to allow others to give the laws a character which secured his own position, without taking harsh measures himself. The two principal instruments he employed for this purpose were Puccio Pucci and Luca Pitti. The family of Pitti had been established in Florence for about a hundred and fifty years, and was destined to make way by its fall for the rising greatness of the Medici. Cosimo had also friends of a different character. Among these was Neri Capponi, who played the part of moderator to his party. Another important friend was Agnolo Acciajuoli, one of a family which reached its highest point of distinction under the Angevin sovereigns of Naples. Agnolo's ancestors had been Dukes of Athens, and of Corinth. The object of his political activity was to favour the rise of his party in Florence, but to oppose himself to the rise of a single family or a single individual. He was therefore not in complete agreement with Cosimo, but was notwithstanding one of the most brilliant and distinguished members of the Medicean party. Another of the same family was Donato Acciajuoli, who was only six years old at the return of the Medici, but who played in early life an important part in state affairs. Other most active supporters of the Medici were the Giugni, who had persistently maintained their devotion to the Guelph cause, the Pandolfini, for whom in later times the painter Rafaelle Sanzio designed a magnificent palace, and the Guicciardini, one branch of which left the party of the Albizzi, to which they had been before devoted, and joined the Medici. From them sprung a few generations later the famous historian Guicciardini. The strength of these families, although they supported Cosimo on the one hand made his position more difficult on the other. He was obliged to keep himself in the back-ground.

The first measure of Cosimo was to fill all the offices with his own adherents. He also took a singular method of excluding the *grandi* from power. He procured the abrogation of the laws which afflicted them with civil disabilities and made them eligible to all offices. The consequence of this was that they were not elected to any office, and were excluded from those offices which had before been specially reserved for them. He raised men to power who were of no consequence or position, and showed the most bitter harshness to his political enemies. Palla Strozzi was banished and compelled to die in exile, while his relations the Bardi were reduced to absolute poverty. Rinaldo degli Albizzi was exiled first to Jesi in the neighbourhood of Ancona, then to Naples, then to Trani on the coast of Apulia. Having no hope of returning to their country except by force, these exiles joined Filippo Maria Visconti in his attack upon Florence. But their plans were shattered by the battle of Anghiari in 1440. They were declared infamous and their portraits were painted hanging with signs of infamy on the walls of the Bargello, the palace of the Podestà. If such was the severity of Cosimo towards his enemies he was not the less anxious that none of his supporters should become too powerful. It is suspected that in 1441 he caused the death of Baldaccio d' Anghiari, a distinguished condottiere leader, in order to weaken the influence of Neri Capponi, who was a great friend of this soldier. In 1444 Cosimo, being Gonfaloniere della Giustizia for the third time in the months of September and October, established a new reform proposed by his friends, called the Balia of the Eight Citizens, with the object of keeping all offices in the hands of the Medici party. This lasted till 1455 when Cosimo, thinking that his power was now sufficiently confirmed, re-established the election of magistrates by lot. Under this new system, which lasted till 1458, his power continued really unimpaired, because the bags from which the lots were drawn only contained the names of his own adherents. In 1458 a revision of the method of rating property was proposed, as the existing rate had not been altered for five-and-twenty years, although during this interval the wealth of Florence had very largely increased. This was naturally resisted by the rich and they had recourse to Cosimo to prevent it. Cosimo did not put himself forward, but he allowed Pitti, who was made Gonfaloniere for the purpose, to take the burden and the odium of opposing the measure. This caused an uproar. The great bell of the Palazzo Vecchio was sounded, the people thronged into the Piazza della Signoria, a Balia was formed like that of 1444, and all the citizens who had opposed the change were tortured or put in prison.

In April, 1459, Pope Pius II came to Florence on his way to Mantua where, as we have heard, he had summoned an assemblage of the princes of Christendom to determine upon a commencement of operations against the Turks, Young Galeazzo Maria, eldest son of Francesco Sforza, was there at the same time, and it is recorded that a giraffe, then a very uncommon animal, was exhibited for his amusement. Whilst the Pope was at Florence a very celebrated man died there, the Archbishop of the town, Antonio, generally called Antonino partly out of affection and partly from his short stature. He lived the simplest life, had no property, and spent his time in doing good and in writing works of morality and devotion. Sant' Antonino now shares with the Virgin and St. Mark the honour of protecting the city of Florence. In 1459 changes again took place in the government with regard to the election of magistrates, which proved a new victory for the Medicean party. Cosimo died at the age of seventy-five, worn out by long infirmities, at his villa of Careggi, near Florence, on August 1, 1464. A few months before he had buried the younger of his two sons, Guiliano, and an infant son of Guiliano's as well. There only remained to him his elder son Piero, who had two sons, Lorenzo, afterwards known as the Magnificent, and Guiliano, one fifteen the other eleven years of age. Cosimo had been accustomed to depend on Guiliano rather than on Piero, because Piero had bad health and had long been a martyr to the gout. Weighed down by these losses he exclaimed as he was carried into his vast and desolate palace that it was too large a house for such a family. Lorenzo the younger brother of Cosimo had died in 1440. His descendants lived in comparative obscurity so long as the elder line lasted, but when this died out in 1537 with Alessandro, a mulatto, the bastard son of Pope Clement VII., Cosimo the head of the younger branch succeeded and became first Grand Duke of Tuscany in 1569.

Cosimo wished his funeral to be simple, but he was too distinguished a man not to be the object of a national mourning. He received the title of Pater Patriae, the Father of his Country, which is inscribed upon his tomb in the Church of San Lorenzo at Florence. He was the great banker of Europe. The name of the Casa Medici had much the same reputation in Europe as the name of Rothschild has in our own day. He lent a large sum of money to our own king Edward IV. But no one ever made a more noble use of his wealth. He performed material services to the most distinguished men of his age. It was in recognition of this that Pope Nicolas V. made him the banker of the Holy See, and in the year of Jubilee 1450 Cosimo held on account of the Pope more than 100,000 ducats. He paid great attention to agriculture, but the magnificence of his taste showed itself principally in buildings. His great palace at Florence in the Via Larga, still exists. Besides this he built numerous

villas at Careggi, at Fiesole, at Trebbio, and at Caffaggi-
volo. He constructed a library at Venice and restored an
Italian college at Pavia. The branch of the Medici bank
at Milan directed by one of the Portinari was famed as
one of the most elegant and sumptuous palaces in the town.
He built or enlarged numerous churches and convents,
notably the basilica of San Lorenzo and the church and
convent of Saint Mark at Florence, the Abbey and convent of San Domenico at Fiesole, and a convent for Franciscans on the hills near his villa. Even at Jerusalem he
established a hospital for poor pilgrims. He said " I know
not the humours of this city. Before fifty years we shall
all be exiled, but these buildings will remain." Cosimo
was a contemporary of many Florentines whose names
are familiar to all who know anything of art, Brunelleschi
who reared into the air the marvellous dome of the Cathedral of Florence, a dome higher and more imposing
than that of Michael Angelo at Rome; Donatello the
sculptor, whose statues have every attribute of life except-
ing those of speech and motion; Luca della Robbia, who
after carving one exquisite frieze of dancing, singing and
playing children, devoted himself for the rest of his life
to modelling saints and virgins in coloured pottery; Ghiberti, who spent the whole of a long life in making two
pairs of gates for the Baptistry at Florence, of which
the second pair are a wonder of the world and are worthy,
as Michael Angelo said, to be the gates of Paradise.
Cosimo stood in the midst of these learned men, who received the new learning as it came like a fugitive from the
East, and distributed its riches through the rest of Europe.
In the convent of S. Mark he founded the first public library
open to the use of all students, he opened another at the

Abbey of Fiesole; the manuscripts in his own private collection formed the foundation of the great Laurentian Library so famous throughout the world. It is scarcely too much to say that if this library did not exist we should be without the best authorities for the text of Æschylus, Sophocles, Appollonius Rhodius, Thucydides, Herodotus and Vergil. His secretary records that his master finished the copying of two hundred volumes in twenty-two months. His treasure-chambers were full of carved gems, vases, coins and jewels; he received the learned Greeks who fled from the advancing Turk, Argyropulos, Chrysoloras and others. He raised the great scholar Marsilio Ficino from the position of a poor and humble youth, and gave him a house in the town, and a little villa at Careggi. Lorenzo has left on record that between the years 1434 and 1461 Cosimo spent 663,705 florins, equal to as many pounds of our money, in alms and buildings and public gardens, and he adds that he thought the money had been well invested and that he was quite content. Such is the man of whom Macchiavelli says that he surpassed all others of his age, not only in authority and riches, but also in liberality and prudence, because amongst all the other qualities which made him the first man of his country, he was above all other men liberal and magnificent.

After the death of Cosimo the most important members of the Medicean party were Agnolo Acciajuoli, Dietisalvi Neroni, and Luca Pitti. They thought that it was very doubtful whether Piero with his ill health would be able to manage so large and cumbrous a business, and they expected to succeed in undermining his influence in order to prepare the way for their own. Cosimo had directed his son to take the advice of Neroni both in public and private affairs, and he recommended Piero to recall a great deal of the money which had been lent lavishly to private citizens, hoping thus to ruin his popularity. He then proceeded to further measures; he formed a conspiracy with the other three, the object of which was to estrange Piero from the Sforzeschi, and to abolish the appointment of offices by the balia, and to have recourse to the lot. This proposition was carried with only five dissentient voices. In November, 1465, Niccolò Soderini became Gonfanloniere della Giustizia, an occasion comparable to that in May, 1376, when Salvestro de' Medici was carried in triumph into the public palace, and laid the foundations of the greatness of his house. Soderini was very likely not actuated by personal ambition, but by the desire to restore liberty and to prevent the predominance of a single family in the State. His party was called "del Poggio" or "the hill", deriving its name from the hill of St. George on which Luca Pitti's house stood, that huge building, once the palace of the Ducal Medici, and now of the Kings of Italy. The Medici party was called the party "del Piano" or of "the plain", names which recall the factions of ancient Greece. Soderini found that he could effect very little. He summoned two meetings of the citizens, one of five hundred and one of three hundred, and sought their advice. But every one had a different plan to propose. He tried to abolish the "Council of a Hundred" a recent creation of the Medicean party, but he could not succeed. He then proposed to examine the accounts of those who had administered the government, but this Luca Pitti would not agree to. His office came to an end before he could do anything except to refill the bags which contained the names of candidates for office. The death of Francesco Sforza on March 8, 1466, seemed to deprive the Medici of their chief support in Italy. During the first six months of 1466 the two parties stood and watched each other. The Hill party knew not where to turn for allies. Milan and the other chief Italian powers were friendly to the Medici, Pope Paul II who had succeeded Pope Pius II was neutral, their only hope seemed to lie in the Republic of Venice which was occupied by its struggle against the Turks. They opened negotiations with Bartolomeo Colleoni, of Bergamo, the great condottiere leader, whose magnificent equestrian statue stands in the Square which fronts the School of St. Mark at Venice. They also thought of inciting René of Anjou to hold in check King Ferrante of Naples, and Acciajuoli did actually unite for the assistance of Borso d'Este, Duke of Modena. He despatched his brother Ercole d'Este with 800 cavalry, 2000 infantry and 1000 archers. They were already on the march when Piero was informed of his danger by the Lord of Bologna and the Duke of Milan. Piero narrowly escaped being killed by the conspirators. A plan had been formed to cut him down as he returned from his villa at Careggi into Florence. There is a tradition that his young son Lorenzo saved his father's life by riding quietly along the roadway as if his father were following, and so keeping the conspirators in expectation, whilst Piero reached Florence by another route. He went immediately to the Signoria and told them of the danger which threatened. He took no strong measures against his adversaries, but even tried to win over Luca Pitti by promising that Lorenzo should marry his daughter and that he should have an important place in the government.

By this means he avoided an outbreak of civil war.

The new priors who entered on their office on September 1, 1466, were all favourable to the Medici. The bell was sounded and the people were summoned to a parliament. The result of this was that the appointment to offices by nomination was restored for ten years, and the heads of the Hill party were sent into banishment: Acciajuoli and his sons to Barletta, Soderini to Provence. The Archbishop, of the family of the Nerini, fled to Rome. Luca Pitti remained in Florence, but his punishment was worse than exile. His palace remained unfinished, his friends who had given him presents demanded them back of him, he died in obscurity, despised and neglected by all men. Thus "the prudence" of the Medici gained its ends. The authority which seemed personal in Cosimo, was strengthened and perpetuated in his son Piero, and marks a new epoch in the history of Florence, bringing the communal government to an end, and preparing the way for the Medicean Principate.

The Florentine exiles did not put up quietly with their defeat. They still continued their negotiations with Venice, and persuaded Bartolomeo Colleoni to join the Lords of the Romagna in campaign against Florence. To meet the general suspicion of danger which hung over the whole of Italy the ambassadors of Milan, of Florence and of King Ferrante formed a league at Rome for twenty-five years on January 4, 1467, giving the opportunity of entering it to Siena, Lucca, Lewis Gonzaga of Mantua, and even to the Republic of Venice of whom they were especially afraid. The Pope did not take part in it, reserving to himself liberty of action. The League of Rome chose Federigo Duke of Urbino as their Commander-in-

chief. The two armies of Colleoni and the league were
arrayed opposite to each other in the neighbourhood of
Imola, but nothing decisive took place. The new Duke
of Milan, Galeazzo Maria, was in the Camp of the League,
and his rank gave him an authority which his experience
did not justify. The Florentines contrived to induce him
to visit their city, where they entertained him with games
and amusements. In his absence the Duke of Urbino was
able to fight a battle. It was long and bloody but
indecisive. The Duke, when he returned to the Camp,
was very angry that an engagement had been fought in
his absence and withdrew his contingent. He had also
heard that Amadeus IX, the new Duke of Savoy, was
invading the dominions of the Marquis of Montferrat his
ally. This Duke, called the Blessed, did much to restore
the prosperity of his country, and was greatly assisted by
his wife Violante, the sister of Louis XI., King of France.
After the departure of the Duke the war continued to
smoulder, but both the Venetians and the Duke of Milan
were anxious that the conflagration should not become
too dangerous. At last on the day of the Purification of
the Blessed Virgin, February 2, 1468, the Pope published
a bull for the pacification of Italy, especially between
Naples, Venice, Milan and Florence ; each of these powers
was to accept the peace within thirty days, Colleoni was to be
made captain general against the Turks with a stipend of
a hundred thousand ducats, and was to restore the territories he had recently captured. Peace was finally made
in May with the exclusion of the Duke of Savoy.

Pope Paul II., of the Venetian family of Barbi, was a
very handsome man, proud of his appearance and fond
of pageants and fine clothes. He desired to assume the

6

title of Formosus on his accession and he laid great
stress on the external trappings of his position. The
jewels on his papal throne were valued at eight hundred thousand gold florins. To save money for this
splendour he turned out the copyists and scribes who had
swarmed in the Vatican during the reigns of his literary
predecessors. They rebelled against this treatment and
shut him up as a prisoner in the Castle of St. Angelo.
Without the culture of a Nicolas or a Pius he was just
as much of a pagan. The Vatican reeked with the greatest
pollution, and the pope celebrated his carnival with representations of gods and heroes, nymphs and Bacchanals.
On the other hand he deserves the credit of having re-
vised the Statute-book of Rome, and having established
judges of the peace to put down the system of wholesale
assassination.

The life of Piero de' Medici was now drawing to a
close. The exiles had lost all hope of returning to their
native land, and gave but little sign of their existence or
of their discontent. Florence was engaged in a short
war with the Pope for the possession of Rimini. Sigis-
mondo Malatesta, Lord of that city, died on October 9,
1468, leaving as his heir a bastard son, Robert. Paul II.
claimed the fief as escheated to the Church, hoping to obtain
it for his nephew, Agostino Barbo. Robert offered to
secure the city for the pope if he might be allowed to
drive out his step-mother Isolta from the possession of it.
The Pope consented, but soon found that Robert intended
to secure the city for himself; a war began in June 1469,
and Florence, Milan and Naples found themselves allied
against the Pope. Federigo of Urbino gained a decisive
victory for the Allies on August 30. The Venetians

were prevented from helping Paul II. by the terrible news of the capture of Negropont by the Turks, and His Holiness at last recognized the succession of the bastard son.

Lorenzo de' Medici was now nineteen years of age. As his father was kept in the background by illness the son came forward to take his place. By frequent travels in Italy he had come to live on intimate terms with the Italian princes. He had been received with royal honours at the courts of Ferrara, of Milan, of Venice, Rome and Naples. He took an active part in public affairs. His literary education had been superintended by Gentile d' Urbino and the Greek Argyropoulos. He had written poetry as a boy. Ficinus had initiated him into the philosophy of Plato. The Medicean Palace was the principal place of resort for literary men and distinguished foreigners. Lorenzo was large and well-formed in body, but an ill-shaped nose and a massive jaw deprived his face of beauty. His voice was harsh, his sight weak, and he was entirely without the sense of smell.

The former league was renewed by the Treaty of Naples on July 8, 1470. It comprised Naples, Milan and Florence as well as many smaller states. The Pope gave it his adherence towards the end of December. After the peace Lorenzo was able to quietly assume his own position. He persecuted one by one the Capponi, the Strozzi, the Pitti, the Alessandri and the Soderini, in short all the families of distinction which were not decidedly attached to the Medicean party. The severity displayed in their banishment and executions formed a strong contrast to the splendours of the Medicean Court. At the age of twenty-one Lorenzo married Clarice, daughter of

Jacopo Orsini, a distinguished Roman noble. To celebrate his betrothal a tournament was held in the square of Santa Croce on February 7, 1469, a very grand and magnificent pageant, which attracted lords and knights from the whole of Italy. Pulci, the author of Morgante Maggiore, a poem which excited the admiration of Byron and inspired Don Juan, gave a minute description of the festival in three cantos. Piero rode out preceded by nine trumpeters and a page with a red and white banner. He was accompanied by two giants in full armour and twelve young nobles on horseback. The dress of Giuliano, Lorenzo's brother's son, was valued at eight thousand ducats. Five pages followed him on horseback, then came drums and fifes, and lastly Lorenzo himself. He was clad half in armour and half in silk, and across his breast was a scarf embroidered with fresh and faded roses and the legend "Le temps viendra" in thickly clustered pearls. On his satin cap sewn with pearls he bore three feathers of gold lace set with diamonds and rubies, and in the middle a pearl worth five hundred ducats. On his shield was a diamond called Il Libro, valued at more than ten thousand ducats. His horse, a present from King Ferrante of Naples, had a saddle cloth of red and white satin also sewn with pearls. His dress worn in the tournament itself was different, and on it were conspicuous the golden lilies of France in an azure field. The victory was probably arranged for him beforehand. He says of himself that though he was young and not very expert, yet he received the prize, a helmet inlaid with silver surmounted by a figure of Mars, the god of war and the ancient protector of the city. These details have been dwelt upon to show how regal the state of the Medici had become and how far it had departed from the republican simplicity of earlier days.

Piero remained almost continually shut up in his villa of Careggi, racked by gout in every limb, entirely unable to move. Before his death he increased the dominions of Florence by the purchase of Sarzana which defended the territory of the republic on the side of Genoa, and rounded it off in that direction. He was never able to acquire the much coveted town of Lucca, which indeed was not united with Tuscany until after the middle of the present century. Piero died on December 3, 1464.

Just a year before this, the Emperor Ferdinand II. made an unexpected expedition into Italy under the pretence of performing a vow which he had made during the siege of Siena in 1462, but really with the object of consulting the Pope on the subjects of Milan, Hungary, Bohemia and the Turkish war. The Pope treated the Emperor with great condescension, and the Emperor was not able to assert himself. Christendom saw for the last time its temporal and spiritual heads walking together through the streets of Rome under the same canopy. Frederick took occasion of publicly depriving Galeazzo Maria Sforza of the Duchy of Milan, and invested a grandson of his own with the fief. The proposed measures against the Turks came to nothing.

The last act of Paul II. was to create his favourite Borso d'Este, Duke of Ferrara. He died suddenly on July 26, 1471. His servants found him dead in his bed; he had not even received the last sacrament. There is no doubt that he died of apoplexy, but the report was that "he was strangled by certain devils who held him fast."

He had carried out nothing of the designs of Pius II., and his only merit was to have increased to some slight extent the material power of the Holy See. His reign appears most favourable when compared with those which followed it. After his death the corruption and the degradation of the papacy proceeded with rapid strides.

CHAPTER VI

DURING the late years of this history we have often had occasion to record the malign influence of the Turks. While cities were struggling together in Italy, and pope and emperor were striving for the mastery, the nomad nation of the Turks, like a black cloud of locusts, or an irresistible torrent of mud, was slowly advancing and obliterating some of the fairest monuments of civilization and of piety. In the present day the sympathies of historians or politicians may be either for or against the Turks. Some admire them, some detest them, others, while condemning them, may feel that it is impossible to set up anything in their place. But four hundred years ago there could be no doubt about the matter, the military virtues of the Turks were equalled or surpassed by those of many European nations, while there could be no question as to their hatred of Christianity and their barbarous and savage character. The countries which were attacked by them were flourishing and prosperous, the coasts of the Levant were covered by the commercial fortresses of the Venetian and Genoese, who occupied the position once held by the ancient Greeks. Bulgaria, since used as a term of reproach, was a flourishing kingdom, the seat of a pure form of Christianity which extended its influence to the furthest limits of Western Europe. Bosnia was governed by a powerful feudal aristocracy. Servia was happy and prosperous under its native princes. Hungary held a proud position amongst the nations of Europe, and Bohemia and Poland played no inconsiderable part in the fortunes of the civilized world. A Slavonic Empire, Christian, civilized and powerful, united with Hungary, side by side with the great Teutonic Empires was then no visionary dream. All this was endangered by the impetuous advance of the Turkish arms. In those days communication of news was difficult, events happening in strange and distant kingdoms were hard to realize. The fate of Constantinople which might long have been foreseen, came upon men with surprise. Yet some of the ablest statesmen in Europe were alive to the danger. It is to the credit of more than one of the popes that they used every secular and spiritual agency to unite the strength of Europe in this great cause. But the popes were generally old men, and were permitted only a short reign; the Emperors were often weak and worthless. Venice, which ought to have stood as the warder of Europe, was occupied with her own ambitions, and when she made the effort it was too late. It has taken the labour of four hundred years of war and diplomacy to redress in part the disasters which were permitted to arise by the sluggish indifference of the age which we are now examining. It will not, it is hoped, be thought foreign to our purpose if we give some account of the origin of those Turks who have played and are destined still to play so large a part in the calculations of European statesmen.

The vast space of Central Asia from the Ural mountains to the sea of China and Japan, from the frontier of India to the ocean of Siberia, is inhabited by a number of nomadic tribes who at one time belonged to the same race and probably spoke a similar language. These are now divided into four great branches who cannot understand each other's language, but who resemble each other very much in manner and habit of life. The first of these are the Mongols, who made their earliest appearance in history under Zingis Khan in the first quarter of the thirteenth century. Even at that time the great bulk of his army was composed of Turks. The Mongols now live to the north of the great wall of China. The second is the Tungusians of whom the most celebrated tribe is the Mantchus who are the present rulers of China. In the third place come the Ugri, a Finnish race. These left their home in Central Asia at a very early period, and extended themselves over the Baltic and the coasts of the North Sea. From them are descended the Finns and the Laps and to them is by many scholars assigned the great race of the Magyars, the conquerors of Hungary. The last and largest of the four races is the Turks, who under different names inhabit a vast extent of country from Lake Baikal to the boundaries of the Greeks and the Slavs. We hear of them from time to time as Turks of Kashgar and Yarkand, as Kirghis or Uzbeks, or Turkomans, as Nogay Tartars, and lastly as Ottoman Turks.

The Turks first appear in history about the middle of the sixth century, when they descended from the slopes of the Altai Mountains and attacked the Avars. They sent an Embassy to the Emperor Justinian and received the envoys of Rome into their camp. About five hundred years later, A.D. 1033, another tribe of Turks or Turkomans conquered Persia, and the dynasty of Seljuk reigned over them for a little more than a hundred years. Towards the end of the eleventh century the Seljukian Empire split up into four parts, and the princes of one of these divisions conquered Asia Minor and founded the Kingdom of Roum. This kingdom is described as extending from the Euphrates to Constantinople, from the Black Sea to the confines of Syria, pregnant with mines of silver and iron, of alum and copper, fruitful in corn and wine, and productive of cattle and excellent horses. The capital of the new kingdom was fixed at Nicæa in Bithynia, distant only a hundred miles from Constantinople, the birthplace of the great creed of Christendom. Gibbon says of this striking change, "the divinity of Christ was denied and derided in the same temple in which it had been pronounced by the first general synod of the Catholics." The date of the consolidation of the Kingdom of Roum is 1084.

The conquest of Jerusalem by the Turks immediately after this gave occasion to the first crusade. The first result of this enterprise was that the Turks were compelled to remove their capital to Iconium, two hundred miles further from Constantinople. The kalifs of Bagdad and the various Seljukin dynasties were overthrown by the invasion of Zingis Khan which has been already mentioned. He retreated believing that he had left nothing but desolation in his track. But a little spark had escaped the deluge and was destined to become a mighty flame. A tribe of Turkomans from the banks of the Oxus had taken service under the sultan of Iconium, the chief of this tribe now ruled over four hundred families in the mountains of Bithynia. His son Ottoman, who should more properly be called Osman, has given his name to the Ottoman

Turks. In the last year but one of the thirteenth century, July 27, 1299, he invaded the territory of Nicomedia. Before his death he was able to hear that his son Orchan had conquered the town of Broussa, and this event which happened in 1326 may be regarded as the real beginning of the Ottoman Empire. It is not necessary for our purpose to follow the development of this empire in detail. A map of Central Europe in 1452 will show that the Osmanlis occupied all the western part of Asia Minor except the mountains of Pamphylia and Cilicia in the South. Philadelphia, which had long maintained its independence, had been forced to surrender it in 1390. The Ottoman Turks occupied the whole of Roumania, Servia and Bulgaria with the exception of the three-fingered peninsula of Chalcidia. The Dobrudska then as now, formed part of the Roumanian territory. Bosnia and Albania still preserved their independence, and Thessaly was a kingdom. The conquest of Constantinople was reserved for Mahomet II. the son of Amurath II.

His capital was at Adrianople. For the attack upon the stupendous walls of Constantinople he prepared a huge brass cannon capable of throwing a stone ball six hundred pounds in weight. A large breach was made in the gate of San Romano. On the evening of May 28, 1453, confused cries of " Allah illa Allah" and of " Kyrie Eleison" ran from the contending armies, and at daybreak on May 29 the assault began. All did their duty, but the Turks were the conquerors, and Mahomet II. entered in triumph the cathedral of Santa Sofia. When the Sultan ordered a search for the person of the Emperor Constantine, his body was found under a confused heap of Christian and infidel corpses.

The fate of New Rome called a blush of shame to the faces of the Christian princes of Europe. If the Emperor of the west could have led a host selected from every European nation from Sweden to Naples the Turks might have been driven back to the Euphrates. We have an animated picture of the feelings of the time in the writings of Silvius Piccolomini. "Christendom," he says, "is a body without a head, a republic without laws or magistrates. The Pope and the Emperor may shine as lofty titles or as splendid images but they are unable to command, and none are willing to obey; every state has a separate prince and every prince a separate interest. What eloquence could unite so many discordant and hostile powers under the same standard? Could they be assembled in arms, who would take the place of General? What order could be maintained, what military discipline could be enforced? Who would undertake to feed so enormous a multitude? What mortal power could reconcile the English with the French, Genoa with Arragon, the Germans with the nations of Hungary and Bohemia? If a small number enlisted in the Holy War they would be overthrown by the infidels, if a large number by their own weight and confusion." When all hope of resistance was at an end the powers of Europe vied with each other in their anxiety to make peace with the conqueror. The brothers of the last Emperor Constantine Palæologos, the princes of Chios and Lesbos, Calojohn of the house of Comnenus all submitted themselves. Servia sent a tribute of twelve thousand florins, the Genoese settled in Galata consented to buy the preservation of their rights from the infidel. The contribution of the island of Ragosa was doubled as a punishment for having received and harboured members

of the Greek Imperial family and Greek men of letters
on their way to Europe. Even the pride of Venice was
compelled to submit. In the capture of Constantinople
forty-seven Venetian nobles had been killed, many taken
prisoners and many Venetian families had lost their property.
The possessions of the republic in Greece were threatened,
and Jacopo Loredano was sent with twelve galleys to the
defence of the Negropont. The fiery-tempered Doge,
Francesco Foscari, would have declared war, but it was
thought better to temporize. The peace of Lodi which
followed on the capture of Constantinople had secured
tranquillity in Italy. Bartolomeo Marcello was sent as
ambassador to the Sultan and agreed to pay a small
yearly sum for the possession of Lepanto and Scutari, and
for security of trade. A resident Venetian consul, termed
a Bailo, was admitted into Constantinople.

This timely submission perhaps preserved Venice from
the fate of Genoa. The Ligurian republic, was, as we
have heard, torn asunder by internal dissensions. There
was no central authority strong enough to defend these
distant dependencies from attack. They were given up
to the Bank of St George only to be lost altogether. Kaffa
in the Crimea had to be surrendered; Amastris, the most
flourishing possession of Genoa in the Black Sea, was
depopulated in order to fill the empty streets of Constantinople. Famagusta, the possession of the Genoese in the
island of Cyprus, was conquered by the family of Lusignan
to be transferred to Venice at a later period. When Mahomet
II. saw that he was secure on the side of the sea, and
had nothing to fear from the intervention of Christendom,
he determined to turn his arms toward the north. Servia
was already tributary, but he wished to subdue it altogether,

and above all to gain the mastery of the great fortress of Belgrade which would thus became the point of departure for future efforts. He did not despair of success. But he was repulsed from the walls of Belgrade by the hero of Hungary, the great general John Hunyadi, the father of King Matthias Corvinus. The only regular troops at his disposition were three hundred Polish crusaders and a few German landsknechts, but with these he was able to put strength into an undisciplined rabble of fifty thousand men. The fleet of Mahomet was destroyed, he was severely wounded, and he retired, leaving 24,000 dead upon the field, and his tents and all his property as a spoil to the conquerors. The defeat took place in July, 1456. Mahomet was driven back to Sofia for a time, but two years later he succeeded in subduing Servia with the treacherous help of the native nobles.

The finest character in this dismal narrative of cowardice and incompetence is Scanderbeg, the ruler of Albania who maintained the independence of his native land during his lifetime. His proper name was George Castriot, and when Albania had been compelled in the reign of Amurath II to submit to the authority of the Sultan he went with his three brothers to Adrianople. Amurath treated him with great distinction and gave him a high command. He concealed his plans till they were well matured, and behaved as a devoted servant of the Porte. But when in 1444 the Turks were retreating before the columns of the Hungarians, he threw off the mask and was received with acclamation by the people. He was assisted by the Venetians, and in the battle of Dibra in the same year he gained a splendid victory, in which twenty two thousand Turks were killed. On the three days October 17—20,

1448, was fought the battle of Kossovo, or the Blackbird field as it is called—certainly one of the decisive battles of the world. After three days' hard fighting the Hungarians were entirely defeated, and even the valour of John Hunyadi could not save them, and Servia and Bulgaria were conquered at the same time. Yet Scanderbeg remained unsubdued. Behind the walls of Croya he laughed at the power of Amurath. All Europe looked on with wonder at his hardihood, and sent him presents and embassies of honour. Amurath II. died in 1451. His son Mahomet II. found Scanderbeg as invincible as his father had found him. In two successive years, 1455 and 1456, he completely defeated the Turkish forces, and in one war took three generals prisoners. Mahomet tried to get rid of Scanderbeg by treachery, but fraud was not more successful than force. He then made peace with him, but this was not of long duration. Year after year the old quarrel broke out again, and always to the advantage of the Albanians. When he died in January, 1467, at the age of 63, his country was independent, while the Venetians were losing one possession after another. Scanderbeg left his territory under the protection of the Venetians, but Mahomet made it a point of honour to obtain the place for which he had so long struggled, and he desired to have Albania as a starting point for the invasion of Italy. The Albanian Scutari was defended by Antonio Loredano with the greatest courage in 1447, and the Turks were forced to retire. But the respite was a short one. Four years later Scutari and Croya were captured by Mahomet II. and their possession was secured to him by the peace of Constantinople in 1479.

One of the transient intervals of peace with Scanderbeg

gave Mahomet the opportunity of completing the conquest of Bosnia. The country was torn asunder by intestine strife, not only political but religious. The king, Stephen Thomas (1443—1459) had wavered between submission to the Turk and dependence on the strength of Hungary. After his death the throne was contested by three competitors. Bosnia, like Bulgaria, was the seat of that rare form of belief called the Paulician heresy, which spreading westwards from the fastnesses of the Balkans had supplied Italy, Germany and Southern France with devoted martyrs. The Pope could not avoid taking part against the heretics, possessed though he was with a fiery zeal against the Turks. The country was completely conquered in the two years 1462 and 1463. The Paulician landowners allowed themselves to be easily converted to the Mahomedan faith, and it is said that the numerous Mahomedan proprietors who offered the keenest assistance to the occupation of Bosnia by the Austrians in 1879 were the descendants of Christian ancestors. Two years later the Herzegovina was incorporated with the Turkish Empire. The Montenegrins withdrew into their mountain fortress and maintained a war of independence against the Moslems for four hundred years until they were recognised by the treaty of Berlin. Wallachia was governed by a despot, Vlad IV., whose. cruelties were worse than those of any Italian tyrant. He is said to have put to death in a few years twenty thousand people of every condition, age and sex. He paid tribute to the Porte, but seeing that Mahomet had determined to conquer him, he made an alliance with Matthias Corvinus. After atrocities far worse than any which in the present century have been witnessed in the east, Vlad was defeated and went to live in Hungary, where he was kept in prison. After his death Wallachia became entirely Turkish.

The brother of the Emperor Constantine Palæologos governed the Wallachians with the title of despot or lord. The tyranny of the Sultan drove them to revolt, and the Peloponnesus was finally conquered in 1461. The proud race of the Palæologi sank into obscurity. The duchy of Athens once held by Walter of Brienne was now in the hands of the Florentine family of the Acciajuoli. They had been at first tributary to the Venetians, but since 1295 had owed allegiance to the Turks. Family quarrels and disputed succession gave Mahomet an opportunity of conquering the country in 1455. Thebes and Bœotia suffered the same fate. The Parthenon, which had been converted into a Christian church, was now turned into a mosque. A Turkish garrison took possession of the Acropolis. Thus in ten years from the time of his accession Mahomet had achieved the conquest of the whole of Greece.

It would be foreign to the plan of this work to trace the development of the Turkish Empire towards the East. Suffice it to say that the Byzantine Empire of Trebizond fell in 1462; Caramania, the eastern part of Asia Minor, was finally subdued in 1473, and that the Crimea including the Genoese emporium of Kaffa was conquered in 1475. But the struggle of the Turks with the great European power of Venice must be described in some detail. The islands of the Greek archipelago were all this time in the possession of various Frankish princes of Italian origin, chiefly Venetians or Genoese. Mahomet saw, that in order to extend his conquests over this region it was necessary to prepare a fleet. The fate of these small principalities was not uncertain, their absorption by the Turks

7

was only a question of time. They attempted to put off
the fatal day by paying tribute and by submission, and
whilst Mahomet was fully employed elsewhere he was
content to leave matters in a state of indecision. In 1462
as soon as he felt himself free he prepared for a powerful attack on Lesbos, then held by a Gattilusi of Genoa, whose
ancestor had married a princess of the Palæologi. An
opportunity was as usual afforded by family dissensions.
Lesbos was besieged and taken by storm on Sept 19, 1462,
and the inhabitants were killed or taken prisoners. The
Venetians were much blamed for allowing this island to
fall without attempting to defend it, but they feared to
bring upon themselves the scourge of the Sultan's power.
Pius II saw country after country and island after island
fall under the grasp of the Moslem, without being able
to rouse Christendom to the rescue. At last in 1463,
stimulated by the loss of Argos, the Venetians were persuaded to declare war. Argos and Corinth were soon
taken and lost again. The last sight which gladdened the
eyes of the dying pope was the sailing of a Venetian fleet into
the harbour of Ancona. It is true Paul II. was a Venetian
but Turkish diplomacy was then, as now, skilful in sowing
dissension between rival powers and in preventing union
for a common object. King Ferrante received a Turkish
embassy at Naples, and the Court of Milan accepted
presents from the Sultan. An alliance with Scanderbeg
gave the Venetians hope for a time, but their plans were
shattered by the defeat of both fleet and army at Patras
in the spring of 1467. Barbarigo, their general, was taken
prisoner and Vittore Capello, their great admiral, died of
a broken heart. The death of Scanderbeg in the same
year was another blow. The Venetians offered Mahomet II

peace, but he refused to accept it and the war continued. The conquest of the town of Œnos by a new Venetian admiral named Niccolò Canale roused Mahomet to a desire for vengeance. He determined to direct all his strength against Negropont, the chief possession of the Republic in Greek waters. This island, called Euboea in ancient times, lies along the north-east coast of Attica and is joined by a bridge to the mainland. The second and final storm took place on July 11, 1470, and on the following morning the island was taken. The inhabitants were treated with the utmost cruelty. The fate of this island produced scarcely less effect in Europe than the taking of Constantinople. Canale, the admiral, whose hesitation was thought to have lost the island, was sent into exile, and Pietro Mocenigo was appointed his successor. For several years the war continued in desultory fashion. Mocenigo succeeded in burning and plundering some towns on the coast of Asia Minor and in assisting the inhabitants to avenge themselves upon the Turks. But this kind of warfare was almost as disastrous to the Venetians as to their enemies. Commerce was interrupted, and the very purpose for which *emporia* had been established in the East ceased to have any existence. In 1471 the Turks carried the war into the Italian territory. They crossed the river Isonzo, pressed on to the Tagliamento and the Piave, and wasted fields and villages with fire and sword. At last peace became a necessity for the existence of the Republic. For fifteen years they had attempted to defend their hard-won possessions. Their commerce was now destroyed, the Moslem was ravaging their vines and mulberries, the coast towns of Albania and Dalmatia were threatened with destruction, their last possessions in the Levant were slipping from their hands, and Venice itself was wasted with a destructive plague. The nobles began to desert the sinking ship, and the Government had no other course open to it but to send Giovanni Dario with full power to treat for peace. The peace of Constantinople was signed on January 26, 1479. The conditions were hard. The Republic was forced to surrender Scutari and Croya in ˉAlbania, the islands of Lesbos and Negropont and the mountains of the coast of Morea, as well as to pay an indemnity of 150,000 ducats, and a yearly sum of 10,000 ducats as a compensation for customs and tolls. The Venetians by these means rescued their remaining commerce, secured the towns which still remained to them and were allowed to establish Bailes or Consuls in various parts of the Turkish states.

A short account of the manner in which the island of Cyprus passed into the hands of the Venetians may fitly conclude this chapter. In the year 1191 the island of Cyprus had been given by Richard Cœur de Lion to Guy de Lusignan in exchange for the kingdom of Jerusalem. It continued in this family till the death of John II., which took place in 1458. John left two children, a legitimate daughter, Carlota, and an illegitimate son, James. Carlota married, first, John Duke of Coimbra, and, secondly, Lewis Duke of Savoy. He was crowned in the cathedral of Nicosia on October 7, 1459, as the king of Cyprus, Jerusalem and Armenia. James with the help of some Egyptian mamelukes conquered the kingdom and drove Carlota out of it. The Genoese, who had an establishment at Famagusta, took the part of Carlota: the Venetians supported the side of James. Marco Cornaro, a Venetian settled in Cyprus, assisted James with money to conquer the island, and gave him his niece, Caterina Cornaro, in marriage, with a large dowry. She had previously been declared the daughter of the Republic and crowned as Queen. James by this means became the son-in-law of the Republic. The marriage took place in 1473, and a child was born in the same year, which was regarded as king of Cyprus under the name of James III. The infant, however, scarcely lived a year, and from 1474 to 1486 the island was regarded as Venetian. The islanders were worse off than ever, they had repulsed Carlota for fear of falling under a Savoyard king, but they now found themselves under the dominion of a Venetian Queen. A rebellion broke out in Cyprus and Mocenigo was compelled to conquer the island. Caterina after her husband's death lived partly at Venice and partly at Asolo where her palace still exists. The island remained in the possession of Venice although the titular Queen survived till 1510.

CHAPTER VII

AFTER the death of Piero de' Medici in 1469 Lorenzo succeeded practically to the government of the State. He felt the great burden which lay upon him and made use of the counsel of Soderini and others. Guiliano was of a quiet disposition and fond of pleasure, so that the chief burden of government fell upon Lorenzo. The government of Florence was arranged in the following manner. There was a Council of a hundred which elected officers called *accoppiatori,* who in their turn chose the Gonfalonieri. As Lorenzo was not satisfied with this arrangement he drew the bonds of power still tighter and on July 3, 1470, secured the election of new *accoppiatori,* who united to the previous body formed a Council of forty which elected the Great Council of two hundred. By this measure, which was carried when Agnello della Stufa was Gonfaloniere of justice, the lordship of Lorenzo began to assume a legal aspect. At the same time the Consiglio del Commune and the Consiglio del Popolo were abolished ; the office of Capitaino del Popolo was also done away with, and the position of the podesta became far less important than before. With respect to external relations, Lorenzo saw that no reliance was to be placed on the Venetians or on the Pope. The Venetians were, as we have seen, being hard pressed by the Turks, and were anxious to increase their possession on the *terra firma* of Italy in proportion as they lost them in the East. The Popes were generally old and capricious men and a sudden and unexpected death might at any moment change the policy of the papal curia. Therefore the surest alliances of Florence lay with Milan in the north and Naples in the South. The Medici were the great bankers of Italy as they were its richest inhabitants. Not only were they the depositories of wealth, which made it the interest of many Italian princes that they should not become insolvent, but they were the resource to which the hard-pressed and impecunious naturally turned in time of need. The archives of the Medici doubtless contained many begging letters in which the suitors were among the most powerful potentates in the world. Gian Galeazzo Sforza consolidated the Florentine alliance by a visit to their city in the autumn of 1471. He was accompanied by the principal personages of Milan, and by Bona of Savoy, his wife. Historians describe with minuteness the number and splendour of his retinue, and of that of his consort; the knights, the pages, the led horses, the very kitchen knaves dressed in gold and silver. This exhibition of royal splendour is not without significance. The centre of it was the son of a Condottiere leader, the grandson of a peasant adventurer, while the visit was made to a republic which could no longer feel shocked that a prince should visit one of its citizens in princely guise. When the Duke entered the Medici palace in the Via Larga he was astonished at the wealth and splendour of its collections, and felt that he could not hope to rival it. The more serious

Florentines were indeed disgusted that, the visit being paid in Lent, the feastings and junketings which accompanied it did not always respect the limit of the precepts of the church.

· After the death of Paul II. eighteen Cardinals came together in conclave on August 6, 1471, and three days afterwards elected as Pope the Cardinal of St. Pietro in Vincoli, Francesco della Rovere. He was born at Albizzola near Savona, the son of a poor sailor. He was general of the Franciscan order and was very learned on questions of scholastic theology. He was now fifty-seven years old, and was of a hot-blooded and determined nature. Sixtus IV., for this was the title he assumed, was inexperienced in politics, but he imitated his predecessors by contemplating a crusade against the Turk. But he was carried on by the irresistible tide of events, and during his reign the papacy began to assume a worldly character which was only surpassed in the time of Alexander VI. Under him we find a terrible development of that vice of nepotism which did so much to discredit the character of the popes, and which yet was almost inseparable from the part of a worldly sovereign. We must not consider this nepotism as merely the amiable weakness of an old man for his relations. It has also its political side. Without some such assistance the Court of Rome could not have held its own among the powerful and ambitious courts which were growing up around it. As the Roman *curia* under Calixtus III. had been Spanish, and under Pius II. Sienese, so under Sixtus IV. it became Liguerian. A few months after his accession he elected to the cardinalate Giuliano della Rovere, bishop of Carpentras, son of his brother Raffaele, twenty-eight years of

age. He was at a later period to become Pope under
the name of Julius II. At the same time he gave the
Cardinal's hat to Pietro Riario, son of his sister Bianca.
Girolamo, the brother of Pietro, was destined to pursue a
political career and to found a state as a man of arms. On
Pietro his uncle lavished all the resources of his favour.
He made him patriarch of Constantinople, Archbishop of
Seville, Florence and Mende, and gave him so many
benefices that his income amounted to 60,000 florins.
Two other nephews, brothers of Guiliano remained laymen.
Leonardo married a daughter of King Ferrante, and was
made prefect of the town of Rome, and Giovanni was
united to a daughter of Federigo, Duke of Molino. Girolamo Riario received as his bride Catherine Sforza, the
illegitimate daughter of Galeazzo Maria, and the lordship
of Imola was purchased for him by his indulgent uncle.

The life of Cardinal Riario was a short but a merry
one. No words can exaggerate the profuse and childish
luxury of his court at Rome. This is shown by the re-
ception he gave to Leonora of Arragon, natural daughter
of King Ferrante, who passed through Rome in June, 1473,
on her way to marry Hercules, Duke of Ferrara. The
square of St. Apostoli was converted into a banqueting
hall. The princess reclined like Cleopatra on the costliest
tapestries. At the banquet the waiters were clothed in
silk and the seneschal changed his dress four times. The
banquet was served with wild boars roasted whole in
their skins, goats, hares, fishes covered over with silver,
peacocks in their pride, pheasants, storks, cranes, stags, a
bear served up, skin and all, with a stick in his mouth, a
mountain which gave birth to a living man who came
out, looked at the people and went in again. Other dishes

represented the history of Atlas, the story of Perseus and
Andromeda and the labours of Hercules. Barley sugar
castles full of meat were stormed and their contents
thrown to the people outside, while sailing ships discharged their cargo of sugared almonds.

Cardinal Giuliano despised the folly of his cousin, but
there was some danger in it nevertheless. When Riario
went to Milan in 1473, where he found a fit companion
in the Duke Galeazzo, he entered into plans of far-reaching
ambition. A design was formed to make Galeazzo Duke
of Lombardy at the expense of the Venetian territory,
and in return Piero was to be made Pope. Sixtus was
either to be forced to abdicate or to be killed. On his
way back from Milan Cardinal Riario stayed at Venice,
where he was received with great honour, but he died
immediately on his return to Rome, Jan. 5, 1474, it is
said in consequence of his excesses. There was some
talk of poison having been administered to him either at
Venice or Florence, and this suspicion may have preju-
diced the Pope against the two cities. During the two
years of his Cardinalate the young man had spent 200,000
gold florins and was considerably in debt. His tapestries,
his silver plate, and his furniture which was valued at not
less than eight thousand ducats, passed to his brother
Girolamo. Leonardo della Rovere died in 1476, and his
brother Giovanni was made prefect of Rome in his place.
This growing degradation of the papacy was not witnessed
by the best and wisest of the Cardinals, Bessarion, who
died at Ravenna on November 19, 1472. He was as
upright and robust a man as he was a diligent and
learned scholar. He left a great collection of manuscripts,
which he gave to the library at Venice. He was born a

member of the Greek church, but became reconciled to the Latin church at the Council of Florence.

The luxury and pride of the new Italian princes, whether men of Milan, Florence or Rome, were not likely to pass without exciting energetic opposition. The Cardinal Riario, if he did not die of poison, might perhaps have fallen a victim at no distant period to private or public vengeance. The years 1476 and 1478 witnessed two murders of princes, both perpetrated in church, both with the design of satisfying private animosity and of overturning intolerable tyranny. The Duke of Milan was murdered in the church of San Stefano in Milan, the conspiracy of the Pazzi slew one of its victims in the cathedral of Florence. The cruelties of Galeazzo Maria Sforza almost exceed belief. A priest who had prophesied that he had only eleven years to reign, was starved to death by the Duke's orders, a man who dared to write a letter to the Duke's mistress had his two hands chopped off. Another offender was shut up in a chest and buried alive. A peasant who had killed a hare was made to eat it, skin and all, and died in consequence. The Duke enjoyed nothing so much as being present at executions. His lust exceeded all limits, and he took as much pleasure in the disgrace of his victims as in the gratification of his passions. In the time of Duke Francesco a certain scholar named Cola Montano had come to teach at Milan. He had a great enthusiasm for the history of Ancient Rome. He painted the effeminacy of Galeazzo in the darkest colours, and hinted that in a purer and more heroic age he would have met the rewards of his deserts. He sent some of the most distinguished of his scholars, among them Girolamo da Olgiate, to Bartolomeo Colleoni to learn the trade of arms, but they were immediately recalled. In 1474 Montano was imprisoned under the suspicion of having written some epigrams against the Duke, and this made him more bitter than before. In the following year he returned to Milan and met Giovanni Andrea Lampugnano. After this he quitted the city never to return. He was absent at the time of the Duke's murder, and therefore could have taken no part in it, but it is certain that the ultimate inspiration of the deed came from him. Lampugnano and Olgiate found an ally in Carlo Visconti, they met in the garden of the church of Sant' Ambrogio, devoted themselves under a solemn compact to the holy work and called upon the Saint to assist them in their enterprise.

The Duke Galeazzo Maria had just been engaged in a military expedition in the territory of Vercelli, and had concluded a league with Louis XI. of France with the assistance of Philippe de Commines, the celebrated historian. He returned to Milan on December 20, 1476, the eve of St Thomas's day, and had passed the season of Christmas in the usual festivities. On the day of St. Stephen, December 26, he desired to hear mass in the castle of Porta Giovia where he resided, but his chaplains had already gone to the church of St. Stephen and the bishop of Como could not satisfy his wish. He went to the church on horseback accompanied by the envoys of Ferrara and Mantua. He was clothed in silk and gold and had unfortunately no breastplate. As he entered the church Lampugnano went before him to clear the way. He then knelt down as if to ask a favour and plunged a dagger into his stomach. Olgiate stabbed him in the neck, Visconti under the shoulders. He died immediately, and was buried the same evening without ceremony in the Cathedral. Lampugnano attempted to fly, but his feet becoming entangled in the dresses of the ladies who thronged the entrance of the church, fell and was killed by the Duke's guards. The other two escaped, but were soon captured and executed. Olgiate who was only twenty-two years of age was torn to pieces with hot pincers. He gloried in his crime, and boldly declared that the Judge before whom he was shortly about to stand would pardon his other faults for this one act of virtue. It is reported that his last words were "Collige te, Hieronyme: stabit vetus memoria facti, mors acuta, fama perpetua." "Courage Girolamo, the memory of your deed will remain for ever; death is bitter, but fame is eternal." When Sixtus IV. heard of the death of the Duke he said: "To-day the peace of Italy is dead."

The conspiracy of the Pazzi was a product of various causes. In this plan was the desire to get rid of a "tyrant." This was an unlovely and unlooked-for result of the study of antiquity. The same feeling had driven Stefano Porcario in 1453 to form a conspiracy against Pope Nicolas V., and it caused the murder of Galeazzo Maria to be received in Florence with a certain degree of approbation. The principate was consolidating itself. This had been shown as early as 1474 by the harsh measures which were taken to suppress the revolt of Volterra. Relations had also become strained between the Florentines and the Pope, but the exact reasons of the quarrel remain in obscurity. The expedition of a condottiere general, Carlo Fortebraccio da Montone, son of the famous Braccio, in 1477 for the conquest of Siena is supposed to have had something to do with it. The Sienese suspected that the Florentines had connived at the enterprise, and they claimed the support of the Pope, Ferrante and the Duke of Milan. They revenged themselves by capturing the Castle of Montone on September 27. The Pope accused the Florentines of having made Montone master of Perugia and of having stirred up the war with Siena. At any rate, in February, 1478, there was a close alliance between the Pope and King Ferrante for the advantage of Girolamo Riario. Ferrante was to have Siena, perhaps Riario was to have Florence. Traitors were not wanting in Florence itself. One of the most powerful of the Florentine families was that of the Pazzi, who stood only second to the Medici in consideration and wealth. Cosimo had taken care to marry the sister of Lorenzo to Guglielmo de Pazzi. His elder brother Francesco was sullen, jealous and discontented, and watched eagerly for an opportunity of overturning the rival family. This local jealousy was fostered by the Court of Rome under the influence of Girolamo Riario, who was always stirring up his uncle to overthrow the power of the Medici. Francesco Pazzi was made the banker of the Holy See instead of the house of Medici. There was also another cause of quarrel. On the death of Filippo de' Medici, Archbishop of Pisa, in 1474, Sixtus IV. appointed Francesco Salviati to the vacant see. Salviati was a Florentine but not of the Medicean party, and Lorenzo refused to give him the possession of the Cathedral. The Pope had also wished to make him Archbishop of Florence, but Lorenzo obtained this dignity for his relative Rinaldo Orsini.

The conspirators found an instrument ready to their hands in the person of Gian Battista de Montesecco, a mercenary soldier in the service of Count Girolamo Riario. It is from his confession written down at Florence on

May 4, 1478, of which there is no reason to doubt the correctness, that we derive the best information as to the details of the conspiracy. The confession is especially important as throwing light on the question as to exactly how far Pope Sixtus IV. was implicated in the plot. The guilt of Girolamo's murder was generally ascribed to the Pope, but it is certain that he limited himself to the desire of a change in the government of Florence, and that he expressly forbade the shedding of blood. He said "I do not desire the death of anyone on any account, because it is not consistent with our office to consent to the death of anyone: and although Lorenzo is a villain, and is on bad terms with us, yet I do not wish his death on any account, but only a change of government." On Girolamo suggesting that the Pope would at least grant absolution after the deed, if it could not be effected in any other way, Sixtus replied, "Thou art a beast," and turning to Montesecco, told him that he must wrest the government from the hands of Lorenzo and that then "we will make of that republic what we desire, and it will aid in a great purpose of ours." Whether Sixtus ought not to have known that a change of government was impossible without murder is another question, and we must condemn him for being an accessory before the fact. The conscience of Montesecco was not appeased, and he asked the Count on another occasion if it was really true that his uncle consented to the crime. Girolamo answered "Do you not know that we can make him do anything we please." Troops were now brought up from the Romagna and from Arezzo to take the necessary measures when the deed was done. The plan was finally matured in the villa of the Pazzi at Montughi, another young cardinal being present, Raffaele Sansoni, sister's son to Girolamo Riario, who had been recently raised to the purple. The other conspirators were two of the family of Salviati, both bearing the name of Giacomo, Bernard di Bandino de' Baroncelli, Antonio Maffei of Volterra, a papal scribe, who wished to avenge in the person of Lorenzo the desolation of his native city. Stefano Bagnone, the chaplain of Giacomo de' Pazzi and Jacopo di Poggio Bracciolini, also Rinaldo and Gulielmo de' Pazzi the latter of whom had married a sister of the Medici.

It had been determined not to carry out the design unless both brothers were present, and the first plan was to effect it at a banquet given by Lorenzo to the new Cardinal Sansone, in the Medici villa at Fiesole, now the Villa Mozzi, but it was put off because Giuliano could not be present on account of ill-health. Politian tells us this, who was himself present at the banquet as the tutor of Lorenzo's son, then a boy of seven years old. It was then determined that the murder should take place on Sunday, April 26, in the Cathedral of Florence at the moment of the elevation of the host. In the morning Montesecco entered Florence with thirty mounted arquibusiers and fifty foot soldiers. The Archbishop Salviati went to the public palace with some armed men to drive out the priors. Montesecco had been told off to kill Lorenzo, but he refused, and Antonio of Volterra and Stefano Bagnone were put in his place. At the given moment, when it was assumed that both brothers were kneeling in adoration, Bernado Baroncelli, Francesco de' Pazzi and others fell upon Giuliano. At the first wound he attempted to escape, but his strength failed him, he fell to the ground and was soon despatched. Antonio of Volterra stabbed Lorenzo in the neck, but he defended himself with the assistance of the Cavalcanti family, fled into the sacristy on the gospel side, now decorated with the doors of Sansovino, and held his own against his assailants. The young Cardinal Sansoni, only seventeen years old, looked on in wonder at a scene of which he probably understood but little. The town rose to the cry of *Palle! Palle!* not for freedom, but against the murderers.

While this was going on, the Archbishop was at the public palace talking with the Standard Bearer of Justice, and waiting for the moment when the uproar in the street should announce that the deed was done. The Standard Bearer suspected him from his talk and arrested him. At the same time Giacomo de' Pazzi, occupied the gate of Santa Croce with Montesecco and his arquebusiers. He then went into the great square to rouse the people and to assist his nephew Francesco, who had been wounded. Finding that all was lost he first retired to his house, and then fled by the Santa Croce gate. The Archbishop Salviati and some others of the conspirators were hanged from the windows of the public palace, and the same fate befell Francesco de' Pazzi, who was dragged from his house naked and bleeding. The rest of the conspirators were executed. Montesecco was beheaded on May 4. Baroncelli fled to Constantinople, but was surrendered and executed December 29, 1479. Niccolo Vespucci alone escaped. Giovanni de' Pazzi was buried in the family chapel in the church of Santa Croce. A heavy rain fell on that day, which was taken to signify the displeasure of heaven that so notorious a malefactor should be buried in holy ground. His body was disinterred and laid behind the Murate. The rain continuing, his corpse

8

was again dug up, and after being dragged ignominiously through the city with scornful songs was thrown into the Arno. It was never seen again, and it was said that the devil had taken it. The property of the Pazzi was confiscated, the square in front of their palace received a new name, and the remaining members of the family changed, for the time at least, their arms and their appellation. The family still exists at Florence at the present day.

Giulano was the darling of the populace. He died unmarried, but left an infant child who was adopted by Lorenzo and who forty-five years afterwards became Pope under the name of Clement VII. He justified the conspiracy of the Pazzi by enslaving Florence and placing a dynasty of spurious and degenerate Medici on the throne. The conspiracy only served to increase the reputation of Lorenzo. Guicciardini concludes his account of the conspiracy with the following words: "Such was the end of civil dissensions and discords, one party is exterminated, the head of the other becomes lord of the city; his supporters and adherents become his subjects, the people and the state are enslaved, the principate becomes hereditary." Gino Capponi observed that all the great conspiracies which took place in Italy from the middle of the fifteenth to the middle of the sixteenth century ended in the same way, the Porcri, the Pazzi, the Fieschi, the murderers of Galeazzo Sforza, of Alessandro de' Medici and of Pier Luigi Farnese, the principates were not overthrown and the conspirators lost their lives. It is said that the young Cardinal never forgot the horror of that terrible hour. The pallor of terror clung to him until his death. He had been imprisoned on the day of the murder and was not set free till June 12.

The effect of the conspiracy on the Roman court was unexpected. Sixtus IV., instead of expressing his indignation at the crime which had been committed by his friends, launched the thunder of the Holy See against the city of Florence. He complained that an archbishop had been murdered, and a Cardinal legate imprisoned. He laid the city under an interdict and joined himself with King Ferrante for the destruction of the Medici. It is fair to say that his conduct roused the indignation of the Christian world. Venice, herself in the anguish of a terrible struggle against the Turks, Milan, Ferrara and Rimini, promised their assistance to Lorenzo. Louis XI., always well disposed to the Medici, gave his special sanction to the league, and sent the historian Philippe de Commines to represent him at Florence. He desired to summon a council of the church at Orleans and sent letters of expostulation to the Pope. The Emperor and Matthias Corvinus of Hungary also sent ambassadors to Rome to warn the Pope from his purpose. It is not necessary to follow minutely the fortunes of this war. Ludovico Sforza, the brother of the murdered Galeazzo Maria, called Il Moro, or the Moor, from his dark complexion, had seized the inheritance of his nephew, and there was some danger of his making terms with King Ferrante and so breaking up the alliance with Florence. Lorenzo determined on a bold course of his own motion, and without communicating his design he sailed to Naples, where Filippo Strozzi, belonging to a distinguished Florentine family, had a considerable business, and in three months he had produced such an effect on King Ferrante by his courtesy and manners, that peace was made between Florence and Naples. The Pope was furious at the news and determined to prosecute the war more vigorously than ever. But in 1480 the admiral of Mahomet II. conquered the Ionian Islands, subduing them with difficulty. He then suddenly crossed the narrow sea and began to threaten the coasts of Southern Italy. This probably disposed Sixtus to recognize the peace made between Lorenzo and Ferrante, which was solemnly published on the day of the Annunciation, March 25, 1480. The city of Otranto was besieged by the Turks on July 28, and was captured on August 11, the greater part of the inhabitants being put to the sword. The Turks then began to ravage the lands of Lucca and Brindisi. The Pope and the King now began to feel in earnest that the Sultan was knocking at their doors. The Pope prepared to fly for refuge to France. It was thought that Mahomet II., as lord of Constantinople, might claim for himself the whole inheritance of the Empire and stab the heart of Christendom by aiming a blow at Rome. However, on May 30, 1481, this victorious Sultan suddenly died. The conquest of the Ottoman Turks were checked for a moment by his death and Otranto was recovered. The terror inspired by its loss had disposed Sixtus IV. to forgive the Florentines. In December, 1480, they received solemn absolution for their offences. The doors of St. Peter were closed, the papal chair was placed in the loggia. The Florentine ambassadors having confessed their sins, knelt before the Pope and were touched by the sword of discipline and absolution. The gates were thrown open and they were once more allowed to enter a church.

Even before this final pacification, Lorenzo had taken care to modify the government of Florence so as to secure his own power. The councils of the hundred, of the people, and of the commune approved the election of thirty citizens who, together with the Priors, were to elect a Balia of two hundred and ten citizens of the age of at least thirty years. The thirty, the two hundred and the executive government were charged with making a scrutiny by which they were to select forty-eight other citizens chosen equally from the four quarters of the city. As the council of thirty might have the appearance of being too oligarchical, the *signoria*, that is the Priors and the Standard Bearer of Justice, determined a few days later to add to them forty other members. This was the origin of the council of seventy, which during the whole of Lorenzo's principate continued to elect the Priors and the Standard Bearer. This council proved a useful instrument of personal government in the hands of the Medici.

The four last years of the life of Pope Sixtus IV. were mainly occupied by two enterprises, the war against Ferrara and the attempt to exterminate the family of Colonna. The war against Ferrara, in which Venice was the Pope's ally, was begun by Sixtus IV. with the main object of securing a temporal principality for his nephew, Girolamo Riario. It was for this that he stirred up the cupidity of Venice, intending afterwards to cheat her for his own advantage. Naples, Milan and Florence acted together to protect Ferrara. The war raged most hotly in the South and in the North. On August 20, 1482, was fought the battle of Campo Morto in the midst of the deadly swamps of the Pontine Marshes. Rinaldo Malatesta of Rimini defeated Alfonzo duke of Calabria, eldest son of King Ferrante, at the head of the Neapolitan army. The result of this battle was that the Pope became tired of the war, and being threatened by the Emperor with another Council of Basel, and being afraid of the aggrandisement of Venice, he changed his policy and joined the alliance of Naples, Florence and Milan. The alliance was published on April 30, 1483. The war with Venice continued for some time longer. During its course the Republic made overtures to the House of France urging the young Charles VIII. to undertake the conquest of Naples, and to the Duke of Orleans the acquisition of the Duchy of Milan to which he laid claim as representing the family of Visconti. Peace was eventually concluded at Bagnolo in the neighbourhood of Brescia in August, 1484. The limits between the Milanese and the Venetian territory were laid down as those fixed by the peace of Lodi in 1454. Conquests on either side were to be restored with the exception of the Polesina, which remained in the possession of Venice. The Duke of Ferrara promised to make no more salt at Comacchio, which had been one of the chief causes of the quarrel.

The peace of Bagnolo was the occasion of great rejoicing at Venice, but it was received by the Pontiff with different emotions. When he heard the news on August 11 he was very seriously ill of gout. He was deeply affected and said that he had undertaken the war for the security of the church, and that he was deeply distressed that he had not succeeded in obtaining it. On the following day he died.

As we have said, the last year of his life was also occupied by a war with the Colonna of whom the Orsini were the hereditary rivals. The Orsini were adherents of the pope, the Medici and the league, whereas the Colonna were friends of King Ferrante. Now that the pope and king were friends it was rather difficult to find a pretext for war, but one was discovered in a strip of disputed territory. Open war did not begin till May, 1484, when Girolamo Riario and Virginio Orsini attacked the houses of the Colonna. They took them after a stubborn resistance, and captured Lorenzo Colonna, who had his head cut off on the last day of June. Five days before Marino had fallen into the hands of the pontiff, and on the last day of July Capranica also fell. That once powerful family was nearly ruined. The unexpected death of the Pope put an end to these designs. Count Girolamo Riario abandoned his war against the Colonna and in the first moment of terror took refuge in the Castle of Spoleto. He then returned to Rome while his wife shut herself up in the Castle of St. Angelo. The Colonna recovered Marino and Capranica and returned to Rome four days after the Pope's death, while the Orsini withdrew in their turn. For a few days it was impossible to perform the obsequies of the dead Pope, but the city became gradually quieter. On August 25, Girolamo's wife surrendered the Castle of St. Angelo to the Cardinals who met in conclave on the following day. There were twenty-five present, of whom the most influential were Marco Barbo and Giuliano della Rovere. Much authority was also possessed by Ascanio Sforza, brother of Ludovico the Moor. Barbo, finding that he could not procure the papacy for himself, joined with Giuliano della Rovere in procuring it for a Genoese, by name Gian Battista Cibo. He took the title of Innocent VIII. He was an inoffensive man who wished no harm to anyone. Perhaps the most remarkable thing about him is that he was the first Pope openly to recognize his children, of whom he had two, Franceschetto and Teodoridi, born whilst he was still a layman. Cardinal

Guiliano della Rovere, afterwards Pope under the name of Julius II., exercised a great influence at the papal court and involved the Holy Father in the intrigues of Europe. The only events which disturbed the serenity of Lorenzo de' Medici's declining years were the war between Florence and Genoa for the recovery of Sarzana which had been seized by them, and a certain participation in the Barons' war of Naples in which Lorenzo helped King Ferrante to put down his rebellious nobles, who on their side were countenanced by the Pope. This war of the Barons was a last attempt to preserve the feudal system against the encroachments of royal power and is analogous to the similar struggle which engaged the chief energies of Louis XI. of France. The family circumstances of Lorenzo were most prosperous. His daughter Maddelena was married in 1488 to the Pope's son, Franceschetto Cibo, but the marriage was saddened by the death of his faithful wife Clarice. His eldest son, Piero, was united about the same time to Alfonzina, daughter of Roberto Orsini, of the branch of Bracciano. His second son, Giovanni, was nominated Cardinal in 1489 at the age of twelve. This was done in *petto*, that is, in the breast of the Pope or secretly, and the appointment was not to take effect until three years afterwards. The boy was brought up at the university of Pisa, together with Cæsar, the son of the Cardinal Roderigo Borgia, one of the most notable and infamous characters in Italian history. They were both intended for the ecclesiastical condition, but their destiny was very different. Giovanni became Pope Leo X., and Cæsar Borgia died an exile, fighting in Spain. The solemn opening of the bull in the Abbey of Fiesole, the gorgeous ceremonial in the church of our Lady of the Flower, the departure of the boy cardinal for Rome all took place in March, 1492, only just before his father's death. Before he went his father took an affecting leave of him. He foresaw his own approaching end and felt anxious about the future of his son.

In a long letter which he wrote to him at this time he recommends to him piety and gratitude to God for the benefits he had received. He says: "You are now entering upon a scene of greater danger. I know that in going to Rome, which is the seat of all wickedness, you will find it very hard to carry out what I have advised you. But I remember to have seen among the cardinals some men of saintly life; follow their example, although there is but little virtue at the present moment in the sacred College." He recommends him again and again to adorn himself with the virtues which are becoming to a true Cardinal. "Use not too much silk or gold, prefer rather the charm of antiquities and beautiful books, and let your suite be noted rather for its courtesy and its learning than for its numbers."

After many years of suffering Lorenzo died at his villa at Careggi in April 8, 1492, at the early age of 43. His relations to literature and art do not strictly belong to political history. But it is difficult to imagine Lorenzo the Magnificent separated from Pico della Mirandola, from Politian and from Marsilio Ficino. He had grown up in a circle of learned men, drawn to his palace by the munificence of his grandfather. Ficino, who owed everything to the protection of the Medici family, was an ecclesiastic who endeavoured to harmonize science and faith, Platonism and Christianity. He edited a Latin translation of the whole of Plato's works, which was published in 1482 at the expense of Filippo Valori. Christoforo Landino translated Pliny, and lectured not only on Homer and Virgil, but on Petrarch and Dante. The first Florentine edition of the Divina Commedia, published in 1481, contains a commentary by him. Lorenzo's own poems were of a light and amorous character, he extended his patronage to Pulci, the author of the Morgante Maggiore. Another of the Medicean circle was Politian, whose proper name was Angelo Ambrogini da Montepulciano. Seldom has the world known so versatile an intellect. He wrote verses in Greek, Latin and Italian; he was a poet, a philologist, and a philosopher of the school of Ficino. He translated Hippocrates, Galen and Herodian and began a version of the Iliad. Giovanni Pico of Mirandola, was as his name implies, not a Tuscan, but with Ermelao Barbaro he enjoyed the hospitality of the Medicean House. He came to Florence in 1484, about the age of twenty. He was a Platonist of the school of Ficino, but he was also an eclectic, as is shown by the nine hundred theses which he proposed to defend at Rome. Thirteen of them were found to be heretical, and the Pope forbade the controversy. Lorenzo founded a museum of antiquities and collected a valuable library. He profited much by the sale of the library of Matthias Corvinus in 1490. He used to spend thirty thousand ducats a year on books. His patronage of art extended itself to Sangallo the architect, Verocchio the sculptor, the painters Lippino Lippi and Domenico Ghirlandaio. The mighty name of Leonardo da Vinci is also connected with that of Lorenzo. By his assistance Leonardo studied the remains of ancient art in the Medicean garden of St. Mark.

The malady from which Lorenzo had so long suffered

began to grow much worse at the beginning of April 1492. His last days were enriched by the conversation of his son Pietro, of Ficino, of Pico, and above all of Politian. Presages announced the coming catastrophe; above all the dome of our Lady of the Flower was struck by lightning. Fra Girolamo Savonarola, of whom an account will be given in a later chapter, came to schrive him in his dying hours. We do not know for certain what passed between them. It is said that before Savonarola would give him absolution he asked three things of him, to have faith in God, to restore what he had wrongly taken, and to give back liberty to his country, and that the dying man assented to the first two but refused the third, upon which absolution was denied him. The story is inconsistent with the account given by Politian, the intimate friend of Lorenzo, and it is probable that the tyrant received absolution from the monk. Pope Innocent VIII. did not long survive him. He died on July 25, 1492.

CHAPTER VIII

CHARLES VIII IN ITALY

THE year 1492 is an important date not only in the history of Italy, but in the history of the world. The expedition of Charles VIII., King of France, into the Italian peninsula is generally regarded as the close of the middle ages and the beginning of modern times. From that event it becomes possible to regard the history of Italy as a whole, and to survey the entire system of European states from a single point of view. This year, as we have seen, witnessed the death of Lorenzo de' Medici, and of Pope Innocent VIII. The one removed an influence which had preserved peace in Italy and prevented suppressed passion breaking out into wild excess; the other was followed by the accession of Alexander VI., the Pope who has helped to give a meaning of horror to the name of Borgia. The same year saw the final expulsion of the Moors from Spain, which allowed that country to assume a leading place in the affairs of Europe, while the following year is signalized by the discovery of America by Columbus.

The immediate cause of the expedition of Charles VIII., which wrought so momentous a change, lay in the circumstances of the duchy of Milan, and to the history of

Milan we shall now recur. After the murder of Galeazzo
Maria in 1476, his son, Gian Galeazzo, was proclaimed
Duke, being at that time eight years old. Gian Galeazzo
had a brother, Erone, a year younger than himself, and
two sisters, one Bianca Maria, betrothed to Filibert of
Savoy, and the other Anne, who was intended to marry
a prince of the Court of Ferrara. The Duchess Bona
assumed the guardianship of her son in January, 1477,
and her most trusted minister was Cicco Simonetta, a
Calabrian, who had been secretary to Galeazzo Maria and
to Francesco Sforza. The murdered Duke had left five
brothers. Of these Filippo Maria and Ottaviano were in
Milan, and three others had been banished, Ascanio to
Rome, Ludovico Il Moro and Sforza Maria, Duke of Bari,
to France. On returning to Milan they found the Duchess
and Simonetta established in their places. They immediately formed a party against their sister-in-law, but by
the mediation of Ludovico Gonzaga, Duke of Mantua, and
the assistance of the Pope and the Florentines, peace was
for the present preserved. The uncles obtained not only
an annual pension, but a fortress and a palace in Milan
for each. The young Duke was solemnly crowned, with
the approbation of the Emperor, on St. George's Day,
April 23, 1478. Just before this, Giuliano de' Medici had
been murdered in the conspiracy of the Pazzi, and in the
war which ensued the Duchess lent assistance to the
Florentines. The Pope and King Ferrante succeeded in
stirring up the Swiss to fight against the Duke of Milan.
The men of Uri crossed the St. Gothard pass into the
Valle Levantina: Bellinzona, an old possession of the Visconti, was besieged, and the battle of Giornico, fought in
November, 1478, was a severe defeat for the Milanese.

About a year after this Ludovico Il Moro, who was in open alliance with the King of Naples, managed to come to terms with his sister-in-law, and entered Milan. He soon persuaded her to dismiss her faithful servant Simonetta, who was imprisoned at Pavia for a year and then beheaded. On his tomb in the Church of St. Aporlinare were carved the following lines:—

> "My country's faithful servant and my Lord's,
> I perished by the guile of treacherous words."

Ludovico then proceeded to sow dissension between the young Duke and his mother, and eventually drove her away from the capital. On November 3, 1480, Ludovico Il Moro was solemnly appointed guardian of his nephew and regent of the duchy. From this moment Ludovico, already Duke of Bari, after the death of his brother, was virtually Duke of Milan in everything but name.

Nothing of any great importance happened for several years. In October, 1488, the city of Genoa was formally given up to the Moor, who received the banner of St. George, the sceptre, the keys, and the seal of the Commune. Thus perished the independence of that ancient republic. The young Duke of Milan had been betrothed at a very early age to a Neapolitan princess, Isabella, the daughter of Alfonzo, Duke of Calabria. As he grew up to manhood King Ferrante demanded the fulfilment of the contract, but under various pretences Il Moro continued to put it off. At last he could defer it no longer, and on February 1, 1489, the fair Neapolitan princess was received with all honour in the Castle of Milan, and the marriage was celebrated. The young couple established themselves at Pavia, and early in 1491 a son was born to them who received the name of Francesco Sforza. Isabella was endowed both with courage and with wisdom, but her husband, although of mild and excellent character, had been purposely left uneducated, and had no experience in affairs. The Moor was very sorry that he had ever allowed his nephew to marry, and he determined to conclude a double alliance with the house of Este. He married Beatrice, daughter of Ercole, Duke of Ferrara, and gave his niece, Anne, to the Duke's eldest son. This made matters worse. Beatrice was devoted to pomp and luxury. The two brides quarrelled with each other. Isabella was compelled to live with her husband in the dull imprisonment of Pavia, whilst Milan was full of wealth and hilarity. Tournays, jousts, and pageants were the order of the day, the machinery for which was often designed by the cunning hand of Leonardo da Vinci. Isabella complained to her grandfather, but without effect.

Ludovico had the keenness to perceive that his power needed strengthening. He bethought him that the right of the Sforzas to the duchy of Milan had never been formally confirmed by the Empire, and he thought that this confirmation might be conveniently effected in his own person. He therefore entered into an arrangement with Maximilian, son of the Emperor Frederick III., by which he promised his niece Bianca in marriage to Maximilian, on the condition that he, when Emperor, would grant Il Moro the investiture of the fief. This agreement was, of course, kept secret for the present. The support of Germany, however, was not sufficient. King Ferrante would certainly take the side of his son-in-law. So he turned for assistance to the quarter whence assistance had often come before, and persuaded Charles VIII., King of France, to revive his claims on the throne of Naples and march into Italy.

Charles VIII., the son of Louis XI., was thirteen years of age when his father died in 1483. During his minority the government of France had been conducted by the strong hand of his sister, Anne of France, commonly called Anne of Beaujeu, from the title of her husband. When he came of age he married, by a sudden change of policy, Anne of Brittany, and thus united to the crown the last great province which stood apart from France and saved it from the clutches of the house of Austria. We have a description of him as he appeared at this time from the Venetian Ambassador, Contarini. "The king is mean in appearance and ugly to look at; his great lack-lustre eyes see but little; he has a hooked nose, disproportionately large, and thick lips which he always keeps open. He is continually making awkward ungainly gestures with his hands, and is drawling in his speech. I may be mistaken, but I think that he is of little use either in body or mind." The claims of Charles to the throne of Naples were of two kinds. In the first place, he was descended in the female line from Charles of Anjou, King of Naples. The eldest son of Charles, called Charles II., or The Lame, or, in Italian history, Carlo Novello, had a daughter, Margaret of Anjou, who married Charles of Valois, the father of King Philip VI., from whom Charles VIII. was lineally descended. Again, Charles, Duke of Maine, nephew and heir to René of Provence, had, on his death in 1481, left all his dominions to Louis XI., from whom the claim passed to his son Charles VIII.

In order to obtain a free hand for his Italian expedition, Charles made peace with his enemies who were likely to interfere with him. He contracted the treaty of Étaples with Henry VII. of England, he yielded Roussillon for the sake of peace to King Ferdinand of Arragon, and he allowed Margaret of Austria, also for the sake of peace, to take back with her to Germany the sovereignty of Artois and Franche-Comté. The French people thought that the crown of Naples, if it was ever won, would be dearly bought by these sacrifices. The papal throne was at this time occupied by Roderigo Borgia under the title of Alexander VI. His election was unexpected. The principal cardinals at the death of Innocent were, besides himself, Raffaelle Riario and Giuliano della Rovere, the two nephews of the late Pope, and Ascanio Sforza, the brother of Ludovico Il Moro. Barbo, whom the Venetians hoped would receive the tiara, had died shortly before, and his countrymen believed that he had been poisoned by Ferrante of Naples. It is said that Borgia owed his election to bribery, and that four mules laden with silver were seen to enter the palace of Ascanio before the conclave. This story does not come from an impartial source. His character has been much disputed, and he had undoubtedly some good qualities. But after making all allowances for the character of the defects of the Renaissance, it is difficult to avoid the conclusion that his reign marks the lowest level of papal morality. Guicciardini tells that the King Ferrante predicted that Borgia would prove the curse of Italy, and in that he was not mistaken. The historian allows him good sense, eloquence, and capacity for affairs, but complains that these qualities were obscured by his dissolute life, his want of uprightness, modesty, truth, honesty, faith and religion, his insatiable avarice and ambition, his cruelty, and his unbridled anxiety for the advancement of his sons, who were as bad as himself. The Pope had five children, four sons and a daughter; their mother's name was Vanozza Castanei. The eldest son Piero Luigi was created Duke of Gandia by Ferdinand of Arragon. He died young, and was succeeded in his dukedom by his brother Giovanni. Cæsar Borgia came next. His father made him Archbishop of Valencia immediately after his accession, although he was not yet in orders, and shortly afterwards Cardinal. The Pope's daughter Lucrezia, of world-wide fame, was at this time a graceful, lively child of twelve years old with beautiful golden hair. She had been betrothed to a Spanish nobleman, but she was married at the age of thirteen to Giovanni Sforza, bastard son and successor to Costanzo, lord of Pesaro, who was a nephew of Francesco Sforza. The marriage was celebrated with great pomp on June 12, 1493. The Pope was present at the banquet, the ball, the play which followed and the songs, as well as the Cardinals and the Ambassadors of Venice, Milan, Ferrara and France. Previously to this, in April, 1493, an alliance for five-and-twenty years had been signed between Rome, Milan and Venice, to which the young King of France was invited to accede. Alexander's youngest son was Gioffredo. He married the daughter of Alfonzo II. of Naples, and received from him the principality of Squillace, in the south of Italy. The character of Lucrezia Borgia has been most unjustly abused. Her contemporaries describe her as high-minded, sensible, strong in character, highly accomplished, speaking and writing Spanish, Italian, French, Greek and Latin. The

plans of Charles VIII. were not unknown to King Ferrante. He sent Ambassadors to France to meet the coming
danger, but they were of no avail. He tried in vain to
obtain assistance from the Pope, who only replied that
the French were also good Christians. He also turned
to Venice, and even to England. A wiser counsel was
to attempt to rouse Piero de' Medici from his state of
torpor, and to urge him to arm the Duke of Urbino.
On January 17, 1494, he addressed one last despairing
appeal to Alexander, but a week after this the aged
monarch was dead. Ferrante and Lorenzo had been the
two princes who preserved the balance of power in Italy,
and now that they were gone ruin was inevitable. Ferrante was succeeded by his son the Duke of Calabria,
under the title of Alfonzo II. He was a man of no
courage or ability, and was proud, cruel and insincere.
His relations with Ludovico Il Moro were naturally of the
most bitter character.

Charles VIII. did his utmost to secure allies in Italy.
The two Marquises of Saluzzo and Montferrat on the
Italian border, promised their aid; Il Moro was able to
secure to him the advantage of the Genoese fleet; Venice
rejected his overtures, and remained neutral. Florence
adhered firmly to the alliance with Naples. But Piero de'
Medici was not a man of great ability. Fra Girolamo
Savonarola thundered from the pulpit of the Cathedral
that God was preparing some great punishment for the
sins of his country and of the Roman Court. The advance
of the French was too completely a fulfilment of his own
prophecies for him to call out the full energy of patriotic
zeal. The Pope, although he was in alliance with Milan,
yet began to become alive to the danger of foreign con-

quest. He invested Alfonzo with the kingdom of Naples in May, 1484, and a few days afterwards his son Gioffredo was married to Alfonzo's daughter Sancia. At the same time the Cardinal Giuliano della Rovere, having been summoned to do homage to the Pope at Rome, had taken refuge in France, and it is said that his advice gave the final impulse to the hesitating Charles. Charles had arrived at Lyons at the beginning of March; he left it on July 22, and a month later reached Grenoble. Here his queen left him, and he pursued his march to Italy alone.

Charles passed the Mont Genevrè on September 2, and entered Piedmont on the following day. His army was composed of 90,000 men; his navy of 450 ships. His most formidable arm, the artillery, was drawn by light horses instead of the oxen of the Italians, and was furnished with moveable carriages. It is difficult to exaggerate the importance of this event; it was a new attempt to conquer Italy by a foreign force after a lapse of many years. It was very different from those expeditions of the German Emperors to be crowned at Rome with which the Italians were familiar. To the French it was the discovery of a new land. They knew nothing of the wealth of art and culture with which Italy had adorned herself during two hundred years. The leader of the expedition was a weak, ill-shapen young man of twenty-two, who seemed incapable of commanding so brilliant an army, but his was only the arm to execute—the head which planned and directed the exploit was that of Ludovico Il Moro. Charles entered Asti on September 9. The Cardinal Giuliano and the Duke of Ferrara were awaiting his arrival. Thither came the Duke of Orleans to bring news to his cousin of his recent victory over the Arragonese fleet, and thither came

also the usurping Duke of Milan and Beatrice his wife.
Here the King fell suddenly ill. However, in a few weeks
he recovered, and after visiting his ally, the Marquis of
Montferrat, at Casale, came to Pavia, where on October 14
he visited the unfortunate Gian Galeazzo on his bed of sickness. The Duke was hot with fever, racked with a con-
suming cough, and evidently near his end. He recommended
to the King his young son Francesco Sforza, Count of
Pavia. However much the entreaties of the unfortunate
young man and of his wife Isabella may have touched
his heart, it did not change his policy. He was with the
Moor at Piacenza when, a week later, he heard of the
death of Gian Galeazzo, perhaps poisoned by his uncle.
Ludovico hastened to Milan, where he secured his election
as Duke.

The Pope, the King of Naples, and Piero de' Medici
in vain attempted to rouse Venice to action. She preserved
a complete neutrality and refused to lend the King 50,000
ducats, even at the request of Philip de Commines. As
the army passed through the Romagna the camps of the
French and the Arragonese were always one in advance of
the other, but the only engagements were insignificant
skirmishes. Caterina Sforza, lady of Imola, declared for
the French. The French now entered the Apennines by
the pass of Pontremoli, at the southern foot of which stood
the fortified town of Sarzana, which belonged to the
Florentines. Piero Capponi had, when he was sent as
ambassador to France, advised the Medici to conclude a
French alliance, but they hesitated to take so decisive a
step. Now Piero de' Medici, on his own authority, went
to the King, who was lodging in an abbey near Sarzana,
and yielded everything that he asked for. He promised

him 200,000 ducats and the immediate surrender of Sarzana, Sarzanella, Pietra Santa, Libra Fratta, Pisa and Leghorn as a pledge for the payment of the money. The King promised to restore them at the end of the expedition. The cowardice of Piero roused the Florentines to indignation. Capponi cried that it was now time to get rid of the government of children and to recover liberty. A new embassy was sent, of which Savonarola formed part. They found the King at Pisa, which he had entered on November 8 with 3,000 cavalry. The Pisans were only too glad to purchase the freedom of their city. They threw down the sitting lions, which were the emblem of Florentine supremacy, and cast them into the Arno. When Piero de' Medici returned to Florence he found the citizens united against him. He tried to approach the Signory, but the door of the Public Palace was shut in his face. His enemies rose in tumult; the party of the Medici were defeated in the streets, and the three brothers, Piero, Giuliano, and the Cardinal Giovanni, were driven from the town. After the departure of the Medici the citizens exiled in 1434 were restored, including the Pazzi; Lorenzo and Giovanni, sons of Pier Francesco de' Medici, were allowed to return, being thought to be on the popular side.

On November 17, 1494, Charles VIII. entered Florence. A canopy was supported by four Florentine doctors, and under this rode the King on a magnificent horse. His coat was cloth of gold, his cloak of blue, and on his head he wore an enormous white cap, so that he appeared as if he were nothing but horse and cap, being a little man, with a smiling face and a hooked nose, and plenty of soldiers round him. He bore his lance in rest as if he were entering a conquered town.

The terms finally arranged between the King and the people were that the Medici should remain in banishment and Florence should be free, the fortresses should be held by the French till the end of the war, and that the town should pay 20,000 gold florins in three instalments, towards the expense of the expedition. The King at first proposed much harder conditions, but Piero Capponi tore the paper in two and said, "Since you demand dishonourable things you shall sound your trumpets and we will ring our bells." From Florence Charles issued a proclamation, declaring that his real object was to march against the Turks, and that he only asked for a passage through the Roman territory. Alexander was in the greatest embarrassment. He knew how insecure his position was, that it was believed that he had obtained the tiara by simony, and that all his enemies were ready to rise against him. However, he boldly refused the passage. He forbade the King to advance any nearer. He fortified the buildings of Rome; he even packed up and prepared for flight. But the patrimony of St. Peter was undefended. Charles left Florence on November 28, and reached Siena on December 2, where he was joined by Cardinal Giuliano della Rovere. He reached Viterbo on December 4. He was received in a friendly manner by the Orsini, and lodged in the Castle of Bracciano. Alexander at last saw that resistance was hopeless. He sent away the Neapolitan garrison from the city commanded by the Duke of Calabria, son of Alfonzo, and came to terms with Charles. The King was to enter the city, but not to cross the Tiber into the Borgo, that is, the part occupied by the Vatican and St. Peter's.

The solemn entry took place on December 31. No one

was waiting for the army at the gates, because the appointed day was January 1, 1495. The King was attended by eight cardinals, among whom were Giuliano della Rovere and Ascanio Sforza. The procession lasted from three in the afternoon till nine at night; the greater part of it was conducted by torchlight. It must have been a wonderful sight; the motley Swiss with their huge broadswords and plumes, the ugly little Gascon archers, the gallant French cuirassiers, the thirty-six bronze cannon each eight feet long, the King, the most hideous of the human race, at the head of his forty thousand troops. There was some talk of deposing Alexander; in which case the world would never have heard of Cæsar Borgia, but the King had not strength of mind enough to effect it. The Pope shut himself up in the Castle of St. Angelo, and Rome was plundered by the French. At last, on January 15, 1495, a treaty was made with the Pope by which he surrendered to Charles Terracina, Civita Vecchia, Viterbo and Spoleto. Cæsar Borgia was to accompany the King in his enterprise against Naples. Gem, the brother of the Sultan Bajazet, who had been since the death of Mahomet II. bandied about like a shuttlecock amongst the princes of Italy, was to remain with Charles. Ostia continued in the possession of Cardinal Giuliano, and an amnesty was accorded to the disaffected cardinals. The effect of this treaty was to make Charles master of the States of the Church. The following day the Pope left the Castle of St. Angelo and returned to the Vatican, where the King came to do him homage. In return the Pope conceded the cardinal's hat to Briçonnet, Bishop of St. Malo. Pope and King then heard mass together in St. Peter's. One thing Alexander steadily refused—

to grant to Charles the investiture of the Kingdom of
Naples.

On January 28, Charles VIII. left Rome accompanied
by Gem and Cæsar Borgia. He marched along the Via
Latina, the same which Charles I. of Anjou had followed
two hundred and twenty-nine years before. His enterprise might to many have seemed Quixotic. Alfonzo had
the reputation of being the chief captain of his time, and
enormously wealthy. But, as Philip de Commines has
said, "Cruel men are always cowards." Alfonzo shut
himself up in his castle in a state of abject terror. The
waves as they beat against the foot of his palace walls,
the leaves as they rustled in the wind, seemed to repeat
the burden: "France, France." On January 21 he resigned the crown, and his son Ferrante II. or Ferrantino,
reigned in his place. The new King could make no
resistance. There was no fighting except a sharp skirmish
on the frontier. Ferrantino fled to Isernia, and Charles
entered the capital on February 22. A few days later
the unfortunate Gem died; the French falsely said poisoned by the Pope. Gem was the elder of the two sons
of Mahomet II. and if he had succeeded to the throne,
being a poet and a man of letters, he might have carried
out his father's design of fusing together the various races
of which the Turkish dominion was composed. But
Bajazet, being the first to hear of his father's death, seized
the crown. On June 20, 1481, the two brothers met in
battle on the banks of the river Jenischen. Gem was
conquered and put to flight, and took refuge in Egypt.
After a second trial of fortune, he determined to go to
Europe and to raise the standard of revolt against his
brother. He sought the protection of Pierre d'Oubussan,

master of the Knights of St. John in Rhodes, but he found himself little better than a prisoner, as each European power regarded him as a valuable hostage. D'Aubusson sent Gem to France and Bajazet had to pay a yearly sum of 45,000 ducats for his maintenance. Gem was anxious to escape. Ferdinand and Isabella of Spain, the Kings of Naples and Hungary, were all anxious to get hold of him. At last, after six years' spent in France, he was delivered over to the Pope. He entered Rome on March 13, 1489. In his first interview with Innocent VIII. Gem bewailed the bitterness of his lot, and expressed his desire to return to Egypt to the society of his wife and children. He shed copious tears and the Pope was much affected. After the death of Innocent he was shut up in the Castle of St. Angelo. The death of Gem was a great misfortune to Charles, who had to give up his Turkish plans, and by it the Pope lost forty thousand ducats which he received every year from Bajazet for his brother's maintenance.

Charles had conquered Naples at a single blow, and his success seemed little short of miraculous. But while he was enjoying himself in that delightful city a storm was rising behind him. Already the ambassadors of Ferdinand of Arragon had torn up before his face the treaty of Barcelona, saying that it was broken by Charles's attack on Naples. Il Moro began to be afraid that the Duke of Orleans might claim Milan and that the French might occupy the whole of Italy. Ferdinand of Arragon dreaded the loss of Sicily; Maximilian could not forget that Italy had once owed allegiance in great part to the Holy Roman Empire. Ambassadors from these discontented powers met in Venice, where Philippe de Commines, the historian, represented France. A league was formed, ostensibly against the Turks but containing secret articles for the restoration of Ferrantino. The parties to it were the Emperor Maximilian, Ludovico Il Moro, Ferdinand of Spain, and the Pope. Henry VII. of England entered it a little later. It was to last five-and-twenty years. In the event of a war in Italy each power was to contribute eight hundred cavalry and four thousand infantry, except the Pope, who was only to provide half that number. If Maximilian came into Italy to receive the Imperial crown, Venice and Milan were each to send four hundred men-at-arms. The league was solemnly proclaimed on Palm Sunday, April 12, 1422. This alliance is of great importance, and may be regarded as the first serious attempt to secure the balance of power in Europe. We have reached the end of the Middle Ages.

Charles, after vainly endeavouring to persuade the Pope to recognize him, had himself crowned with great pomp in the Cathedral of St. Januarius on May 12. A week afterwards he set out on his return, leaving about half his army in the kingdom as a garrison. The Pope fled at his approach, but ordered that he should be received with every honour. He re-entered Rome on June 1, when he was offered apartments in the Vatican, which he did not accept. He then proceeded northwards by Orvieto and Siena. Here Savonarola came to him and bitterly reproached him with the excesses of his troops and with the grand opportunities which he had neglected. He desired to avoid Florence, and, passing through Pisa, prepared to cross the Apennines. His object was to reach Asti, where the Duke of Orleans was posted with a large army. Now was the time for Italy to avenge herself. The King was returning with a small force of 15,000 men, having left the bulk of his army to garrison his towns. If the army of the league could intercept him as he crossed the Apennines, he could be completely destroyed and the danger of French domination be crushed for ever.

Four large rivers, or rather torrents, descend northwards from the Apennines into the Emilian plain. One of these is the Trebbia, on the banks of which Hannibal won his celebrated victory over the Romans; the others are the Reno, the Parma, and the Taro. It was at Fornovo on this last named torrent that the army of the league determined to intercept the French King. The battle was fought on July 6, 1495. It did not last an hour. The allied army was four times as strong as the French, but their generals committed two faults. The marshal Gonzaga allowed a large reserve to accumulate on the right bank of the Taro, where they were entirely useless, and these soldiers who did not attack were chiefly occupied in plundering the French baggage. The Italians lost 3,500 men; the French only 200. The King was saved by the excellence of his horse "Savoie," which had been given him by Philippe de Bresse. Charles VIII. arrived at Asti on July 15, having got back much more safely than he could have expected, or than he deserved.

The immediate results of the expedition into Italy were slight. Even before the battle of Fornovo the Pope returned to Rome, and on the very day after it was fought Ferrantino re-entered Naples. He did not enjoy his kingdom long. He died without children on October 7, 1496, and the throne was taken possession of by his gifted uncle Federigo, Count of Altamura. The deposed

Alfonzo was already dead. But the results of the expedition of Charles in Europe were more important. It indeed deserves to be considered as the transition from the Middle Ages to modern times. In the first place, it revealed the Renaissance to France, and, through her, to the rest of Europe. The revival of learning, beginning in Italy, gradually spread to all branches of human inquiry; but it had scarcely touched France until the expedition of Charles VIII. France is undoubtedly a most powerful distributor of culture, and the French genius and language are specially fitted to make the discoveries of other nations the common property of the civilized world. In the second place, as we have already said, the league of Venice against Charles VIII. is the first instance of a general combination of the powers of Europe for a common object. Lastly, this expedition marks the end of Italian freedom. We have yet to trace through a period of five-and-thirty years, the dying struggles of that noble country. But the death blow has been already dealt, and we shall see how state after state gradually sank into that sleep of insignificance which has only been broken in our own age. Perhaps it is a consolation that her final throes are decorated, and in some measure concealed, by the splendours of art and the enthusiasm of chivalry.

CHAPTER IX

SAVONAROLA

In this history we have more than once mentioned the name of Girolamo Savonarola. It will be convenient now to give a more complete account of his teaching and his political views. Let us first mention two salient points in his influence. We have seen that there was in Florence a sharp contest proceeding between the democratic and the monarchical tendencies. Savonarola broke in upon this strife with a strong democratic influence, and we shall best understand him by regarding him from this side. At the same time, from the point of view of general culture, the Medici, as the supporters and distributors of the new learning, wished to form a union between Christianity and Platonism. To this Savonarola was vehemently opposed. While Platonic banquets were being held in the halls of Careggi, Savonarola was thundering in the Church of St. Mark against any admixture of Christianity and Paganism.

Savonarola was born at Ferrara, in the year 1452, a city which the brilliant court of the Este family made as illustrious and as active as Florence itself. His early boyhood coincided with the time when Pope Pius II. was preparing for his fruitless expedition against the Turks.

Savonarola became a Dominican friar at the age of three-and-twenty. At this time he wrote to his father, " The reasons which move me to enter the religious life are these,—the great misery of the world, the iniquities of men, the adulteries, the robberies, the pride, the idolatry, the cruel blasphemies; for the age has come to this, that one can find no one who does good." When he was thirty years of age, the war broke out between the Pope and Venice for the possession of Ferrara which Sixtus IV. desired to convert into a principality for his nephew. The Dominican convent was broken up and Savonarola entered the cloister of St. Mark at Florence, illustrated also by the names of Fra Angelico and Fra Bartolomeo. He found the Florentines at this time strongly opposing the interdict which Sixtus IV. had launched against Lorenzo de' Medici and supporting the Bishop of Carniola in his efforts to call yet another council together at Basel. Up to the year 1490 Savonarola preached in various towns of Italy against the papacy, saying that a renovation of the Church was necessary, which would follow its present misery as spring follows winter. On his return to Florence in the above-mentioned year, he found Lorenzo de' Medici fast friends with Pope Innocent VIII., but it was not consistent with his principles to approve of Lorenzo's method of government, nor of his enthusiasm for pagan culture. As we have before said, he was in politics a democrat, and he regarded paganism as the natural enemy of Christianity. He attempted to reform his order; he did reform the preaching of his age; for a dull explanation of difficult texts of Scripture couched in stiff and cumbrous syllogisms he substituted a stirring appeal to the people in simple homely language. He gradually assumed the style and tone of a prophet. There is no doubt that he considered himself prophetically inspired and thought that he was empowered by Heaven to thunder against the vices of Florence, as Isaiah and Hosea had thundered against the vices of Israel. He dreamed that he had seen a sword suspended in the sky with the inscription, " Gladius Domini super terram cito et velociter",—" the sword of the Lord above the earth speedily and swiftly." He foretold the coming of a new Cyrus across the Alps; no fortress and no sword would be able to stand against him.

Savonarola was a man of small stature but well proportioned. He had a high but wrinkled brow, and blue eyes gleaming from under dark bushy eyebrows. His most prominent feature was his nose, which is familiar to us in the portrait of his friend Fra Bartolomeo, or in the waxen bas-relief which his followers the Piagnoni carried about with them as an object of reverence. He was courteous in his address, accessible to everyone, and marvellous in his power over men. He knew the works of Aristotle and Thomas Aquinas almost by heart, and was probably better versed in the text of the Bible than any theologian of his age.

The descent of Charles VIII. into Italy gave him that honour in his own country which a prophet so often lacks. It seemed as if the king were coming for the very purpose of carrying out the preacher's views. Charles put forward as his two great objects, after the conquest of Naples, the reform of the Church and the expulsion of the Turks from Europe. Alexander VI. did not much care for either of these ideas. He naturally preferred that the Church should remain as it was, and he would have been willing to have placed Gem instead of Bajazet on the throne of Constantinople. But even if Charles seriously entertained these designs he had not the ability to carry them out. He made terms with the Pope, gave up the design of the Turkish war, and left the reform of the Church to Savonarola.

Savonarola saw that political reform must precede religious reform. He has left on record his views with regard to the government of Florence. His principles are based upon the teaching of Aristotle and Thomas Aquinas. He admits that a good monarchy is ideally the best form of government, but it easily degenerates into tyranny which is the worst. The rule of the mob, which according to Aristotle's definition would be called ochlocracy is detestable. The Florentines are too independent to put up with a monarchy, they must therefore have popular institutions.

These once existed in full vigour, but they had been corrupted by the Medici into a tyranny. A republican government is best for the city. But the offices must be filled by the genuine vote of the citizens, and that not of all the inhabitants, which would produce confusion and anarchy, but only of properly qualified citizens who shall form the great council. He looked forward to the entire abolition of party and to the equality of all privileged persons. He made it, as might be expected, a matter of great importance that no one should be admitted to the council who was not a man of good moral character. He promised his fellow-citizens that if they devoted themselves heartily to the common cause they should speedily obtain possession of Pisa. Savonarola did not apparently see that Pisa had as much right to independence as Florence.

T he constitution of December 23, 1494 was drawn up under the influence of Savonarola. Under this there were to be two councils. The first was to consist of all those who had completed the age of twenty-nine years before January 1, 1495, and whose father, grandfather, or great-grandfather had been elected to one of the principal offices of the State, these being Signory, the Standard Bearer of Companies, and the twelve *Buoni Uomini,* or if they themselves had held one of these offices. If the number of these exceeded fifteen hundred they were to be divided into three parts and each part was to hold office for six months.

T he number proved to be two thousand three hundred. Every year additional young members of not less than twenty-four years old were to be added to the Great Council. The Great Council was to elect a council of Eighty, called the *Richiesti della Signoria,* members of which were to be at least forty years old. The Signory, the various Boards, the ten of liberty, and the twenty accopiatori or electors were also to form part of this upper chamber. These twenty accopiatori had been appointed on December 2, 1494, by a *parlamento,* or general assembly of the people, in the great square to choose the Signory and the Standard Bearer of Justice. By this new constitution their power disappeared. Savonarola had considerable difficulty in getting his counsels of peace and pardon accepted. At that time the Otto di Guardia could by six votes send anyone into exile. This was supported by the common people as a security against tyrants, and especially against the party of the Medici, the Pallesci as they were called. Savonarola succeeded in getting a general amnesty passed, and in giving those condemned to death or exile an appeal to the Great Council. It was also part of the friar's plan to do away with the right of calling a *parlamento* or assembly of the whole people in the piazza, which was the recognised manner of changing the constitution. The abolition of this popular right was obtained with some difficulty. In fact the proportion of Florentine citizens admitted to the government by Savonarola's constitution was small. The number of inhabitants of Florence at this time is placed at 90,000, whereas the number of *beneficiati* or persons capable of belonging to any deliberate or representative body was only 3,200.

Whilst Charles VIII. was engaged at Naples, parties in Florence were divided between the King and the Duke, the latter having joined the league of Venice against Charles. Savonarola had supported the King, as he feared that the influence of the Duke might be used to upset the constitution and restore the Medici. As we have seen, Savonarola had an interview with Charles on his way between Siena and Castel Fiorentino, in which, although he reproached him with his shortcomings, he did not altogether repudiate him. At this time he was the most powerful man in Florence, and was consulted upon all matters both public and private. But it was not likely that the Pope would forgive the monk who had endeavoured to overthrow him, or that the people would support him in his attack on the Holy See.

Besides this the Cardinal Ascanio, the brother of Il Moro, was always present to poison his mind against the friar. Alexander VI., by a letter dated July 21, 1495, summoned Savonarola to Rome to give explanations with regard to his preaching. He declined to go, pleading his weak health, and the danger of leaving Florence at so critical a moment. The Pope was at first inclined to accept his excuses, but a second letter of September 8, written in a very different style, suspended him from teaching and preaching, and this prohibition was repeated on October 16. However, in February, 1496, Savonarola ascended the pulpit, saying that he had obtained leave from the Pope. In the meantime the Franciscan friars of Santa Croce began to take part against him. The city was divided between the two parties. The chief among Savonarola's opponents were Piero Capponi, Alessandro da Pisa, Francesco de' Medici, Guidantonio Vespucci and Bernardo Rucellai. They were of aristocratic interests and sympathies. Oppo sed to them, under the name of Piagnoni, were Francesco Valori, Paolo Antonio Soderini, and Gian Battista Ridolfi.

If the first party gained the upper hand, the friar would have to leave the city. But both parties were united against a common foe. They were equally afraid of the return of the Medici from exile and of the destruction of the constitution, and they knew that the friar and his sermons were their best defence against this danger, The effect of the new constitution had been that the aristocracy and the old families lost their power in the state. This was still further intensified by another change. Formerly no one who owed any money to the State could be a candidate or a voter for a public office. They must all be what was called "netto di specchio,"—that is, clear of the account books or "specchio." This condition was now done away with, as the Great Council was too numerous for it to be enforced. At one time as many as seventeen hundred persons were assembled in it.

The Carnival of 1496 showed Savonarola's power in a striking light. The ordinary games and amusements were given up—thousands of children walked in procession through the streets, despoiling ladies of their useless finery, and bringing their money to the Frate to found a Monte di Pieta, or public pawn-broking establishment, where money could be lent to the poor on easy terms. All this increased the bitterness of the friar's enemies. Sickness broke out in the city, there was no employment for workmen, the troops were not paid, and at each of these calamities Savonarola continued to preach that worse miseries than these must precede the desired reformation.

We have seen how much the power of Savonarola depended upon the King of France, on whom he had hung all his hopes of present improvement. There was some talk of Charles returning to Italy in 1496 and repairing his former mistakes. But the condition of Europe was altered. Spain was now a united monarchy, and even the Duke of Milan felt something of the patriotism of an Italian. Maximilian, the Emperor, began to assert himself. He called on the Florentines to submit to him, and Ludovico Il Moro supported his demand.

It was difficult for the Frate to resist his influence. The great desire of Florence was to recover Pisa, but this Maximilian sternly opposed. He even marched into Italy to its defence and prepared to attack Florence. On September 30, by the advice of Savonarola, a solemn procession was held in Florence, in which the picture of Santa Maria Immaculata was carried with great pomp and ceremony. On the morning of that very day, news arrived that a favourable breeze had carried the French fleet into the harbour of Leghorn, escaping the hostile armaments of the Emperor and the League. This was a great triumph for Savonarola and his friends, who argued more boldly than ever that the arm of the Lord was on their side. His preaching took a higher tone. He had a pulpit fitted in the hall of the Great Council, that vast chamber which still excites our admiration, in the Public Palace of Florence. He tried to wean them from earthly objects and from political ambition. "Dost thou wish for peace?" he said, "Serve Jesus." He told them not to place their trust in men but in God—"Ah! my people of Florence, you hang all day on these matters of temporal importance ; let them go. I do not say that you shall not have what I have promised, for that God has said. But is it not enough that God has illuminated you? If Florence were to go to the ground and lose its liberty and all temporal things, would it not be enough that it has the light of God which may lead it into Paradise? Let this suffice, and if you are Christians do not seek for anything but this light."

The Carnival of 1497 was even a greater triumph than that of the previous year. All vanities, all books and pictures which excite idle thoughts were collected and solemnly burnt, and it is to be feared that many valuable works of art perished in the process. The friar was destined to reach a still greater height of power in the State. The Standard-Bearer of Justice for the first two months of 1497 was Francesco Valori, one of the warmest supporters of the Frate. He was a violent opponent of the Medici, a man eager for his cause, simple in manner, silent in speech, but very ambitious. Under his influence a measure resembling a progressive income-tax was introduced, and the age for admission to the Great Council was lowered from twenty-nine to twenty-four, while measures of severity were adopted against the Frate's

opponents. A reaction naturally followed. For the next
two months, March and April, Bernardo del Nero, one of
the Bigi, or Medicean party, was Standard Bearer, and it
was perhaps owing to this that on April 28, Piero
Medici made an attempt to return from exile. He came
close up to the gates of Florence, but was compelled to
retire. This defeat, strangely enough, roused the popular
feeling against Savonarola, because he counselled moderation towards the Medici party, and Piero's attempt made
the citizens too angry to be moderate. The Pope now
wrote to the Signory of Florence, begging them to prevent
Savonarola from saying harsh things of the Holy Father.
After deliberation they determined that no friar should
be allowed to preach on May 4, the feast of the Ascension. Savonarola came down to the Cathedral, accompanied
by a large number of friars, by a large military guard,
and a numerous body of private friends. He mounted
the pulpit and said, "You believed that I should not
come to the pulpit this morning, but you see that I am
come. Perhaps you will say, 'Yes, thanks, friar, to your
guard.' And I tell you that I did not summon this guard,
but that I would have come anyhow, and that I will
always come when the Lord God inspires me. No man
in the world, be he who he may, shall make me stop in
such a case." He went on to protest that he had been
calumniated, but that he always returned good for evil.
"If I thought it better not to preach I would leave off.
I have received no order from the Signory not to preach,
and if I had it is doubtful whether I should have thought
myself bound to obey it." At this moment, two loud
knocks were heard in the Church, which was the signal
for a tumult. The friar fell on his knees and grasped his

crucifix, exhorting the people to hope in Christ. He then descended from the pulpit and, accompanied by his followers, repaired to his own convent of St. Mark, where he finished the sermon. The expressions used by Savonarola had been an open defiance of authority. In consequence of this he was excommunicated by the Pope, partly for not obeying his citation to Rome, and partly for his contumacious words. The Signory entreated the Pope to withdraw his excommunication, but in vain. It was published in Florence on June 11.

At the end of July, traces were discovered of a conspiracy for effecting the return of the Medici to Florence. The members of it belonged to the most distinguished families in the city, and the head of it was Bernardo del Nero, an old man of seventy-five, who had been Standard-bearer of Justice. Others were Niccolo Ridolfi, Lorenzo Tornabuoni, Giovanni Pucci, and Giovanni Cambi. It was proposed to refer the matter to the Great Council, but the cause was finally judged by a *pratica* or committee of a hundred-and-thirty-six persons consisting of the Signory, the sixteen Standard-Bearers of guilds, the twelve *Buoni Uomini*, the Captains of the Guelph Party, the Ten of War, the Eight of the Balia, the officials of the Monte di Pietà, the Conservators of the Laws, the Council of Eighty, with the additional members. The vote was given not personally, but by the separate component magistracies. The five criminals were unanimously condemned to death. There was some talk of a new trial, but Francesco Valori courageously opposed it and they were beheaded in the courtyard of the Bargello. It is not certain what part Savonarola played in this celebrated trial, but the probability is that he would have wished to leave the matter in the ordinary course of law to the decision of the Great Council. At any rate, the effect of what had happened was to give Francesco Valori the greatest authority in the City. The convent of St. Mark became the nucleus of the governing party; every new measure was discussed with Savonarola. A private body of his friends decided on every subject of business before it was submitted of the Eighty. Even when it came before the Great Council the assembly was found to consist almost entirely of the friar's friends. By these means a free constitution had been gradually changed into a party government.

In external politics the party of the Piagnoni always held more or less closely to the King of France, and hoped for his return to Italy. The opposite party were attached to the League of Venice which had intercepted Charles VIII. at Fornovo. Of these, Milan and the Pope were powerful members, and the Pope had recently shown his feeling against France by giving the consecrated hat to Henry VII. of England. The party of Savonarola were very careful to keep the elections to the public offices favourable to themselves; the more so, because they feared the vengeance of the friends of the executed conspirators. The Signory which governed Florence in the last month of 1497 were favourable to Savonarola, and they continued to negotiate with the Pope in his favour. But the friar did not await the result of these interventions, and on the evening of Christmas Day in that year he celebrated mass. At last, on February 11, 1498, he again ascended the pulpit in the cathedral. This is a very important event, as it was a direct denial of the Pope's authority.

In his sermon he spoke of the excommunication, and denied its validity. He said that it had been brought about by the Florentines whose only desire was to do away with good living and the commonweal. He said . that if he did not preach he should be excommunicated by Christ. "To whom," he said, "should you betake yourselves? To those who are blessed by the Pope and whose life is a shame to Christianity, or to those who are excommunicated by the Pope, but whose life brings forth fruit of truth and daily becomes better?" A change now took place in the attitude of the Pope towards Florence. It was believed that Charles VIII. was preparing another expedition into Italy, and the Florentines expected by this means to recover the possession of Pisa, which was the great object of their desire. But the Pope now suddenly promised to give them Pisa, and said that in his eyes its union with Florence would be favourable to the unity of Italy. The Florentines were, on their side, inclined to accept the offer. It would cost them nothing, whereas Charles would demand a contribution in money. On February 26, Alexander wrote to complain that Savonarola, although excommunicated, was performing priestly functions, and asked that he should be arrested and sent to Rome. He, however, continued to preach, and prophesied the terrible retribution that would fall upon his country. "O, Italy, thou shalt be given into the hands of savage people, a barbarous race, who shall only take pleasure in doing you harm, and slaughtering men, and in the sight of blood; they will be barbarians, cruel as lions, and will come from this side and from that. Italy then shall be given into the hands of a strange people, everyone of which will rack his brains to do thee harm and even the worst they can. And it shall be worse for Rome than for any other city. Your property, your treasures, shall be given into their hands." This, many years later, seemed to the Piagnoni a prophecy of the descent of Constable Bourbon and of the sack of Rome.

The Pope's brief of February 26 was referred to a Committee which was favourable to the friar. An ambassador was sent to Rome with explanations, but he found the Pope very angry and he threatened Florence with an interdict. On March 9, in another brief, he attacked the doctrines and the orthodoxy of the friar. The citizens were told that to hear the friar preach was a sin, that they might be absolved if they confessed immediately and promised not to offend again, but that if they continued in their contumacy they would be papally excommunicated and could only be absolved by the Pope. A party now arose of young men of family who were opposed to the friar. The head of these was Dolfo Spini. Party-spirit ran high. Some said that Fra Girolamo was a good and holy man, but that it was safer to obey the Pope; an interdict would destroy the commerce and prosperity of Florence. Others, amongst whom was Francesco Valori, asserted that the Frate was a direct messenger from God, and that the Pope had no authority to prevent his preaching. At last, on March 17, a new committee determined to ask Savonarola to suspend his preaching. He said to the messengers who brought the news, "Is that your will, my lords?" They said, "It is." He replied, "I have another Lord whom I must consult. I will give my answer to-morrow." The next day he preached his farewell sermon. He said that true believers must have recourse first to their confessor, then to the bishop, then to the Pope, but if all these forsake him he must go to Christ, and say "Thou art my Confessor, thou art my Pope." He agreed to obey the orders of the Committee, but declared that some sign from Heaven would soon be given to prove the truth of his mission. Savonarola did not give up the struggle. He persuaded his friends to write to the Florentine ambassadors in France and Spain that the time was come in which a general council ought to be called. He drafted letters on the same subject to the Emperor Maximilian, the kings of France, Spain, England and Hungary. In these he declared Alexander not to be a true Pope. These letters were never sent, but they were written. The schism in the city was not healed. Crowds still flocked to St. Mark's to hear the devoted friend of Savonarola, Fra Domenico of Pesca, who took his place in the pulpit. At last a strange method was adopted for deciding the quarrel. In the year 1063 a monk of Vallombrosa had charged the bishop of Florence with having obtained his see by simony. The charge was rejected by the lord of Florence at that time, but the monk offered to prove his case by passing unhurt through two rows of burning faggots. He did so with safety and the bishop was condemned. Fra Domenico da Pesca now offered to pass through the fire to prove the truth of Savonarola's teaching, and a Franciscan friar of Santa Croce offered to enter the flames with him to prove the contrary; they would both be burned, but the truth would prevail. The authorities of the city doubted for a long time if they should permit the ordeal, but at last they did so. If Fra Domenico was burned Savonarola was to leave the city. Everything was arranged, the gates were closed, the streets guarded, the trial was to take place on Saturday, April 7, the eve of Palm Sunday, at four o'clock in the afternoon. The propositions which Fra Domenico was prepared to defend were these:—the church of God needs renovation; it shall be scourged; it shall be renewed; Florence also after scourging shall be renewed and shall prosper; unbelievers shall be converted to Christ; this shall all come to pass in our own time; the excommunication recently launched against our reverend father, brother Girolamo, is null and void; those who do not observe it do not sin."

The platform necessary for the ordeal was erected in the great square of the Signory. It was forty ells long and five wide, covered with earth and paved with stones so as to resist the fire, a pathway an ell wide was left in the middle and on each side were piled up the faggots and logs of wood. The brothers of the two orders arrived at the spot and took up their position in the Loggia de' Lanzi, on the south side of the square. The Franciscans advanced in silence without ceremony, but Fra Domenico was dressed in full priestly robes and held in his hand a huge crucifix. Savonarola was also clad in a pluvial and carried a pyx with the consecrated host. Some citizens with lighted candles accompanied him. The Dominicans had been celebrating divine service in St. Mark's and marched to the square chanting psalms with a loud voice. An unexpected difficulty arose. The Franciscans demanded that Fra Domenico should take off his robes and dress like a Franciscan. They also would not allow him to enter the flames with the crucifix and the host.

Savonarola would not permit him to go otherwise. The dispute continued till dusk, and the people were disconcerted and confused. The friends of Dolfo Spini, the *arrabiati* and the Compagnacci, as they were called, proposed to seize Savonarola. The feeling of the people was now strongly against the Dominicans; they said that their wish to carry the Host and the crucifix into the flames was an insult to God; the Franciscan had offered to enter the flames alone; the whole thing was a trick and a delusion. On Palm Sunday Savonarola preached in St. Mark's, but those who went to hear him were threatened by the Compagnacci. A Dominican, preaching in the afternoon in the cathedral, was interrupted by loud cries. The tumult spread from the church to the streets. The people rushed to St. Mark's to bring the business to an end. The Signory in vain summoned them to lay down their arms, on the condition that Savonarola should leave the city in twelve hours. They continued to shout against him and against Valori. Valori, who was at St. Mark's, returned with difficulty to his house, and on his way from thence to the Public Palace was met by some of the relations of the men whom he had had executed, and was murdered. The monks defended their convent as well as they could against attack. Savonarola stood before the altar in the midst of his novices with the Host in his hand, the brethren kneeling around him in prayer. Then appeared the messengers from the Signory bidding him to go with them. They guaranteed him against violence and he determined to obey. He took leave of his brother friars in an affecting speech, urging them to remain firm in faith, prayer and patience, and swearing to them before the sacrament that he had never preached anything but the truth. He then proceeded with lights and torches and a large body of soldiers to the Public Palace, where he was thrown into prison.

Savonarola's strength had lain in his opposition to the Pope, an opposition intensified by the different characters of their morality. Florence now desired to be friends with the Pope, and the supernatural foundation on which the friar had attempted to base his mission had broken down. His political enemies rose against him; his religious supporters could no longer defend him.

The days which followed were most painful. Savonarola was examined under torture. We cannot be sure of the authenticity of the confessions thus extorted. It is said that he gave himself up to despair, that he doubted of the reality of his mission, that he confessed that he had always expected some supernatural intervention which never came. It is asserted that he admitted that his object had been the glory of the world, and to have credit and reputation, and that with this object he had invented his prophecies. The Signory which entered upon office on May 1, 1497, was the bitter enemy of the friar. On May 22, he and two friars, his companions, were condemned to death. They were first to be hanged and then burned; their offence was declared to be heresy in denying the Pope to be the true Pope, the perversion of Holy Scripture and the divulgence of the secrets of confession, as well as the causing of dissention and deaths in the city. The last night of Savonarola in prison was spent in a parting colloquy with his disciples. They communicated together and then watched in prayer. After this Savonarola slept peacefully, his hand resting on the knee of Jacopo Niccolini, who had come to comfort him, The other friars were executed on May 23, in the square of the Signory, on the very place where the platform had been prepared for the ordeal. They were di-

vested of their orders; they then received a plenary in-
dulgence from the Pope, which they acknowledged with
reverence. The first hanged was Maruffi, then Buonvi-
cini, then Savonarola. As he mounted the ladder to his
execution he gazed with widely opened eyes upon the
crowd which had thronged to see him die, and called out,
" My people, what have I done to you that you should
treat me thus? " They were all dead before their bodies
were burnt. Their ashes were thrown into the Arno,
but their memory was long preserved, and for many years
reverent and loving hands placed fresh flowers on the
spot where they had suffered, on the anniversary of their
execution.

CHAPTER X

CHARLES VIII., king of France, died of a stroke of apoplexy on April 7, 1493, the very day on which the doctrines of Savonarola were to be submitted at Florence to the proof of fire. Charles was twenty-seven years of age, and had reigned for about fourteen years and a half. He was the last of the direct line of the house of Valois, which had sat on the throne of France for a hundred and nineteen years, he was succeeded by Louis XII., a name full of fate to Italy; before his accession he was known as the duke of Orleans, being descended from Louis, duke of Orleans, son of king Charles V. who married Valentine of Milan.

Before we proceed with the further relations between France and Italy we must retrace our steps and follow with close attention the career of Alexander VI. Charles VIII. had left Italy in a state of the most terrible confusion. It was divided by two parties, the league of Venice between Rome, Venice and Milan, supported by the emperor Maximilian and the king of England, and the French party which consisted of Savoy, Montferrat, Ferrara, Florence, Bologna, and the Orsini of Rome.

Whilst Charles was on his homeward march the emperor Maximilian was at the Diet of Worms, haggling with the Estates for money. Before he returned to the Tyrol, Charles was back again in France and the war was over. But there was some danger lest Charles should return. An embassy was sent to Maximilian to say that Charles was expected every day and that the Florentines were threatening Pisa. After taking counsel with his son Philip, Maximilian determined to march. His plan aimed at something more than to rescue Italy from the hands of the French. He proposed after Italy was pacified to go on to Provence to help Duke René. Philip was to attack France from the Netherlands, Ferdinand of Spain from Roussillon, the invaders were to meet in Lyons, and Burgundy would be recovered for the empire. It should be noticed that in the wars of Europe at this time, German soldiers bore a principal part. German soldiers assisted the Muscovites against the Poles. With their help the Swedes destroyed the forces of the Scandinavian union. Germans fought in England for the House of York, and for Britanny against the crown of France. In Naples, the soldiers on both sides were Germans, and so also were the conquerors of the Hungarians. Maximilian had some reason for believing that if he could unite all these forces under his own standard he would be irresistible in Europe. The reality was a dismal contrast to the dream. The king of the Romans arrived at Monza, at the end of August, 1496, without an army and without money. He hoped to be able to obtain these from the league, but in vain; he found that he could trust neither Sforza nor the Pope. The dispute was chiefly centered round the question as to whether Pisa should be free or whether it should be surrendered to the Florentines. In October Maximilian laid siege to Leghorn, but the French fleet was able to relieve the place and his own ships were destroyed by a storm. He returned to Germany at the close of 1496.

This event and the restoration of the Arragon rule in Naples mark the commencement of the second epoch of Alexander's pontificate. Up to this time, his faults had chiefly been those of indecision and weak self-indulgence; he now seemed to enter upon a deliberate course of evil. His first object was to dispossess the Barons of the Roman state in order to enrich the family of the Borgia. He began with the powerful Orsini. In the wars of Naples they had taken the side of Charles, and their rivals, the Colonna, the side of Arragon. In June, 1496, the Pope confiscated the property of the Orsini and gave it to his son the duke of Gandia, whom he also made standard-bearer of the church. The Orsini at first bowed before the storm. They surrendered all the places which appeared to them incapable of defence, and took refuge in the strong castle of Bracciano, which was formidable not only by its natural strength, but by the lake which lay before it. Help speedily came to them from the north, and the pope's troops were entirely defeated at the battle of Soriano, on January 26, 1497. The Duke of Urbino was taken prisoner and the Duke of Gandia wounded. The plans of the Pope against the Orsini were thus baffled and he was compelled to make peace. He now turned his attention elsewhere. With the help of the great Captain Consalvo, of Cordova, he conquered the castle of Ostia, the property of the noted Cardinal Giuliano, now in possession of Virginio Orsini. He divorced his daughter

Lucrezia from Giovanni Sforza, lord of Pesaro, probably at the bidding of Cæsar Borgia, who now began to exert his baneful influence. He loaded the Duke of Gandia with honours. He gave him the duchies of Benevento, Terracina and Pontecorvo and offered even to mark him out for the throne of Naples. He was to go there with his brother the Cardinal Cæsar to crown Federigo of Altamura. Before they could start on their journey a terrible event occurred. On the evening of June 14, 1497, the Duke of Gandia, Cæsar and their mother Vanozza, together with Cardinal Ascanio Sforza supped together in a vineyard on the outskirts of Rome. It is said that during the banquet the Borgia insulted Ascanio. Cæsar and his mother went away and Ascanio and Gandia were left alone. Gandia then departed, riding a mule, with a single companion. When they reached the piazza degli Ebrei Gandia sent his attendant to the palace to fetch arms. When he returned he saw nothing of the Duke, but the mule was afterwards discovered. Some charcoal burners deposed that they had seen on that night a man on horseback with others on foot mount one of the bridges over the Tiber, and throw the dead body of a man into the river. The man on horseback said to his attendants. "Has it gone to the bottom?" and one of them replied, "Yes, my lord." The charcoal burners looked on to the river and saw the dead man's mantle floating and threw stones to sink it. When asked why he had made no report to the Governor, he replied "I have in my life seen a hundred dead bodies thrown into the river there and no one ever troubled his head about them." The next day the body of the Duke was recovered. It was completely dressed, and had nine wounds and one mortal thrust in the throat. The purse was full of money. The Pope on hearing of it neither eat, drank nor slept for three days. He was altogether inconsolable, and could only say perpetually, " I know the murderer." There can be little doubt that the murderer was Cæsar Borgia, who was very jealous of his brother. He had entered most reluctantly into the ecclesiastical state, which seemed to shut the door to civil honours. The Pope, after a fortnight, gave up all attempt to discover the criminal. After a few weeks' decent mourning, Cæsar went to Naples, and crowned Federigo on August 10. He was the last king of the house of Arragon. The attempts which the pope had made at reform in the first threat of disaster were given up, and there was no more talk of his relinquishing the tiara. Cæsar Borgia became more powerful than ever. He was invested with the fiefs which were to have belonged to his brother, and it was clear that he would soon exchange the Cardinal's hat for a princely coronet.

The summer of this year showed a change in the politics of Europe which was one of the signs of the era. Spain takes henceforth a prominent place in the new family of nations. Ferdinand became anxious to strengthen himself with alliances. He betrothed his daughter Isabella to Manuel, King of Portugal, making it a condition of the marriage that all Jews and enemies of the Inquisition should be driven out of the country. The Jews thus expelled spread over Europe, which they enriched by their industry, and from that time there was peace between Spain and Portugal for a century and a half.

A similar negotiation was begun with the King of England. Catharine of Arragon was married to Arthur, Prince of Wales, and Henry VII. joined the league against

France. The Pope, as has been already mentioned, sent to Henry the consecrated hat and sword. The pretenders Lambert Simnel and Perkin Warbeck were supported by the French party in order to weaken the position of Henry. They also found assistance in Scotland, which was always well disposed towards France. Peace with Scotland was purchased by the marriage of Margaret, daughter of Henry VII., to James IV., the king of that country, an alliance which eventually brought about the union between the two kingdoms. A strong friendship also existed at this time between Scotland and King John of Denmark, who possessed Norway and had claims over Sweden. Thus a league of alliance and friendship extended from the Arctic Circle to the southern shores of Spain and Sicily. The three pillars of the alliance were Ferdinand, Henry and Maximilian. It seemed to threaten the very existence of the French Monarchy. The troops of Maximilian entered France in three bodies, but as we have seen, Charles VIII. died on April 7, 1498, and his successor, Louis XII., was able to break up the league and to place Europe in the same condition as if it had never existed.

The first object of Louis XII., on coming to the throne was to strengthen his position as king. For this purpose he divorced his own wife and married the widow of Charles VIII., Anne, Duchess of Brittany, by which means that appanage was secured to the crown. In order to contract this marriage he required a Papal dispensation, and this gave an opportunity for bringing about more intimate relations between himself and the Pope. On his entry into Paris he proclaimed himself King of Naples and Duke of Milan, King of Naples as heir to René of

Provence, and Duke of Milan as the lineal descendant of the Visconti in the female line. This step had the effect of breaking up the league. Ferdinand joined him against Naples, Venice joined him against Milan. Ludovico Il Moro awaited the onslaught relying on the Turks, the Emperor and the Swiss. We shall see how these props were destined to fail him.

In August, 1498, Cæsar Borgia solemnly laid aside the dignity of Cardinal. This was the easier because he was still a layman and had never received holy orders. He declared that he had no vocation for the priestly state, and that he had become a Cardinal under the compulsion of the Pope. Someone has remarked that these are perhaps the only true words he ever spoke. In October he set out for France with a gorgeous train. He carried with him a treasure of two hundred thousand ducats. The robes of his suite were sewn with pearls, the shoes of his horses were of silver. He was received by Louis XII. at the castle of Chinon with outward courtesy but with inward contempt. He was created Duke of Valence or of the Valentinois, a province on the Rhone. This is curious, because he had before been Archbishop of Valentia, and it has led to some confusion. He soon afterwards married Jeanne d'Albret, sister of the King of Navarre, and thus became a member of the royal house of France. The object of Cæsar was to procure for himself a principality in Italy, and Louis promised to assist him in this as soon as he got possession of Milan. Alexander joined the alliance which the King of France had made with Milan, paying no attention to the protest of the King of Spain. This alliance was effected by the treaty of Angers concluded between France and Venice on February 9, 1499, by the mediation of the Cardinal Giuliano della Rovere. The cause of quarrel between Il Moro and Venice was the possession of Pisa, the Venetians wished it to remain independent, the Moor wished it to belong to the Florentines. But there was no mention of Pisa in the treaty. It only provided that Venice should make war against Il Moro, and in case of success should receive Cremona and the whole of the Milanese east of the Adda. It was the will of fate that the Duke of Milan should find no allies to assist him in this crisis. The neutrality of England and Spain was secured by treaty. Maximilian, who had begun an attack on Burgundy, found himself engaged in a war with Switzerland, Florence was busy with Pisa, and Federigo of Naples had quite enough to do to defend himself. There are few things more remarkable in history than the manner in which Louis XII., finding himself at his accession girt with a threatening ring of powerful foes, contrived to break up their alliance, and even direct some of its force against his chosen enemy.

The war began in August. Trivulzio, the general of Louis XII., took Valenza and Alessandria. As he advanced from the west, the Venetians pressed on from the east. The Guelph party took the side of the French, and town after town fell before them. Il Moro had no safety but in flight. He went first to Como and then into the Tyrol, where he was received with much favour by Maximilian. Louis XII. entered Pavia on October 6. He was accompanied by the princes of Savoy, Montferrat, Ferrara, and Mantua, by the ambassadors of Venice, Florence, Siena, and Pisa, by Guiliano della Rovere, and by Cæsar Borgia. An eye-witness, after speaking of the Duke of Valentinois as a most wicked man, describes him as a young man well made and robust, with fair hair falling over his shoulders, his face lean and pale, his eyes light and fiery, his general appearance combining beauty and grace, with signs of the terrible temper which seethed within. Louis XII. left Milan to return to France on November 7. He took with him Francesco Sforza, a child of eight years old, the son of the unfortunate Gian Galeazzo. He left Trivulzio behind him as a viceroy.

The visit of Cæsar Borgia to the court of France had a profound political effect. The Pope received authority to overthrow the vassals of the Church in Italy. He did not lose time in beginning the work. He made his daughter Lucrezia, Regent of Spoleto, a town which up to this time had never been under the authority of a *signoria*. He drove the Gaetani out of Sermoneta. He declared the great reigning houses, the Malatesta, the Montefeltri, the Bentivogli, to be deprived of their authority. Macchiavelli has praised this design of freeing Italy from a multitude of rulers. Cæsar Borgia who principally effected it, and who is Macchiavelli's ideal prince, is one of the most remarkable characters in history. He was extremely handsome. His terrible lust was controlled by a cold and acute understanding. He had at his command all the arts and devices of secret government, mysterious silence, deceit and delusion, a careful laying of plans, swift action at the proper time, pitiless cruelty, and knowledge of mankind, perhaps rather of their weaknesses and vices than of their virtues. He could use both good and bad means for his purposes. He could be just and generous, but only when it suited his ends. We may be glad that such monsters of inquity, if they now exist, cannot exercise their influence in high places, but find their way eventually to the felon's dock.

Cæsar Borgia began his conquests in the Romagna in November, 1499. He first attacked Imola, which fell an easy prey, and then Forlì, which was defended by Catherine Sforza, "rather a virago than a woman." It yielded on January 12, 1500. After the conquest of these two towns and of Cesena, Cæsar made his triumphal entry into Rome.

In the meantime Ludovico Sforza had been the sport of the most varied fortune. Maximilian could be of no use to him in the Tyrol, so he went on into Switzerland, and persuaded the men of Uri to help him by promising them some extension of territory. He swooped down upon Milan from the slopes of the Alps, surprised Trivulzio, who was defending it, and entered it on February 5. His triumph was of short duration. Louis XII. sent La Tremouille to recover the lost possession. Ludovico was betrayed by the Swiss in Novare. On the night of April 9 the Burgundians and Germans penetrated into the Duke's chamber and said, "You are the King's prisoner." He exacted the promise that he should be taken to Bellinzona. He then dressed himself like a Swiss soldier, and soon afterwards contrived to mix himself up with the sixteen thousand who were there and got out of Novare. But a Grison captain pointed him out to the French. Il Moro, when he was discovered, said, "I surrender myself to my kinsman Monsieur de Ligny. The Duke was first taken to Lyons and then to Loches, where he remained ten long years in prison. His brother Ascanio was also taken to France, but was let out after a short time. Milan remained in the hands of the French and Bellinzona was given to the Swiss.

In the summer of 1500 Rome was horrified by another

fearful crime. The young Prince of Biseglia, the husband of Lucrezia Borgia, was coming out of the church of St. Peter on the evening of July 15, when he was stabbed by an assassin who immediately disappeared. The wounded man was carried to the Pope and named the murderer. Lucrezia, who was present, immediately swooned. The name was not revealed, but it was well known to be Cæsar Borgia. For a month the wounded man lay, tended by his wife and the Pope and surrounded by guards. It was no secret that Cæsar had determined on his death. At last, on August 18, Cæsar entered the apartment, sent Lucrezia away, and strangled Biseglia with the assistance of a paid assassin.

After the conquest of Imola and Forlì, Cæsar turned his arms against Faenza, then governed by Astorre Manfredi, a youth of sixteen, who was the darling of his people. The town was reduced by famine, Astorre was captured by treachery and sent to Rome, where he was imprisoned in the Castle of St. Angelo and put to death. Cæsar received the title of Duke of Romagna, and Alexander did not hesitate to alienate this large province from the Holy See. Bologna was to be the capital, and Cæsar hoped eventually to unite with this principality the sovereignty of Italy. After this, in May, 1501, Cæsar turned his attention to Florence, and threatened to restore the exiled Piero de' Medici, but the Florentines bought him off, and by the intervention of Louis XII. he was recalled to Rome.

A treaty had been signed at Grenada on November 11, 1500, between Louis XII. and Ferdinand of Arragon, who then assumed respectively for the first time the titles of the Most Christian and Catholic King. The object of the treaty was the conquest of Naples by the combined force of the two monarchs and the partition of the kingdom. Calabria and Apulia were to go to Spain, the rest of the country to France. Federigo, a wise and gentle sovereign, beloved by his subjects, was entirely ignorant of the storm which was preparing. In his simplicity he went so far as to request the King of Spain to assist him against France. The treaty was communicated to the Pope, who gave his adhesion to it. The ostensible reason for the conquest was that it might be the stepping-stone to an expedition against the Turks; the Pope's real reason for acquiescence was, that when Spain and France had worn themselves out in the struggle Naples might fall to the lot of Cæsar Borgia. The French army invaded Naples in the summer of 1501. Consalvo da Cordova, to whom the terms of the treaty had been communicated, and who was a subject of King Ferdinand, treacherously betrayed Federigo, who had committed his fortunes to his keeping. Capua was taken by storm with circumstances of great atrocity. Federigo dismayed and thunderstruck at the treachery of his nearest relatives and most trusted friends, threw himself upon the mercy of the French king. Louis XII. gave him the duchy of Anjou and a considerable pension. He died a prisoner at Tours in 1504. His son Fernando preserved the title of Duke of Calabria and Prince of Tarentum. He died in 1559, and the Neapolitan branch of the house of Arragon came to an end.

The conquest of Naples by the French gave the Pope an opportunity of attacking the Barons of Latium. During his absence in the field, he left his daughter Lucrezia as regent in the Vatican. That a woman should be placed even temporarily in the chair of St. Peter is a measure of the degradation and corruption of the Holy See. The property of the vanquished barons was divided between Roderigo, the son of Lucrezia and the murdered Alfonzo, and Giovanni Borgia, a bastard son of the Pope. By these means nearly the whole of the States of the Church came into the hands of the Borgia family. The unfortunate Lucrezia was now compelled to contract a fourth marriage with Alfonzo, son of Ercole d'Este, the Duke of Ferrara. The object of this was to acquire support for Caesar Borgia in the north of Italy. The marriage which took place on December 28, 1501, turned out better than might have been expected, and Lucrezia lived happily with her husband and children. She held a brilliant court at Ferrara. Her beauty, virtue and wisdom were exalted to the stars by the poet Ariosto, the Cardinal Bembo, to whom she sent a tress of her hair still preserved, and seen by Byron and the scholar Aldus Manutius. She died on June 24, 1519, and on her deathbed wrote a touching letter to Pope Leo X, committing her husband and children to his care and her soul to his prayers.

Cæsar Borgia was now tyrant of Rome, and the Pope was entirely unable to restrain him. A Venetian had written a pamphlet against the Pope and his son; he was smothered and thrown into the Tiber. When complaint was made to Alexander he said that the Duke of Valentinois was a good-natured man, but that he could not bear to be abused. " I have often told him," he said, " that Rome is a free town, and that everyone may write and speak here as he pleases; that I am often abused myself, but I take no notice of it. The Duke answered me, 'If Rome is accustomed to unite and to speak in this manner, good, but I will make people who do

this suffer for it." The death of Astorre Manfredi at the
age of 17, and of his brother at 15, was brought about
by Cæsar's orders. Cæsar left Rome in June, 1502, to
continue his operations in the Romagna. He was already
master of a considerable territory; he desired further to
occupy Camerino, Urbino, Florence, Siena, and Perugia,
and to be proclaimed King of Central Italy. The latter
half of 1520 was occupied by the crimes which were
undertaken for this end. The first two towns he gained
by treachery. He then took the title of Cæsar Borgia
of France, by the grace of God, Duke of Romagna, of
Valence, and of Urbino, prince of Arditi, Lord of Andici,
Piombino, Standard-Bearer and Captain of the Holy
Roman Church. His name was extolled by flatterers to
the skies, men of genius like Leonardo da Vinci entered
his service. His attempts on Tuscany failed. Louis XII.
forbade him to touch Florence.

The King of France found himself again summoned
to Italy by the course of events. Since the partition of
Naples peace had never been secured between the
Spaniards and the French. There were disputes about
the boundary, and in this age of bastard chivalry everyone
preferred the occupations of war to those of peace. A
notable incident was the Disfida, or challenge of Barletta.
On November 9, 1502, the Duke of Nemours marched
from Melfi towards Barletta, which was defended by
Consalvo de Cordova, Fabrizio, and Prospero Colonna, and
other Italian lords and barons. The soldiers on either
side vied with each other in deeds of valour. In January, 1502, the Spaniard Diego Mendoza, made some
Frenchmen prisoners. At dinner some hot words arose
between them, and Inigo Lopez de Ayala who defended

the honour of the Italian soldiers against the attack of the Frenchman. It was settled that the question should be fought out by thirteen on each side. The battle took place on February 13, 1503, in a plain between Andria Barletta, and Quadrata. Ettore, Fieramosea the leader of the Italians, returned victorious, bringing with him the Frenchmen as prisoners. It is said that nothing discouraged the French army so much as this defeat, and from that day fortune abandoned them.

The situation of affairs in Europe was at this time remarkable. The two most prominent countries were France and Spain. The heir of Ferdinand and Isabella was their son Juan, who seemed destined to reign over the Spanish portion of that great peninsula which was now united for the first time. He, however, suddenly died, and his posthumous child died also as soon as it was born. Isabella, married to the King of Portugal, now became the heir, and it seemed as if the entire peninsula would be subject to a single ruler. She, however, died, and her son Miguel after her. The inheritance now passed to Juana, the third daughter of Ferdinand and Isabella, who had been married to Philip the Fair, son of the Emperor Maximilian. An heir had been born to them on the day of St. Matthias, February 24, 1500, who was afterwards to reign over half Europe under the name of Charles V. It was the consequence of such a series of accidents that such vast dominions were united under a single crown. As Ferdinand and Louis XII. were at least nominally in alliance, and Philip, the son of Maximilian, was son-in-law to Ferdinand, it need not appear strange that the Emperor should invest the King of France with the duchy of Milan.

Cæsar Borgia did not secure his conquests entirely without opposition. Frightened by his designs on Bologna, his condottiere leaders were against him, and brought him into the greatest danger. The great Macchiavelli, the author of the immortal "Prince," was now in the service of Cæsar Borgia, and has left us an account of these events. He tells us that on the last day of the year 1502, Valentino was marching along the shore which stretches between Fano and Sinigaglia. There met him in the suburbs of the city, Vitellozzo, Paolo Orsini, the Duke of Gravina, and Oliverotto of Fermo. He entered with them into the city. Macchiavelli noticed that the face of Vitellozzo was pale; perhaps the Duke had let a word fall which betrayed his design. Arrived at the castle he called the captains into his room and had them arrested. Vitellozzo and Oliverotto were executed that very night. The Pope did the same to the Cardinal Orsini. Prayers and bribes were squandered in vain to save his life. It was believed that at the very time when the Pope was promising to spare him, the Cardinal had already drunk of the poisoned cup. The Pope immediately seized the castles and possessions of the Orsini, and their property was only to some degree protected by the intervention of France.

In the spring of 1503 the Borgias stood at the height of their power. The Pope was sturdy and strong. The Orsini and Colonna lay conquered at their feet. Cæsar was destined to become King of Romagna and the Marches. France alone stood in the way. But for that power Cæsar would become lord of Pisa, and possibly of the whole of Tuscany. Even this obstacle seemed in a fair way to be removed. The French generals Aubigny and

Nemours were entirely defeated by Consalvo. A French historian remarks that Louis XII. was justly punished for allying himself with such monsters as the Borgias. Alexander was separating himself from Louis and preparing to ally himself with Ferdinand to drive the French from Italy. Louis offered Alexander the possession of Naples if he would surrender Bologna and the Romagna. Alexander was beseeching the Emperor to invest Cæsar with the lordship of Pisa, Siena, and Lucca. La Tremouille lay ill at Parma, but intended when he recovered to march on to Naples with a new army. These complicated intrigues were brought to nothing by an unexpected event. In the early part of August the Pope and Cæsar were supping with Cardinal Adriano, a very wealthy man, in his vineyard. Shortly afterwards they were both attacked by illness. The Pope died on August 18. Cæsar, after lying in the agonies of death, eventually recovered. It has always been supposed that they were poisoned. The corpse of the Pope became rapidly black and was horribly swollen and disfigured. He was buried, after a long interval, on September 3, in a miserable manner, without funeral rites. The explanation usually given is that Cæsar had intended to poison the Cardinal in order to seize his property, but that by accident or design the wine destined for the purpose was handed to the Pope and himself. Some modern historians see in this only a violent attack of autumnal malaria fever. The consequences of this event will be narrated in the next chapter.

CHAPTER XI

UP to the time of his father's death Cæsar Borgia was lord of Rome. He had money and strong castles, many friends, and eight devoted Spaniards in the Sacred College. With these resources he expected to be able to carry any election he pleased for the Papal chair. He told Macchiavelli that he had anticipated everything that could possibly happen on his father's death, only that he had not foreseen that at the time he himself might be dangerously ill. As it was, he got possession of the Pope's treasure before the death was made known. Everything else was plundered by the servants. The Cardinals were in the greatest embarrassment. A French army under Francesco Gonzaga was on the march from the north. The Orsini and the Colonna might at any moment make an attack upon Rome. Cæsar entrenched himself in the Borgo—that portion of Rome which contains St. Peter's and the Vatican, and which is defended by the Tiber and the castle of St. Angelo. He contrived to make a treaty with the Colonna, and so to detach them from their alliance with the Orsini. He also offered to join his army with that of the King of France, to receive in return a guarantee of all his possessions. With the Cardinals he made an agreement to leave Rome in three days. Giuliano della Rovere now returned to Rome after an exile of ten years, together with Ascanio Sforza and Cardinal d'Amboise, Archbishop of Rouen, the minister of Louis XII. At the same time Jacopo d'Appiano returned to Piombino, Pandolfo Malatesta to Rimini, and Giovanni Sforza to Pesaro. The French and Spanish armies were both forbidden to enter Rome.

The French candidate for the Papacy was the Cardinal d'Amboise, the Venetians were in favour of Giuliano della Rovere, who promised to be a "good Italian." The requisites for a Pope at this time were that he should reform Church discipline, should summon a Council, and should conduct a crusade against the Turks. The Italians and Spaniards united against a French Pope, and preferred to choose an old man who would fill the place for a short time. The votes fell on the Cardinal of Siena, Francesco Todeschini Piccolomini, sixty-four years of age and in bad health. He was proclaimed on September 22. Being the nephew of Pius II., he took the title of Pius III. The Venetians had determined to take possession of the Romagna, and conquered Cesena and Faenza without difficulty. Cæsar Borgia returned to Rome with a certain number of troops, and received the protection of the Pope, which was not worth much. But the Orsini made peace with the Colonna, and Cæsar retired into the Castle of St. Angelo, which had been the living tomb of so many of his victims. Pope Pius III., who had been in weak health at the time of his election, and was actually ill on the day of his coronation, died on October 18, 1503. There was no doubt as to his successor. The

thirty-six cardinals who entered into conclave chose unanimously Giuliano della Rovere, who took the name of
Julius II. He was a most remarkable man, sixty years
of age, but full of enterprise and energy, more fitted to
be a great king than a great priest. During his ten years'
exile he had cared more for the interests of France than
of Italy. He had stirred up the expedition of Charles VIII.
into Italy in order to overthrow Alexander VI. He had
promised the Spaniards that if he became Pope he would
make Cæsar Borgia Standard Bearer of the Church.
Macchiavelli says that the only mistake Cæsar ever made
was in allowing him to be Pope instead of the Cardinal
d'Amboise. Julius was not only a soldier of blood and
iron, but a great patron of literature and art. For him
Bramante worked in St. Peter's, Michael Angelo painted
the frescoes of the Sistine Chapel, and Raffaelle made the
apartments of the Vatican glow with colour. The attempt
to produce a tomb worthy of the great pontiff was the
tragedy of Michael Angelo's life.

If the Venetians thought that Julius would make a
compliant Pope they were greatly mistaken. Rimini had
already opened its gates to them, but the Pope bade
them abstain from invading the dominions of the Church.
At the same time he refused to confirm Cæsar Borgia
in his dukedom, and had evidently planned his overthrow.
Cæsar embarked on the Tiber on November 9, and set
sail for Ostia. His supposed object was to go to Tuscany
and to implore the assistance of the Florentines against
the Venetians, but Julius demanded from him the restitution of the Romagna in order to save it from Venice.
When Cæsar refused he was brought back to Rome and
thrown into prison. Here he was compelled to humble

himself before Guidobaldo da Montefeltro, Duke of Urbino, whom he had so ruthlessly driven from his capital. In the beginning of the year 1504, he was released from prison on the condition of delivering up his fortresses. Just before this, on December 28, 1503, the French had been seriously defeated by the Spaniards under Consalvo on the banks of the Garigliano. Piero de' Medici was drowned by the swamping of a boat at the mouth of the river. When Cæsar found that he could no longer depend upon the French, he turned his attention to their rivals. He took refuge with Consalvo da Cordova at Naples. The Great Captain appeared at first to receive him in a friendly manner, but afterwards treacherously delivered him to Spain. He spent two years in confinement at Medina del Campo, and was then allowed to live with his brother-in-law, the King of Navarre. He fell in his service on March 12, 1507, in a petty conflict with his vassals. So perished one who is justly regarded as one of the greatest monsters of an age fruitful in evil characters. He was relentlessly cruel, and allowed no obstacle to stand in his way, yet he was not only admired but loved by those who knew him well. Macchiavelli represents him as the incarnation of political wisdom, but we may reasonably doubt whether this wisdom went much beyond a calculating cunning. Had he been a really great man he would have thrown himself into his dukedom of the Romagna, and either held it against all comers, or perished in the struggle. He may have conceived the idea of the Unity of Italy, but greater political wisdom would have shown him that he was not taking the best means to effect his object.

We have seen that Julius II. ascended the Papal throne

at a great crisis in the history of Europe, and especially of Italy. Naples was in the hands of Spain, and Milan in those of France, and on the rivalries of these two great powers hung the destinies of the peninsula. The smaller states were powerless. Florence was entirely occupied by the war with Pisa. In 1502 she had entirely changed her constitution by abolishing the rapid succession of magistrates who held office for two months only, and electing Piero Soderini Standard Bearer for life. Perugia, Siena, Lucca, Bologna held their independence only on sufferance. Julius restored to their possessions those Roman barons who had been driven out by the Borgia. Amongst these were the Colonna and the Orsini. The Pope also established his nephew, Francesco Maria della Rovere as heir to the Montefeltri in Urbino. He also favoured the triple alliance between France, Spain and the Empire concluded at Blois on September 22, 1504. By this treaty Naples was to pass to the Archduke Philip, and Louis XII. was to have the investiture of the Milanese. Charles, the son of Phillip, was to marry Claudia, the daughter of the King of France. For the moment, there was peace in Italy with the exception of the war between Florence and Pisa. But a league was made between the Pope, the Emperor, the King of France, and the Archduke Philip to recover from the Venetians the territories which they had conquered. This remained for the moment without practical result. Under the present condition of Europe it was impossible for an energetic sovereign like Julius not to desire to imitate in some degree the policy of Cæsar Borgia, and to establish a solid temporal princedom in the centre of Italy. For this purpose it was necessary to extinguish the petty lords who stood in his way, and the cities which principally arrested his attention were Perugia and Bologna. He entered Perugia as a conqueror on August 13, 1506; he then proceeded to Cesena, where, on October 1, he published a bull deposing Giovanni Bentivoglio from the government of Bologna, at the same time excommunicating him. Finding that the help of France was given to his rival, the unhappy victim surrendered himself with the promise of life and revenue, and on November 11 Julius entered Bologna in triumph. He stayed there the whole winter, and on Palm Sunday, March 13, 1507, he reached Rome, received with every sign of rejoicing which the imagination of the Renaissance could invent.

At this time Ferdinand the Catholic was at Naples. He had heard on his journey of the death of his son-in-law Philip, son of Maximilian, husband of Juana, called the Mad, and father of Charles V. He returned hastily, passed by Ostia without going to Rome to visit the Pope, and landed at Savona, where he met Louis XII. They remained together for three days, but it is not known what agreement they arrived at. It is supposed that they took into consideration the reform of the Church, the league against Venice, and the fate of Pisa. Venice was at this time occupying some towns in the territory of Lombardy and of Naples which were claimed by France and Spain. The Pope had determined, ever since the moment of his accession, to abate the pride and restrain the ambition of the Venetians by wresting from them the conquests which they had made in the Romagna. At an early period he had created three French Cardinals and one Spaniard, the famous Ximenes, in token of his desire to bring the two rival powers into harmony. As

early as March, 1504, he had sent representatives to the
courts of France, Spain, and the Empire to stir them up
to an attack upon Venice. At that time Louis XII. and
Maximilian were not on terms of intimate friendship, and
the Emperor is supposed to have favoured a plan by
which Il Moro should be restored to the throne of Milan,
and some addition of territory should be granted to the
Swiss. His views on these matters were altered by the
death of his son Philip. The heir to Spain and the
Empire was his grandson Charles, a weakly child of seven
years old. He wished to secure to him the quiet possession of his inheritance, and one step in that direction
was to re-establish the power of Germany and its influence
over Italy. Maximilian desired to receive the Imperial
crown at Rome. He made known his intention of doing
so to the Imperial Diet assembled at Constance in 1507.
The Pope was not in favour of this expedition, while
France and Venice were strongly opposed to it. Switzerland, in the Diet of Zurich, alone declared its consent.
On February 3, 1507, Maximilian was proclaimed in
Trent " Roman Emperor Elect," a title which was afterwards used by his successors, as it appeared to relieve
the Emperors of the necessity of being crowned in Rome.

The project of a journey to Rome was given up, and
a war was undertaken against the Venetians, who, with
the support of France, had refused the Emperor a passage through their dominions. Maximilian was every-
where defeated; Gorizia and Trieste were added to
the Venetian dominions, and in June, 1508, he was, with
great reluctance, forced to accept a three years' truce.
Venice was at this time in a critical condition. She had
by degrees lost her possessions in the East before the

advancing Turk, and had only the shreds of her former power left. Her commerce also was passing from her. The discoveries of the Portuguese, the opening of the new road to India, were events destined to carry the course of the world's traffic into other lines. Venice determined to make up by an Empire in Italy for what she was losing in the East, and she dreamed that she might be the saviour of the peninsula, who should bring together state after state in long-desired unity. Had she followed out this design with frank and open magnanimity, it is possible that she might have been able to effect at least a considerable portion of it. But she attempted to gain her ends by conquest, and so roused the determined opposition of powerful enemies. She was then the mistress of great resources. Her fleets had kept the French from Genoa, the Spaniards from Naples, her army had defended Milan. She lay, a bulwark against the invader, before the Alps of Tyrol and Carinthia. She was mistress of Verona, the key of Italy, to those who entered her by the valley of the Adige. She possessed Brescia, Bergamo, Cremona, and part of the duchy of Milan. She also owned Friuli, which was coveted by Austria, and some towns on the coast of Italy of which Spain demanded the restoration. In the Romagna she held Ravenna, Faenza, Cervia, and Rimini. She possessed something which every other power wished to have. Pope Julius was especially wroth with the Republic of St. Mark about his territory in the Romagna. He said one day to the Venetian Ambassador, "I will make Venice into a fishing village." "And we," replied the envoy, "will reduce you again to the status of a petty priest if you are not sensible." The outcome of all these jealousies was that a league was formed

against Venice at Cambray on December 10, 1508,
the object of which was the destruction of Venice and
the partition of her possessions. Besides the gains of the
powers already mentioned, Hungary was to have Dalmatia,
and Cyprus was to pass to the House of Savoy. The
league was formed between the Emperor, France, Spain,
and the Pope, but the latter did not sign it until all hope
of gaining the towns in the Romagna by other means had
been lost. The Florentines were induced to join it by
the promise of Pisa. The league of Cambray is a serious
blot on the reputation of Julius II. He consented to
invite the great powers of Europe as invaders into Italy
in order that he might recover a few towns of no great
importance. Venice prepared to withstand her enemies
with courage. The burden of the war fell upon Louis XII.,
as Maximilian was slow in collecting his forces. The
famous battle of Agnadello was fought on May 14, 1509
and nearly destroyed the Republic. It is said that the
killed amounted to 20,000, nearly all Venetians. Peschiera,
Cremona, Brescia and Bergamo fell, and the keys of Verona,
Vicenza and Pavia were delivered to the representatives
of the Emperor. The very completeness of the victory was
to a certain extent an advantage for the Venetians, as
it brought into contrast the ambition of Louis XII., and
the sluggishness of Maximilian, who was not supported by
Germany. When the Emperor at last in July reached
Italy in person he found that an accommodation was
already in progress. The Venetians, in their despair,
offered to the Pope and the Spaniards the towns which
they coveted, and when the Pope hesitated about grant-
ing peace talked of appealing to the Turks. Julius thundered with his bulls on the other side. In the din of the

conflict Pisa, after a long resistance, surrendered itself to the Florentines. Venice was saved by the jealousy of the allies, who were opposed to her, and by the slowness of the Emperor. Maximilian was driven back from the walls of Padua. The Pope began to be more disposed towards peace. He said to the Venetian ambassadors, "If Venice ceased to exist we should have to create another." He came to terms in February, 1510. The Venetian ambassadors received solemn absolution, as the Florentines had received it from Sixtus IV. The ceremony took place in St. Peter's on the second Sunday in Lent, February 24, 1510.

Julius was not contented with being the most powerful man in Italy, he wished to become the most powerful man in the world. The peace between the Pope and Venice was a great blow to Louis XII. He and Maximilian continued the war. Julius sent the golden rose to Henry VIII. of England, who had succeeded his father a few weeks before the battle of Agnadello, he also granted the investiture of the kingdom of Naples to Ferdinand the Catholic, although he was still bound in a league of amity with Maximilian. In August, 1510, he attacked Ferrara which was an enemy of Venice. Louis lost all patience. In September he summoned a Synod at Blois and renounced all dealings with the Pope. Julius replied by expelling the French embassy from the Papal court. He pursued his conquests in the Romagna in person. It was not a matter of astonishment to the Italians that the Pope should fight in person at the head of his army. He was carried into Mirandola, the city of Pico, through the first breach made in the walls. After this, being unable to ride on horseback, he was conveyed from town to town in a carriage drawn by four oxen. In May, 1511, he suffered a great blow by the loss of Bologna, which he had left under the charge of Cardinal Alidosi, a worthless favourite. Exasperated by the vices of his government the people rose in tumult, pulled down the statue of Julius II., which Michael Angelo had placed over the portal of the cathedral to commemorate the conquest of the city, and cast out of its materials a cannon and a bell, and recalled the Bentivogli to their ancient city. The Cardinal fled to Julius at Ravenna and laid the blame on the young Duke of Urbino, who, he said, had reached the town too late to save it. The Duke enraged at this, cut Alidosi down in the public street and killed him with his own hands, none of the Cardinal's retinue daring to defend him. Julius was beside himself with rage and despair; the world seemed to darken around him. Bologna was lost, his nephew had disgraced him, he was threatened by a schism and a council. The rebel Cardinals, among whom the principal were Adriano da Corneto and Bernardino Carvajal, who had deserted Julius on his breach with France, retired to Pisa, where they prepared to summon a council. They said that as Julius had always refused to do this, the king of France had a right to call one in his place.

It is said that at this time Maximilian had serious thoughts of making himself first coadjutor of the Pontiff, then actual Pope, and at last priest or saint. It is not known whether he was serious in this design, but there is evidence that he had collected 300,000 ducats to purchase the votes of the Cardinals. It is scarcely likely that he would have succeeded in securing the obedience of the world. The Pope, on his return to Rome, summoned a council to meet at the Lateran, which was the most effective answer to his enemies. In the middle of August he fell suddenly ill, and in a few days a report spread through Italy that he was dead. His attendants plundered his palace; they scarcely left the linen in his bed. The Romans determined to make an effort to restore the ancient liberties of the Republic which the Ecclesiastics had usurped. Pompeo Colonna, who was afterwards Cardinal, and Roberto Orsini placed themselves at the head of the movement. A new Pope was to restore popular rights, to raise four Romans to the purple, and to surrender the castle of St. Angelo for ever to the people. But Julius suddenly awoke from his lethargy. There was a general panic in the Court and in the city. Colonna retired to his estates in the Campagna and collected partisans for the French cause.

After his recovery Julius II had only one thought, to drive the French out of Italy. As the League of Cambray had been formed against Venice he would now form another league for this purpose, which should be called "The Holy League." This new alliance between the Pope, Spain, and Venice was proclaimed in the church of Santa Maria del Popolo on October 5, 1510. It was open for Henry VIII. and Maximilian to join it if they pleased. Raimondo da Cordova was made commander-in-chief. Money alone was needed; Switzerland would supply soldiers in plenty. Julius had given the Cardinal's hat to Schinner, bishop of Sion. The Swiss had hitherto fought in the cause of France. Schinner now enlisted them in troops for the service of the Pope. Just a month after the publication of the Holy League, the schismatic Council held its first sitting in Pisa. It was a mere shadow of the Council which had sat there a century before. It comprised two archbishops, fourteen bishops, and a few abbots, who were all placed under the Pope's ban. The Pisans closed their cathedral, and the council soon transferred itself to Milan. In the war of the League which now ensued, the soul of the French army was Gaston, Count of Foix, and Duke of Nemours, sister's son to Louis XII. Gaston speedily conquered Bologna, Bergamo, and Brescia. This last conquest was sullied by a terrible slaughter. " The unhappy city was quickly sacked," says a contemporary, " and all its male inhabitants were either killed or taken prisoners, a thing cruel indeed but almost necessary." Gaston tried to save the convent of nuns from attack, but was unable to do so. This took place on February 19, 1512, and appeared to be a realization of the prophecies of Savonarola. Gaston had been ordered to fight a decisive battle before the Swiss could have time to descend from their mountains, or Henry VIII. to land in Normandy, and before Maximilian had declared himself. The conquered territory was to be preserved for the future Pope, and Naples was to be attacked by the victorious army of the French. With this intention he appeared before the walls of Ravenna. On the low swampy ground where the Roman fleet had once ridden at anchor was fought on April 11, 1512, the terrible battle of Ravenna, one of the bloodiest on record, a battle fought on Easter Sunday between the Most Holy Pope and the Most Christian King. Gaston had under him 8,000 French and Italians, 5,000 Gascons, 5,000 German mercenaries, together with splendid cavalry and artillery. The army of the League which contained the veterans of Consalvo, was commanded by Cardona. On one side was Cardinal

Sanseverino, clad in full panoply of mail; on the other Giovanni de' Medici, the luxurious epicurean, afterwards Pope Leo X. The artillery fire lasted two hours. Then the French cavalry completely routed the Spanish. Giovanni de' Medici was taken prisoner. Giuliano de' Medici, afterwards Pope Clement VII., fled for safety. The struggle between the German and Spanish infantry was terrible. Just in the flush of victory, as he charged with " French fury" in the final encounter, Gaston de Foix was killed. He was only twenty-two years of age. He has left a brilliant name in that chivalrous time, but impartial judgment cannot acquit him of needless cruelty. The victory of the French was complete. Ravenna was plundered for four days. Rimini, Forlì, Cesena, Siena, Imola opened their gates. Rome and Naples would not have been safe if there had been a general competent to lead on the troops. But Gaston de Foix had fallen at the moment of greatest need. This battle is remarkable, among other things, as marking the transition from the mediæval to the modern methods of fighting. Cannon were largely used, but pikes, spears and halberds were no less efficacious. The chivalrous nobility of France, Italy, and Spain appeared in full armour. The battle was undoubtedly won by the steadiness of the Swiss and German infantry, who held their own against a storm of onslaught.

When the news of the defeat reached the Vatican the consternation was very great. The Cardinals counselled peace, the Pope prepared to fly, but he soon recovered courage, and sending for the ambassadors of Spain and Venice, told them that he would risk 100,000 ducats and his tiara to chase the French from Italy. He was really saved by the Swiss. Cardinal Schinner was not ungrateful for his elevation. He got together a force of twenty thousand mountaineers and sent them over the Alps to invade the Milanese. The French were forced to retreat into Lombardy, and to give up all idea of marching against Rome. The Pope felt so secure that he was able to open the Lateran Council on May 2. There were present at the first sitting fifteen Cardinals, thirteen Patriarchs, ten Archbishops, fifty-six Bishops, two Abbots, four Masters General of Orders, the Florentine Pietro Squarcialupi, senator of Rome, and the ambassadors of Spain, Venice, and Florence, Girolamo Vich, Francesco Foscari and Antonio Strozzi. The Council was opened with an ostentatious display of military pomp. A fortnight later the Pope was able to announce the renewal of the Holy League. Henry VIII. of England had promised to support the power of the Papacy which he afterwards did so much to destroy, and Maximilian also agreed to join in driving the French out of Italy. Thus by skilful diplomacy a brilliant victory had been turned into a disastrous defeat. Cardinal Schinner recovered Cremona and Lodi, and entered Milan at the end of June. The victory of Ravenna bore no fruit. Giovanni de' Medici escaped from prison, and the French retreated from Italy.

Pope Julius was now again at the height of his power, and it might seem that he had recovered it by the direct interposition of Providence. Bologna drove out the Bentivogli and made its submission to the Pope, Alfonzo of Ferrara was solemnly reconciled with him. A congress of the allies was held at Mantua, at which were present Raimondo de Cardona as Spanish Viceroy and the representatives of the Emperor, the Pope, the Venetians, the Swiss, and the Florentines. The possession of Milan

was secured to Massimiliano Sforza, the son of Il Moro,
a boy of fifteen. The fate of Florence was more difficult
to determine. At this time, as we have seen, Piero
Soderini was Standard Bearer for life. The League
wanted money, and Florence, under its present rulers,
was not able or not willing to grant it, whereas much
more might be expected from the Medici. King Ferdinand had given an uncertain voice with regard to the
destiny of Florence, but Cardona demanded the deposition
of Soderini and the recall of the Medici. When these
conditions were refused, and the negotiations for money
dragged on slowly, the war against Florence was declared
to be the business of the entire League. Pirato was
besieged by the Viceroy and taken on August 29. The
sack of the city by the "infuriated dogs" of Spain is one
of the most terrible events in Italian history. A contemporary says, "The sack was universal, of all property, of
all persons, and of all places, sacred and profane. Of
the rapes, incests and adulteries which followed I will
not speak for shame." Florence was ill prepared for
defence. A sedition broke out which had been long
brooding. A number of young men went to the palace
crying that they wanted no more of the Standard Bearer.
On August 24 Soderini left the Public Palace, and on
September 1st Giuliano de' Medici entered Florence. Cardinal Giovanni followed, and then his nephew Lorenzo.
Giuliano, the second son of Lorenzo the Magnificent, was
regarded as the head of the house after Piero's death,
but Cardinal Giovanni was really the soul of the government. A conspiracy of the Piagnoni to restore liberty to
Florence which broke out in February, 1513, under the
leadership of Agostino Capponi and Pietro Paolo Boscoli,

was easily suppressed. Niccolo Macchiavelli was imprisoned in consequence of it. He had lost all his offices at the change of government. Parma and Piacenza now submitted themselves to the Pope, the first time that they had been under papal dominion since the original donation of Pepin. The Madonna di San Sisto of Raffaelle, which was painted for a church in Piacenza, is a standing memorial of the Divine favour which those cities might expect who sought for the mediation of the Pope by accepting his authority. But these very successes had within them the germ of future dissensions. Venice was discontented with her share of the plunder, Maximilian did not approve of the aggrandisement of the Papal See. He was also desirous to obtain the duchy of Milan for his grandson Charles, a project which was strongly opposed both by Julius and the Swiss, who were now a considerable power in Europe. Matthew Lang, Cardinal and Bishop of Genoa, came to Rome in November, 1512, to attend the Lateran Council as representative of the Emperor. This secured the countenance of the Emperor for this œcumenical council in opposition to the schismatical council which had now removed from Milan to Lyons. The Emperor and the Pope also agreed to make common cause against Venice, who refused to surrender the important towns of Verona and Vicenza. Julius II. now stood at the height of his power. He had established the authority of his Council, had driven the French from Italy, gained the friendship of the Emperor, and enlarged the states of the Church. He ruled with undisputed sway over the fairest provinces in the heart of Italy. There is some reason for believing that his next enterprise would have been to turn his arms against the Spaniards and to recover Naples. Just at this juncture he died. He fell ill with fever at the end of January, 1513, and could not be present at the fifth session of the Lateran Council held on February 16 in that year, in which were promulgated the famous constitutions for the abolition of simony in the election of the Popes, one of the most important events of his reign. He gave orders for his burial, lamented the sins and offences of his life, and with his last breath absolved the signory of Venice and the Duke of Ferrara from censure. A vain attempt was made to rescue him by a draught of melted gold. He died in the night between February 20 and 21. All Rome felt that a mighty spirit had departed. Julius II., besides being one of the greatest of Popes, was one of the most conspicuous princes of his time. But whatever may have been his eminence in the Councils of Church and State, it is impossible to dissociate his memory from the names of Bramante, Raffaelle and Michael Angelo. All these he employed in turn on the great work of St. Peter's, a building which was planned as the emblem of a new era and a new Church. Bramante made the design for the mighty temple, Raffaelle decorated the Vatican with undying frescoes, Michael Angelo raised, as he said, the dome of the Pantheon in the air as a symbol of a church which was to embrace the whole of Christianity. Also the great tragedy of the sculptor's life was to have projected the gigantic monument of Julius, too vast a conception ever to be realized. Instead of that majestic dream, the figures of prophets and virtues, the sarcophagus raised aloft by Titanic representations of heaven and earth, all that marks the burial place of Julius is a small slab in a chapel of St. Peter's, while the most notable fragment of the monument, the horned Moses, with its cataract of beard, is to be sought in a distant church. Julius had no successor. The sceptre of the temporal power fell from the grasp of weaker hands. The building of the Cathedral of St. Peter's laid taxes upon the Catholic world, which could only be met by the sale of indulgences, an abuse which roused the indignation of Christianity and stirred up the revolt of Luther.

CHAPTER XII

LEO X

THE conclave for the election of a new pope met on March 5, 1513. The time of meeting had been hastened to prevent the interference of the schismatic cardinals, and the outbreak of tumults in Rome. The twenty-five cardinals who were present were divided into two parties, the old and the young. The first might think of electing Rafaello Riario, sister's son to Sixtus IV, the Cardinal whom we remember as a young man struck for ever with a deathly paleness by his presence at the conspiracy of the Pazzi in Florence. The younger party, however, were determined to choose Giovanni de' Medici. He had indeed weighty claims, his house was illustrious and wealthy, he was the enemy of France, his character was good according to the standard of those times, he was a great patron of literature and art and was known to be remarkably generous. His palace was the centre of the Italian culture of the late renaissance, and he turned no one away without a gift. He was only thirty-seven years of age, but he was known to have an incurable disease. He was elected without difficulty on March 10, as the other party withdrew their opposition, and took the name of

Leo X. The title was singularly inappropriate: there was nothing of the Lion in that soft, gentle and self-indulgent nature. His election was, however, hailed with joy throughout Italy. It was regarded as the beginning of a golden age. His first act was to appoint as his secretaries Bembo and Sadoletus, the most distinguished Latinists of the age.

He chose April 11, the anniversary of his capture at the battle of Ravenna, for the day of his coronation and of his solemn procession and ride from the Vatican to the Lateran palace. A more splendid spectacle had never been seen in Rome, at least in later days. The vassals of the church were all assembled: the Duke of Urbino, Alfonzo of Este, Duke of Ferrara, the hero of Ravenna. Leo rode on the white Arab steed which had carried him in the day of battle. The streets were decorated with the full magnificence of the pagan renaissance. The talent of Rafaelle and his scholars was at Leo's disposal to devise statues, inscriptions and triumphal arches. Some of the finest statues of antiquity were set up before the houses, Ganymedes, Apollos, figures of Bacchus and Venus. The fountains flowed with wine, servants scattered gold and silver among the crowd. A lofty arch erected by the banker Agostino Chigi bore this inscription:

> " Olim habuit Cypria sua tempora, tempora Mavors
> Olim habuit, sua nunc tempora Pallas habat."

" Love and war have had their time, wisdom now claims hers," — a delicate allusion to Alexander, Julius and Leo. The Pope must have smiled still more when he saw that close by this arch a goldsmith had placed a statue of Venus with this legend, in better Latin, "Mars fuit, et Pallas, Cypria semper ero." Lust indeed was not likely to fail in the court of the renaissance. When after a passage of many hours the procession arrived at the Lateran, the palace was found guarded by a joint battalion of Colonna and Orsini.

The beginning of Leo's reign was certainly auspicious. He set free from prison Niccolo Macchiavelli, and Nicolo Capponi, his father's biographer, who had been confined since the conspiracy of the Boscoli. He recalled the exiled Soderini from Ragusa. He wrote to his brother Giuliano and to the king of France, that the dearest wish of his heart was union and peace among the Princes of Christendom. The schismatic cardinals Carvajal and Sanseverino surrendered themselves, and all the states of Europe declared their obedience—except France. Still the situation was full of anxiety. The two pressing needs of Leo X. were to preserve intact the inheritance of Julius, and to keep the king of France away from Italy. War was not long in breaking out. Two leagues or alliances stood opposed to each other face to face. The league of Blois signed in March, 1513, between Louis XII. and the Venetians for the recovery of Milan, and the league of Mechlin or Malines between Henry VIII. and Maximilian to which Spain and the Pope afterwards gave their adhesion. Among the objects of this league were to defend Milan and the Church and to attack the king of France in his own country. Swiss mercenaries, the best infantry of those days, were to be hired with papal gold. The war began and was destined to continue for a long time. Milan was the prize of victory, and its possession seemed to determine the mastery of the world. The struggle was fought out in the broad plains of Lombardy, where Swiss infantry, French men-at-arms, Spanish arquebusiers, Italian cavalry and artillery, and German landsknechts wrestled together

in endless conflict. The battle of Novara was fought on
June 6, 1513. The French generals Trivulzio and La
Tremouille were completely beaten and were compelled
to repass the Alps. Dominitianus Sforza was established
in the possession of his capital. At the same time Louis
XII was being hard pressed by the English in his own
country. On August 16 was fought the battle of Spurs,
which cost the French the possession of Picardy. Swiss
troops were also laying siege to Dijon. These reverses
induced Louis to make peace with the Pope. In December, 1513, he solemnly renounced the schism of Pisa and
gave in his obedience to Leo X. as the rightful occupant
of the Holy See. Such was the brilliant close of the first
year of Leo's reign.

It soon appeared that in the matter of nepotism Leo
would be little better than his predecessors. The court
of Rome which had been in turn Spanish and Ligurian
became Florentine. Leo made his brother Giuliano and
his nephew Lorenzo, the son of Piero, Patricians of
Rome, and he seemed anxious to create for his brother a
principality in central Italy. He raised to the cardinalate
Giulio, the bastard son of his brother Giuliano, after falsely
declaring his legitimacy, and thus paved the way for his
becoming Pope under the title of Clement VII.

It ought to be mentioned that in the spring of 1514 Pope
Leo exercised, for perhaps the last time, the faction which
has long been accorded to the Holy See, when the world was
not yet divided between Catholic and Protestant—of being
the supreme referee of disputed questions between the
sovereigns of Europe, and the enforcer by spiritual means
of the sanctions of International Law. At this time
the progress of maritime discovery was chiefly due to the

enterprise of Spain and Portugal. There was some danger
of their conflicting claims clashing and producing a serious
European war. Alexander VI. had therefore, either as
the acknowledged arbiter in such questions, or because
all newly discovered islands were held to belong to the
Pope, drawn an imaginary line between the conquests of
the two countries, with the idea that one should pursue
their discoveries to the East and the other to the West.
The ships of the two nations had, however, unexpectedly
met on the other side of the globe and a new arrangement became necessary. Pope Leo received a Portuguese
embassy with Tristan d'Acunha at its head, bearing the
treasures of the East to lay at the Pontiff's feet. An
elephant was now seen in Europe for the first time since
the destruction of the Roman empire. Leo solemnly
secured to the Portuguese the possession of the lands
which they had discovered and made an award which
was calculated to prevent disputes in future.

The history of Italy now becomes involved with those
struggles for the balance of power in Europe with which
we are familiar in modern times. The defeat and death
of king James IV. of Scotland at Flodden Field on November 9, 1513, deprived Louis XII. of an important ally.
This led to his making peace with Ferdinand at the close
of 1513, with Maximilian in the treaty of Orleans in
March, 1514, and with Henry VIII. in the treaty of London, August 9, 1514. Louis was anxious to marry his
daughter to the young Archduke Charles, but it did not
suit Leo's purpose that France and the empire should be
so closely connected, and the marriage did not take place.
Wolsey on his side was anxious for an alliance between
France, England and the Pope against Spain and the

empire, and with this view Louis XII. married Mary the
sister of Henry VIII. just at the time of the peace of
London. But this marriage had no result. Louis died a
few months afterwards and was succeeded by his nephew
Francis I. on January 1, 1515. Leo was too cautious
to commit himself. He saw that the strength of
the papacy lay in holding a just balance between France
and Spain. He even secretly encouraged an alliance between
Spain, the Empire, the Swiss and Milan for the defence
of that duchy. With two leagues before him he was able
to join whichever he pleased. At another time he sent
a nuncio to the Venetians to detach them from the French
alliance. They replied that they were well disposed to
the Pope, but that it was for his advantage to be on
good terms with France, because it might assist him
in claiming the Kingdom of Naples for his brother
Giuliano.

Francis I. was now twenty years of age, a brilliant
prince, full of ambition. The world had seldom seen two
such monarchs side by side as Francis I. of France and
Henry VIII. of England. A third was soon to be added
to them in the person of Charles V. On his succession
Francis assumed the title of Duke of Milan, and asserted
his claim to that duchy. With the object of enforcing
it he renewed the alliance with England and Venice. Leo
was in hesitation as to which side he should take. Giuliano
had just married Filiberta of Savoy, which seemed to favour
the French alliance, and if Francis would have given
Naples to Giuliano in exchange for Milan, it is possible
that Leo would have joined him. But Francis wished to
keep Naples for himself and so in July, 1515, Leo definitely
joined the alliance between the Empire and Spain. At

the same time he made Wolsey a Cardinal in the hope of detaching Henry from the French alliance.

The strength of the league consisted of thirty thousand Swiss soldiers, whom Macchiavelli calls, "the masters of modern warfare," but the French were successful against them. Frioulozi, crossing the more southern passes of the Cottian Alps with his heavy artillery, surprised Prospero Colonna and defeated his army, so that the frightened Leo cried for peace. Francis I. in person marching from Turin advanced against the Swiss. A battle raged at Marignano, between Milan and Pavia, for two days, September 13 and 14, 1515, at the end of which the French were victorious and the Swiss infantry lost its prestige for ever. Milan passed into the hands of the conqueror. Francis might now, if he had pleased, have advanced to the conquest of the rest of Italy, with better hopes of success than Charles VIII. But he was afraid to have his two rival powers of England and the Empire in his rear. The terrified Pope hastened to change his policy. He met Francis at Bologna on December 8 where he held a conference which lasted two days. His passage through Florence rivalled his brilliant entry into Rome. For this occasion the unfinished façade of the cathedral was temporarily completed by Sanscovino and Andrea del Sarto. Francis assumed an attitude of humility. He had the assurance to tell Leo that he had journeyed over mountains, woods, rivers, and streams of fire, and made his way through the legions of the Swiss only to submit himself in lowly reverence to the godlike man; he laid his power, his riches, his army, his fleet, his kingdom and himself at the feet of His Holiness. The result of the meeting, however, did not correspond with these professions. The

Pope had to surrender Parma, Piacenza, Reggio and Modena, and to content himself with the duchy of Urbino. Francis also took the opportunity of extracting from the Pope a *concordat* which has since formed the basis of the liberties of the Gallican church. By this the King of France had the right to nominate to vacant sees, while the Pope received the revenues during the first year. In accepting these terms Leo perhaps chose the best way out of his many difficulties, but all hope of driving the French from Italy was lost. On March 17, 1516, Giuliano de' Medici, Duc de Nemours, died. The Pope transferred his interest to his nephew Lorenzo. King Ferdinand the Catholic had died previously on January 23. After he had secured the unity of Spain by the expulsion of the Moors, the ruling principle of his life had been antagonism to French ambition, which he believed, with some justice, would never be satisfied with anything short of the Empire of the world. Ferdinand was succeeded by his grandson, Charles I. of Spain, and Charles V. of Germany, a youth of sixteen. It was probable that before long he would also succeed to the dominions of his paternal grandfather Maximilian, who was now growing old, and this union of possessions would make him the most powerful monarch in Europe. The war which had been begun by the league of Cambray now came to an end and after an eight years' struggle Italy might hope for quieter times. On August 16, the treaty of Noyon was signed between Francis, Henry VIII. and Charles, by which the fate of Italy was left undecided. This was followed by the treaty of Brussels signed on December 3, by which Verona was surrendered to the French and by them handed over to the Venetians. Before this on

November 29, the thirteen Swiss Cantons had made the perpetual peace of Fribourg with the French.

This peace was only of a short duration. Europe was seething with mighty forces which no one completely understood, and which no one could master. All were conscious of the presence of a new age, and each tried to grasp eagerly and prematurely the advantages which the new age would bring forth. As early as February, 1517, Leo X. invited the assistance of Francis I. for the recovery of the Duchy of Urbino, and the Medicean state of Florence was naturally comprised in the arrangement. Shortly afterwards a treaty was signed at Cambray between the three great potentates, Charles, Francis and Henry for the partition of the North of Italy. Venice, Florence, Pisa, Leghorn and Siena were to be formed into a state under the name of "The Kingdom of Italy," which was to be given as an Imperial fief either to Charles V. or to his brother Ferdinand, while the rest including Lombardy, Genoa, Asti, Piedmont, Mantua, Montferrat, Verona, Piacenza, and Lucca were to go to Francis, also as an Imperial fief under the name of "The Kingdom of Lombardy." Leo besides was afflicted by domestic troubles. His enemies were those of his own household. The most powerful of these was Cardinal Raffaello Riario, who rode about Rome with a suite mounted on forty horses. Another young Cardinal, Alfonzo Petrucci, formed a plot to kill the Pope and to change the government of Rome. He had more than once brought a dagger with him into the consistory, but his courage failed him. He then attempted to use poison, but was betrayed to the Pope, tried and executed. At the same time the Cardinals Raffaello Riario and Adriano were both put into prison. Adriano, strange

to say, was of Bath and Wells in England. He
escaped to Venice, but returning to Rome at the death
of the Pope he was murdered by one of his own servants.
In order to secure himself against similar attacks Leo
created thirty-nine cardinals at once, of various states and
of different ranks in the ecclesiastical hierarchy. Some of
them were distinguished, but they were most of them
friends and adherents of the Medici. The ceremonies
attending this creation, and the war with Urbino which
now came to an end, cost the pope enormous sums, and
plunged him heavily into debt. Still he was in the possession of outward prosperity; the states of the Church
were consolidated and at peace; Lorenzo was married to
Maddalena, daughter of John II. Lord of Latour-Auvergne;
the Lateran Council was closed, having devoted its last
sittings to the possibilities of a crusade against the Turks.
Yet on the other side of the Alps a storm was arising,
more serious than any which had as yet stricken the
foundations of papal obedience. The money required for
the Pope's necessities was supplied by the sale of indulgences and this sale raised the indignation of Luther.
On the eve of All Saints, October 31, 1517, he fastened
on the door of the Cathedral of Wittemberg the ninety-
five theses by which he challenged the authority of the
Pope. Luther, born at Eisleben in 1483, had visited
Rome in 1510, had made his pilgrimage round the seven
basilicas, and had climbed the Sacred Staircases on his
knees. He now refused to obey the Pope's citation to
Rome, he attended the Imperial diet at Augsburg with
the safe conduct of the Emperor and the Elector of Saxony,
and appealed against the authority of the Pope to a General
Council.

Together with the Reformation which brought about a condition of war in Europe which lasted till 1648 and indeed for some time afterwards, arose a political struggle for the possession of the Empire. Maximilian strained every nerve to secure it for his grandson Charles, who he hoped would some day recover both Milan and Burgundy as ornaments of the Imperial crown. His rival was King Francis I. Maximilian pressed Leo to crown Charles king of the Romans in Germany, but before this could be accomplished Maximilian died at Linz on January 11, 1519. With him passed away a remarkable figure. He stands astride the mediæval and the modern world. He so far comprehended his peculiar position, that he took pains in his political conduct, by reconstruction of the army, and by constitutional reforms, to prepare the old fabric of the Empire to meet its new conditions and responsibilities. In the contest for the Imperial crown Leo, as might be expected, played a double part. He thought that the raising of either of these two powerful monarchs to the Imperial throne, would not contribute either to the security of the Apostolic See or to the interests of Italy. The Pope would have preferred the Margrave of Brandenburg but he would not accept Frederick of Saxony, the protector of Luther. Charles was elected Emperor at Frankfort on June 28, 1519. When Leo saw that his election was inevitable he did his best to secure his friendship. Charles was, it is true, a stranger to Germany, but he was grandson of Maximilian, a descendant of the Imperial line of Hapsburg, and was the best bulwark that could be found against the ambition of the French and the onslaught of the Turks. The great Empire of Charles V is the common source from which most of the arrangements of our modern states have arisen. Before this time the two great powers in Europe were the Church and the State, the Pope at the head of one and the Emperor at the head of the other. Both these powers were weakened or destroyed by the Reformation, and in their place a new antagonism sprang up, the antagonism between Protestantism and Catholicism represented mainly by the Germanic and the Romanic nations. France stood at the head of one section, Germany, herself divided, at the head of the other. The political life of Italy sank into comparative unimportance.

At the age of nineteen Charles ruled over Spain, Flanders, Naples, Sicily and Germany, and styled himself King of the Indian Islands and of the Oceanic continent. A struggle with France was inevitable. Leo, as usual, knew not which side to take. His flatterers advised him to throw himself in the arms of Charles, but his instinct forbade him as he dreaded the effect of his overweening power in Italy. At the same time an alliance with Germany was rendered easier by the death of his nephew Lorenzo, Duke of Urbino, who had married a Frenchwoman. His wife had died six days before in April, 1519, after giving birth to a daughter, who at a later time became famous as Catherine of Medici, the wife of one French king and the mother of three others. She was the last legitimate scion of the elder house of Medici. One son remained, Alexander, afterwards Duke of Florence, from 1534 to 1537. He was a mulatto, and his mother was a negress. It is certain that he was a bastard, but it is not certain whether his father was Lorenzo or Giulio, probably, however, the latter. Macchiavelli urged Leo X. to take the opportunity of restoring liberty to Florence, but he refused as he had been too much accustomed to regard Florence as the private property of his house.

It is strange that Pope Leo X should, like the Emperor Augustus of Rome, have lost one after the other those whom he had expected would be his heirs. But this loss did not make him less anxious to increase the possessions of the Holy See. He aimed at the wresting of Parma, Piacenza and Ferrara from Venice and he was ready to ally himself with that power which would best further the execution of his views. For this purpose he entered into communication both with Francis and Charles. Charles assumed the crown of the Holy Roman Empire at Aix-la-Chapelle on October 23, 1520, on the very same day that Soliman the Magnificent girt himself with the sword of Mahomet at Constantinople. Charles had some difficulty in persuading the citizens of Castile and Arragon to accept a sovereign who was a Fleming by birth and education, and he was greatly in want of allies. Henry VIII. had married his aunt Catherine of Arragon, but nevertheless on the Field of the Cloth of Gold he had met Francis I. and embraced him with all affection, although he was the most formidable rival of Charles. In order to counteract this friendship Charles took care to meet Henry VIII. at Rouen and by loading his minister, Cardinal Wolsey, with riches and honours, believed that he had fully attained his end.

The Emperor Charles V. summoned his first diet to meet in Worms on January 6, 1521. Germany was then on fire from one extremity to the other with the agitation produced by Luther. He had been excommunicated, as we have heard, on July 15, 1520, and had appealed to a Council. Charles was at this time extremely anxious

14

to secure the friendship of the Pope. They both needed
each other for the ends they had in view, the driving
of the French from Italy and the establishment of the
Sforza in Milan. Just before the meeting of the diet,
Leo renewed his excommunication against the rebellious
monk. At Worms Charles stood for the first time face
to face with the German nation. The younger and more
alert spirits would have wished him to place himself at
the head of Germany and to resist her two deadliest
enemies, France and the Papacy. But Charles was not
disposed to break entirely with the ancient church. His
views were rather to repress the storm of anarchy in
Germany which threatened to break up the old civil and
religious polity, to extinguish the authority of the Turks
in the East and to curb the ambition of France in the
West. France provoked him to war and he was ready
to meet her. It is perhaps fortunate that the Emperor
did not head the German Reformation. Being left to
itself it became a popular movement, and was in the
end more completely successful. Luther appeared before
the Diet of Worms on April 17 and 18, 1521. Here
he withstood the Emperor surrounded by his brilliant
court. " I cannot do otherwise, God help me! " was his
cry. The edict launched against him was dated May
26, when many of the estates had gone away and
Luther himself was in safety. Charles did not act a
sincere or single part with regard to Luther. On the
one hand he was anxious to ingratiate himself with the
Pope, and perhaps to satisfy his own conscience by
condemning him, on the other he felt that it would be
unwise to crush him entirely as he could be used from
time to time as a useful check upon papal authority.

The Reformation in Italy had a different character to that in Germany. Its principal effect was to bring into prominence the hatred felt against the temporal power of the Pope. Macchiavelli and Guicciardini the two foremost political characters of their time both considered the temporal power of the popes as the curse of Italy, and Guicciardini tells us that although circumstances forced him into the service of the popes, yet that his nature would have led him to prefer Luther, in the hope that if he did not entirely ruin, he might at least seriously impair, the accursed tyranny of the priests. Such were the aspirations of Italian patriots who desired that Italy might take her proper place among the kingdoms of the world. But Italy was not ripe for such an effort and there were no materials for forming or for continuing temporal sovereignty. Centuries were destined to elapse before their hopes were finally realized.

On the same day on which the bull against Luther was issued, a league was made between the Pope and the Emperor. The conditions were that Milan and Genoa should be taken from the French and be given back to their legitimate rulers, Francesco Sforza, the younger brother of Massimiliano, and to Antonietto Adorno. After the French had been driven out Charles promised to give Piacenza to the Pope, and to help him to conquer Ferrara. On the other hand the Pope was to invest Charles with the Kingdom of Naples, to crown him Emperor, and to support him in the war against Venice. It was to be left open for the Swiss and the English to join this league if they pleased. It was not so easy to hire Swiss soldiers as it had been. Cardinal Schinner did his best to assist the Pontiff, but Zwingli told his

countrymen: "The Cardinals wear large cloaks and red
hats, shake them and ducats fall out of them, wring them
and your own blood drops out." France seeing that a
breach with Charles was inevitable, declared war against
him, and attacked his possessions both in Luxemburg and
Navarra with very little success. It was in the battle of
Esquiros in the war of Navarra on June 30, 1521 that
Ignatius Loyola received the wound which had so important
an effect on the fortunes of the Catholic Church. It was
in the enforced retirement of the hospital that he conceived the idea of founding the Society of the Jesuits.
The King of France had no allies in Italy except the
Duke of Ferrara, the republic of Venice and some of the
smaller Italian despots. Wolsey, although he did not
give up the hope of mediating between the two contending powers made a treaty with Charles V. on August 25
at Bruges. Milan was captured on November 19 and
only a few towns were left to the French. The Pope
was so overjoyed at the fall of Milan that he said that
it was of more value than the papacy itself. He talked
of creating Cardinal Giulio de' Medici, Duke of Milan, and
of making Francesco Sforza Cardinal in his place. Piacenza and Parma soon followed the fate of Milan. But
Leo was unable to enjoy his triumph. News of the
conquest of Milan was brought to him on November 24 in
his villa of Malliano. The next day he returned to Rome
and was received by the populace with great rejoicings,
the shaking of olive branches, the blowing of trumpets, and
the firing of guns. A consistory had been summoned on the
following Wednesday, November 29, and the Pope intended to go in person to the church of Santa Maria del
Popolo to return thanks for his victory. But the night

before he felt unwell, and on December 1, 1521, he died. One effect of his death was to ruin his friends, as they had lent him large sums of money which now would never be repaid. After the enormous expense of his court he did not leave enough money to pay for his funeral. It was necessary to use up the old candles prepared for the obsequies of Cardinal Riario. The name of Leo X. is generally held in honour as the great hero of the renaissance, who continued the work of Lorenzo and Cosimo de' Medici, the sovereign under whom culture and refinement reached its zenith in Italy. This side of his career belongs rather to literary than to political history. As a politician we must judge that Leo X. was little better than his predecessors. He filled the papal court with his relations, he did not succeed in driving out the French from Italy, he dealt no serious blow to the Turks; he did not secure either the unity of Italy or the peace of Europe. He shewed no courage in great crises, he left the church a prey to the Reformation. If he cannot be accused of employing the arts of Macchiavelli in temporal matters, he must plead guilty to the charge of defending the Holy See with those weapons of deceit and double dealing which under the name of *finesse* and economy have brought so much discredit on the career and the reputation of the Jesuits.

CHAPTER XIII

THE SACK OF ROME

THE election of a new Pope appeared to contemporary politicians as the decision between the conflicting claims of Charles V. and Francis I. to the mastery of Europe. Every device of persuasion, fraud, and violence was used to affect the result. It was said that there were eighteen candidates. Charles's ambassador, Manuel, was horrified at what he saw at Rome. He said that Hell itself could not contain so much hatred and so many devils as there were amongst the Cardinals. The candidates who had the best chance were the Spaniard Carvajal, Wolsey the Englishman, and Giulio de' Medici. Charles would have been very glad to accept Giulio but he had too many enemies to succeed. The States of the Church were in a flame when Giulio consented to give his support to some other Imperial candidate and the choice fell upon Hadrian of Utrecht who was elected on January 9, 1522. It was difficult for the conclave to make up their minds to elect an unknown foreigner, and Cardinal Farnese came very near to obtaining the papacy. The people of Rome received the news with a howl of execration, but the Imperial party were in the greatest delight. The new Pope was a Fleming, son of a ship builder at Utrecht, named Boyens. He was born in 1459, he had been a tutor to Charles V. and was then Vice-chancellor of the University of Louvain. He afterwards became bishop of Tortosa, and Cardinal, and on the accession of Charles to the throne of Spain was made regent of that country in his absence. Charles was naturally delighted at the election and sent immediately to say that he hoped to receive the Imperial crown at the hands of his former tutor. In return the Pope gave him similar assurances of good will. Hadrian heard of his elevation at Vittoria, but he delayed his departure until a fleet should be ready in Barcelona to convey him across the dangerous seas.

In the meantime the war between the French and the Imperialists was continuing in Northern Italy. Milan, as we know, had been taken, and Genoa was sacked. Anarchy and confusion reigned in Rome itself, and there was some apprehension lest a second Avignon should be established in Spain. To make matters worse, the plague had broken out in the eternal City. It is a curious proof of the heathen sympathies of the time, that in order to stay the pestilence, an ox, consecrated with magic rites, was led by a Greek through the streets to the Colosseum and there solemnly sacrificed, the Roman clergy not offering a word of objection. Hadrian set out from his see at Tortosa on July 8, 1522, and a month later sailed from Tarragona. He had no interview with Charles before his departure, which was looked upon as a sign of independence. He landed at Genoa and did his best to spare the town. He reached Rome at the end of August. On his arrival he refused all pagan honours. His entry into his capital was simple, partly on account of the plague, partly because Leo had left the treasury poor. His life was certainly a great contrast to that of his predecessors. He hated the unholy pomp; the naked statues, the glaring frescoes; he reluctantly submitted to endure the splendours of the Vatican, and longed for a lodging in a quiet house and garden. Pope Hadrian VI, for his title was a repetition of his christian name, was a handsome man of imposing and serious mien. He lived in the simplest manner. He rose before daybreak to pray, and spent the rest of the day in study. His needs were supplied by a single servant whom he had brought with him from Spain. His expenses were a ducat a day which he paid overnight to his chaplain for the morrow. He spoke no Italian, and little of anything else, and Latin with a foreign accent. He gave no encouragement to artists, and it is well perhaps that Raffaelle had died in 1520. The great frescoes begun by his predecessors remained unfinished on the walls. Poets and fine writers were driven from the Vatican. Sadolet went to his bishopric of Carpentras, saying that Rome was Rome no longer; Castiglione retired to Mantua. Perhaps the reputation of Leo X. has been intensified by the contrast with his successor. Hadrian found nothing to succeed to but debts. He dismissed the idle crowd of menials which thronged the galleries of the Vatican. He filled the court with Flemings and gave his chief confidence to men of his own nation.

The objects which Hadrian had nearest at heart were those which had for some time formed part of the programme of every new Pope. He desired to give peace to Italy and to the world, to lead a crusade against the Turks, to stamp out heresy and to reform the church. He began by setting himself to stop the sale of indulgences.

But in none of these objects was he successful. He effected something by restoring Alfonzo of Ferrara to his dominions, but he could not reconcile the great powers. Indeed on June 19, 1522, Charles and Henry had met at Windsor and entered into an alliance against France. Although Belgrade had fallen, and Soliman was threatening Rhodes, there was little hope of organizing an expedition against the Turks. The attempts of the Pope to reform the church were equally idle; the evils which caused the mischief were too deeply rooted. There was no abuse which had not many defenders personally interested in maintaining it. Hadrian's own simplicity of life served only to set off in stronger contrast the unbounded luxury of the cardinals. He had too little sympathy with the tastes and passions of his predecessors, the breach between him and them was too abrupt. He stigmatized the great group of the Laocoon as one of the idols of the heathen, and made the Belvedere of the Vatican, the depository of the finest statues from antiquity, almost inaccessible. His efforts to stem the reformation were not destined to be more successful. Luther was, it is true, imprisoned on the Wartburg, but his writings were disseminated throughout Germany. Hadrian would have been glad to have reformed the Church, but how was such a work to be begun? The war against the Turks fared no better. The knights of St. John in Rhodes in vain implored help from Europe; only three papal ships went to their assistance. They had possessed the island since 1309; they left it for ever, four thousand strong, on January 1, 1523. It was impossible to compel the three great rivals Charles V., Henry VIII., and Francis I. to sink their differences, and make a truce. Francis refused to yield up his claims to Milan and Naples, and Charles would not desert the league formed for the humiliation of France. The troubles of Hadrian were still further increased at this time by a conspiracy which was formed against the government of Giulio de' Medici at Florence. It was supported by Cardinal Soderini, the leader of the French party in the Sacred College, and the king of France was privy to it. It was hoped that France would assist by attacking Florence and sending a fleet against Sicily. The Pope, therefore, seeing that Francis was beyond the reach of his advice was forced slowly and reluctantly to take the side of the Empire and England. On August 3, 1513, a league was signed between Charles, Henry, Milan, Florence, Genoa, Siena, Lucca, and the Pope, and was published two days later in the church of Santa Maria Maggiora. Lannoy, Viceroy of Naples, was named general of the league. It was directed against the enemies of Italy, but the Turks were forgotten, and its true objective was Francis I.

The chances of Francis I. in resisting his enemies were made far worse by the sudden revolt and desertion of Charles, Duke of Bourbon, Constable of France. He was one of the most powerful of the vassals of the crown, and had been allowed to preserve almost royal independence. He was descended in the seventh generation from Robert, Count of Clermont, brother of Philip le Hardi and son of Louis IX. who had married Beatrice of Burgundy, heiress of Dampierre-Bourbon. Charles, himself of the line of Montpensier, had acquired the Duchy of Bourbon through his wife Suzanna, heiress of the elder line. Constable Bourbon had ambitious views for his own advancement, and aimed at independent sovereignty. His

treachery became at last too open to be concealed and
he fled to take refuge with Charles. Francis, however,
did not interrupt his preparations and marched upon
Susa. Hadrian was heart-broken at the overthrow of his
cherished plans, the security of the peace of Europe, the
crusade against the Turks, and the Council for reforming
the church. He died on the very day that the French
army crossed the Ticino, September 4, 1523. He was
one of the most virtuous popes that ever occupied the
papal throne, but he strove in vain to stem the tide of
corruption. He was the last pope who was not an
Italian. He is buried in the German church at Rome
and on his monument are inscribed these words: " Proh
Dolor! quantum refert in quod tempora vel optimi cujus-
que in virtus incidat."

"Alas what a difference do the circumstances of their
time make to the merits of even the best man."

The conclave summoned to elect a new pope after the
death of Hadrian lasted fifty days. As before, it must be
regarded as a trial of strength between the three great
potentates of Europe, Henry VIII., Francis I. and Charles V.
Cardinal Wolsey, the nominee of the first of these monarchs,
had no chance, because the Romans were determined to
have an Italian pope. Cardinal Farnese was the French
candidate, while Giulio de' Medici was supported by the
Emperor. Giulio was at last chosen on November 18,
1523, it is said mainly by the influence of the Condottiere
leader, Prospero Colonna, who was in his turn influenced
by the Duke of Serre, the representative of Charles. The
new pope took the name of Clement VII, and reigned
till 1534, a date which transcends the limits of this
present work. The election was received with joy, and

the people looked forward to the prospect of a brilliant court. The bastard son of the murdered Giuliano was now forty-six years of age; he was of a serious and energetic character, and the greatest hopes were entertained of him. He recalled to his court the men of letters whom Pope Hadrian had exiled, and bade fair to renew the glories of the age of Leo.

Clement VII. had taken an active part in the formation of the league against France, but he felt that as pope he should display at least some appearance of impartiality. He could not declare himself as openly as he had done when Cardinal. The war continued in Lombardy, but fortune began to abandon the French. Milan was held by Prospero Colonna in the name of the Emperor, but was closely invested by the French, who occupied the territories of Legnano, Monza, Cassano, and Melegnano. The last mentioned place was held by the chevalier Bayard, the hero of French romance, the knight "without fear and without reproach." He captured Lodi, and went on to attack Cremona, but failed in the attempt and had to return to Monza. Colonna, now over eighty years of age, died on December 28, 1523, and was succeeded first by Lannoy, who was summoned hastily from Naples, and then by the Constable Bourbon, who was made lieutenant-governor of Lombardy. As a Frenchman taking service under a German Emperor he may be regarded as the last of the Condottieri. In the beginning of the next year the French again suffered defeats. Bayard was beaten at Robecco on January 25, 1525, the castle of Cremona was taken, the allies passed the Ticino on March 2 and Bonnivet, the French commander, retired to Novara. Defeats again followed on the Sesia, and

Bayard was taken prisoner at Ravisingo, after receiving a wound which caused his death in a short time. The French army existed no longer; a few scattered and demoralized bands of troops re-entered France, more or less protected from insult by the Swiss. Lodi, Pescara and Novara fell.

Pope Clement was by no means unfeignedly pleased at this result. He did not need the Emperor to obtain a permanent footing in Italy; therefore he opened up negotiations with France and tried to detach Venice from the league. Nicholas Schomberg, Archbishop of Capua, was despatched as legate to France, Italy and Germany to endeavour to conclude a truce. This, however, had no effect and on May 25 Henry VIII. and Charles V. renewed their ancient league, engaging themselves to invade France from different sides. Bourbon was base enough to invade his own country, and had been induced by the English ambassador, Richard Pace, who visited him at Moncalieri to take an oath of allegiance to the Emperor. As he marched along the shores of the Mediterranean town after town fell before him, and he at last undertook the siege of Marseilles. Francis, having to avenge the disgrace of his arms, collected a force of forty thousand men and marched in person at its head. He crossed the Alps and descending into the Lombard plain, found Milan in a defenceless state, the garrison having been withdrawn into the neighbouring towns. On October 26, 1524, the French entered the long contested capital in triumph and immediately began to lay siege to Pavia.

By this unexpected change of fortune Clement VII. found himself in the greatest difficulty. He naturally wished to preserve the integrity of the papal dominions and of Florence, and he may be credited with some desire to restore peace to Italy. When Charles had conquered he had negotiated with him and he now entered into overtures with France. Venice also began to seek the protection of France which some time before she had so basely deserted. It is difficult to forecast the ultimate object of negotiations which were never brought to a conclusion, but it is probable that Clement wished that Milan should remain in the hands of the Emperor, and that Francis should have possession of Naples. He therefore granted a passage through his dominions to John Stuart, Duke of Albany, who was sent by Francis into the South of Italy and excused himself to Lannoy, the Viceroy, on the ground that he was obliged to bow to circumstances. He afterwards made a league with the French king under the condition that Parma and Piacenza should pass to the Holy See, Florence should remain untouched, the Church should be supported, and that a war against the Turks should be begun. Charles V., when he heard of this, was beside himself with anger. He declared that he would come to Italy in person to revenge himself upon his enemies and that he would make Venice, Ferrara and the Pope pay dearly for their duplicity. It was no time now, he said, to speak of Luther. The French army was still engaged in the siege of Pavia, but the king idled away his time in the park of Mirabello, and left the whole conduct of military affairs to Bonnivet. Fortune at this time smiled upon the French at sea. Varagine Lago di Moncada, the admiral of the Imperial fleet, was conquered and taken prisoner by Andrea Doria. But this did not prevent a serious disaster on land. The duty of Francis was obviously to raise

the siege of Pavia and to meet the Imperial army before
it would receive reinforcements. This course of action
was pressed upon the king by La Pelise, La Tremouille,
and Thomas de Foix, but he continued to confide in
Bonnivet. Lodi was still in the possession of the Imperial
troops. They marched out of the town on January 25,
1525, passed over the fatal field of Marignano, and ap-
proached Pavia to attack the besieging army. For some
weeks the armies lay in the presence of each other, the time
being occupied by skirmishes which generally ended to
the disadvantage of the French. At length, on February
24, 1525, the decisive battle of Pavia was fought. It
was very hardly contested, as both sides knew that the
possession of Italy was at stake. The king thought that
he had won the day by the prowess of his splendid
cavalry, but the result was changed by the steadiness of
the Spanish arquebusiers. The bravest nobles on the
side of France had fallen, the King himself was wounded.
When Francis saw that the battle was lost he attempted
to fly, but he was conspicuous from the splendour of his
attire. His surcoat of silver, his white plume had been
noticeable in the thickest of the struggle. He was borne
down by force of numbers and compelled to surrender
himself prisoner. He refused to give up his sword to
the traitor Bourbon; he said, "I know no other Duke of
Bourbon but myself." He would only submit himself to
Lannoy, the appointed Viceroy of Charles V. He was
in a terrible condition, bleeding so as scarcely to be
recognized. His plume, his girdle, his order of St. Michael,
his silver coat of mail had been stripped off him by the
soldiers, as they said, for keepsakes. Bourbon and the
rest of the victorious generals could scarcely refrain from

tears. It was indeed a remarkable scene, only paralleled by that other tragedy of our own days when the Emperor of the French surrendered his sword to the future Emperor of Germany. The French army was entirely destroyed, out of 36,000 men 12,000 lay dead on the field. The chief among the French nobles were taken prisoner, Thomas de Foix, Montmorency, and the King of Navarre. From Pavia couriers hastened to Spain, Germany, England and Rome. Francis in sending the news to his mother, the Duchess of Angoulême, said, "All is lost except life and honour."

When Charles V heard in Madrid that the King of France was his prisoner, he grew pale. He was overcome by the greatness of his good fortune, he allowed no extravagant signs of rejoicing, but sought for help in prayer, and looked forward to a European crusade against the Turks. Clement VII. received the news with dismay. He could scarcely believe it. The Colonna and the Spanish party were triumphant. The Pope felt himself in much the same position as that in which Julius II. had been after the battle of Ravenna. The Imperialists were eager to march immediately upon Rome, but Lannoy thought it better policy to make terms with Clement and to force money out of him. Florence had to pay 100,000 florins, and a large sum was demanded from Venice. Charles had a dread that Francis might be taken to Naples, but the King persuaded Lannoy to conduct him to Genoa instead, as being better for his health. From this port he would be removed by sea to Spain, and it is possible that he expected to be rescued by the fleet of Andrea Doria. He landed at Palamos on June 17, and then proceeded to Barcelona. Charles gave orders that he should be confined in the castle of Madrid, where he arrived on August 17.

The battle of Pavia had brought Europe into a serious crisis. France lay exhausted; England threatened her with invasion; the Emperor conceived plans of attacking Lyons and Avignon. Germany was overthrown by the Reformation and by the rising of the peasants. The papacy was tottering to its fall. It was natural that Clement should favour the formation of a league against this preponderance of strength, his object being to unite the powers of Italy, Venice, Florence, and Milan under the protection of England. Relations between England and Charles had became strained because the King of England would not consent to the Emperor's occupying a portion of France. Wolsey had not forgiven Charles for cheating him, as he believed, out of the papacy. He listened to the proposals for forming "a lyge for the defence and liberties off Italye". The projected alliance was to include England, France, Italy, Scotland, Portugal, Hungary, Navarre, Lorraine, Guelders and Switzerland. At the same time a very obscure conspiracy was begun by Morone, the secretary of Francesco Sforza. Even after the publication of numerous documents the whole matter remains in the greatest uncertainty. It appears that Morone invited Pescara, the conqueror of Pavia, to commit a great act of treason, to betray Charles, restore the dukedom of Milan to the Sforzas and to receive the Kingdom of Naples as his reward. It is not certain how either Morone or Pescara were guilty in this arrangement, it is certain that they both betrayed each other to the Emperor. Pescara listened to the suggestions of Morone, but said that nothing could be done without the adhesion of Venice and the Pope. He then invited Morone to a conference and had him arrested. Pescara died shortly afterwards on December 3, and by his last testament ordered that Morone should be set at liberty, perhaps being afraid of the revelations which he might make. His successor, the Marchese del Vasto, did not dare to assume the responsibility of executing his wishes. Pescara at his death was only thirty-six years of age—he left behind him the highest reputation as a general. His widow, Vittoria Colonna, devoted her poetical powers to the celebration of his virtues.

Francis I. was still a prisoner in the castle of Madrid and it was difficult to determine on what terms he should be released. In any case it was probable that he would remain an enemy to Charles for life. The Duchess of Alençon, sister of Francis, came to Madrid in September 1525, partly to take care of her brother who had fallen ill, and partly to discuss terms of accommodation with the Emperor. The renunciation of all claims to possessions in Italy was easily agreed upon, but Charles demanded not only the complete restitution of the Duke of Bourbon to his estates, but also the concession of all his other claims, besides the annexation of the Duchy of Burgundy by the Emperor. This Francis could not assent to. There was also some talk of the marriage of the King, who was a widower, to Eleonora, sister of Charles V., who was herself the widow of the King of Portugal. The duchess returned to her brother having settled nothing. The negotiations were then taken up by Gabriel de Gramont, bishop of Tarbes. Francis offered to pay the enormous contribution of three million crowns, and to marry Eleonora, giving her the duchy of Burgundy as a dower. These terms were not accepted. Francis then abdicated in favour of the Dauphin, with the Duchess of Angoulême as regent. At last on December 19 the terms were concluded. Francis renounced his claims to Italy, Arragon, Catalonia, Roussillon, Flanders, Artois, and Burgundy, and agreed to marry Eleonora. The treaty of Madrid, as it was called, was solemnly sworn to by the King and the French plenipotentiaries on January 14, 1526, but the day before he had signed a protest declaring that he yielded to force, and that his arrest was to be regarded as null and void. Charles was advised not to release Francis before he had obtained possession of Burgundy, but he ratified the treaty on February 11 and ten days afterwards returned to France, leaving behind him as hostages two of his sons, the Dauphin aged eighteen and a half, and the Duke of Orleans who was under seven. The Duke of Angoulême, the youngest, remained with him. Macchiavelli said of this treaty, " I shall always say that if the King acts as a wise man the Emperor is mad.' Francis touched the soil of France again on March 9 and of course did not ratify the treaty. The states of Burgundy refused to detach themselves from France. Eleonora, sister of Charles V., had been promised in marriage to the Duke of Bourbon. When she became the wife of Francis I. Bourbon was invested with the Duchy of Milan by the Emperor, and Francesco Maria was deposed. The establishment of a Frenchman on an Italian throne caused great indignation in Italy. Francis, when he found himself safe in his own dominions, formed the league of Cognac on May 22, 1526. The contracting parties were France, Venice and the Pope, but, as a formality, leave was given both to Charles V. and Ferdinand his brother to join if they pleased. The object of the league was the liberation of the King's sons from Spain on payment

of an adequate sum of money, and the preservation of
the Duchy of Milan for Sforza. The King of France was
to retain the county of Asti in Italy, and his ancient
suzerainty over Genoa. There were two final articles, one
as to the conditions under which Charles V. should be
allowed to retain possession of Naples, and the other
intended to place Florence firmly under the principality
of the Medici. This was a second Holy League. The
Pope solemnly absolved Francis from his sins, and Henry
VIII. of England was named protector of the league, in
the hope that he would shortly join it. A pope once
more stood at the head of a league the object of which
was the enfranchisement of Italy. Charles was surprised
at this energetic resistance, and sent Jago di Moncada to
explain his views, and if possible to disarm his enemies.
He tried his powers of persuasion on the Pope, but Clement
was not willing to desert his allies. It was necessary for
the success of the league that the armies of the several
allies should act in strict combination. But each of the
members distrusted the other. Milan was attacked, but
with little success, and Sforza was compelled to surrender
himself to Bourbon. But a rising in Rome struck the
league in its most vital part. The old feeling of the
Ghibellines for the Empire was not extinct. The Colonna
was against the Pope and attacked Rome. Although
Clement VII. was a far better pope than Leo X. he was
much more unpopular. The Pope was forced to retire
with his Swiss guard into the castle of St. Angelo, and
the Vatican was left defenceless. The palace was plundered by the troops of the Colonna to the value of
300,000 ducats. The Pope could not maintain himself in
the fortress of St. Angelo, because it had been disarmed.

He was compelled to submit, received the tiara from the hands of Moncada, made a truce with Charles and promised to withdraw his troops from Lombardy. The conduct of the Pope was not calculated to stimulate the Emperor to a more active persecution of Luther. At the diet held at Speyer in 1526 it was determined that until a general national church assembly could be convened, each German province should practice that form of worship which the local government should sanction. While Germany was thus breaking away from the allegiance to the papacy, the Turks had become masters of Hungary. Soliman the Magnificent having gained the victory of Mohacz on August 29, 1526, in which King Louis II. lost his life.

Clement VII. probably never intended to keep the truce with Charles V., and scarcely needed the arguments of Henry and Francis to induce him to break it. On the other hand the Emperor determined upon vigorous measures. He despatched Lannoy to Naples whilst an army was collected in Germany under Georg Frundsberg, an ardent partisan of Luther; who had done much to secure the victory of Pavia. Frundsberg was prince of Mindelheim, the principality which after the battle of Blenheim was given by the Emperor to the Duke of Marlborough. The bulk of his army was composed of pious *Landsknechts*, at this time the most powerful infantry in Europe, stronger than either the French *hommes d'armes* or the Swiss. They formed a kind of organized military republic, the duties and obligations on either side being carefully drawn up and guaranteed. They were generally armed with a long lance which they carried over their shoulders and were clad in a striped dress of different colours, but their arms and uniforms were very much varied. They consisted of Swabians, Franconians, Bavarians, and Tyrolese, all of them young, strong and active. Frundsberg was determined to march on Rome, and it is said that he carried with him a golden cord with which he intended to hang the Pope. In November, 1526, he marched over the little-known passes lying between the lake of Garda and the lake of Idro until he descended into the territory of Brescia. At the same time Lannoy sailed to Naples, and began to invade the papal territory from the South. On December 21 he had marched as far as Frosinone. The *landsknechts* came on with irresistible force. They were at one time decoyed by the Marquis of Mantua into a trap and were very nearly destroyed. Encompassed by swamps and ditches they were attacked by the Duke of Urbino and Giovanni de' Medici, captain of the Bande Nere, or Black Bands, but they escaped by their marvellous steadiness. They were greatly assisted by Alfonzo, Duke of Ferrara, who after much hesitation now determined to join the Emperor. He sent Frundsberg money, provisions and cannon. On November 27 Giovanni de' Medici was wounded close to Governolo by a shot from an arquebus in the same leg in which he had been wounded two years before at Pavia. He was carried to Mantua where his leg was amputated, but he died on December 30 in the arms of Pietro Aretino, at the early age of twenty-eight. He was the great grandson of Lorenzo, younger brother of Cosimo "Pater Patriæ;" his mother was Caterina Sforza. Someone has called him a mixture of hero and fawn, but he was the last hope of Italy and of the Pope.

Frundsberg had reached Firenzuola, between Parma and Piacenza on December 14. Here he was joined on February 7 by the Constable Bourbon who came from Milan. Their army was now 30,000 strong, an immense force for those days. It comprised 16,000 *landsknechts*, 5,000 Spaniards, 2,000 Italians, 500 men-at-arms, and 1000 light cavalry. A fortnight afterwards they set out on their march, their destination being either Florence or Rome. Terror reigned in the Eternal City and the civic militia was called out after a disuse of many years. The invading army had now reached San Giovanni in the immediate neighbourhood of Bologna, when a mutiny broke out which nearly brought the expedition to an untimely end. The soldiers were in want of arms, money and provisions. The Spanish soldiers heard a rumour that a truce had been signed with the Pope, and clamoured for pay. The disorder spread to the *landsknechts*. Frundsberg tried to pacify them and told them that in a month all would be well, but they would not listen and levelled their spears at him. This broke his heart, he sank down on a drum and never spoke again. He was first carried to Ferrara and then to Augsburg where he died a year and a half afterwards. He was one of the greatest of German soldiers, and in different parts of his character resembled both Cromwell and Wallenstein. A few days after this Clement made a truce with Charles: the Emperor was to have Naples, Sforza was to be restored to Milan, and the Pope was to pay the army of Bourbon 60,000 ducats on the condition that it retired from Italy. These terms were ratified by Lannoy and were carried by Cesare Fieramosca to the army. But they refused to accept them and Fieramosca nearly lost his life. The Spaniards said that they had committed many sins and needed to be absolved at Rome. At the end of March the army resumed its march. Lannoy went to Florence to

see what arrangement he could effect. It was agreed
that 150,000 ducats should be paid to the army and that
it should retreat on receipt of the first instalment. The
money was supplied by melting down church and public
plate. Lannoy went to visit Bourbon in person, who was
encamped in the Casentino, but the Constable raised his
demands to 240,000 ducats. It is evident that he
always intended to plunder first Florence and then Rome.
Lannoy was so ashamed of having effected nothing that
he would not return to Florence, but retired to Siena.

Clement was now in great straits. When he felt certain that the march of Bourbon would be stopped, he had
dismissed the Bande Nere and left himself defenceless,
but when it became evident that the attack was inevitable he again joined the league of Cognac which he had
previously left. The Constable now advanced to Arezzo,
a position from which he could equally threaten Florence
and Rome. The Duke of Urbino barred the way to
Florence but left the road to Rome open. Bourbon now
suddenly declared to his troops the object of his march.
They marched by way of Siena, Montepulcaino and
Montefiascone, reached Viterbo on March 2, where they
were received by the Knights of St. John. They crossed
the Monte Cimnio, drove the papal troops out of Ronci-
gliano and encamped at Isola Farnese, the site of the
ancient Veii, three hours distant from Rome. From this
point the Constable sent a trumpeter to demand a free
passage into the Neapolitan territory, while some *landsknechts* attempted to cross the river in boats. The next
day, May 5, 1527, the Constable established his head-
quarters at the monastery of St. Onofrio, on the Janiculan,
the place in which were spent the last days of the poet

Tasso. His army of 40,000 men now surrounded the city in a half circle, the Germans on one side, the Spaniards and Italians on the other. A council of war was held which determined on an assault. The attack began in the grey dawn of May 6, the Germans advancing upon one side, the Spaniards and Italians on the other. They had no cannon and were forced to make their scaling ladders out of vine stakes. The walls of the city were covered by a thick mist. Bourbon in person, his coat embroidered with silver, urged on his warriors on horseback. Soon seeing them waver he leapt from his horse, seized a ladder, mounted it and beckoned with his hand. A ball struck him in the stomach. He cried out, "Ha! Notre Dame, je suis mort!" "Our Lady! I am dead," and fell. The Prince of Orange covered him with his cloak and he was carried into a neighbouring chapel, a dying man. Benvenuto Cellini, the famous sculptor, claims for himself the honour of having fired the fatal shot, but the fact rests upon no other evidence than his own.

The fall of their leader inspired the besieging army with a new courage and they stormed the walls in a resistless flood. The Pope fled from the Vatican along the wooden bridge into the Castle of St. Angelo, covered with a bishop's mantle, and about three thousand people took refuge in the same place. It was a misfortune for the Pope that the Constable was killed. Had he lived he would have spared the city and after exacting a large tribute marched on to Naples or Venice. As it was, the army could not be restrained. The last defence was made at the bridge of San Sisto. The victorious soldiers remained in the ranks during the day, but at midnight they broke up to plunder the city. The sack of Rome was permitted

for three days, but when Filibert of Châlons, Prince of
Orange, who had succeeded Bourbon in the command of
the army, attempted to put a stop to it he found that he
was unable to do so. It continued for twelve days longer,
and then only ceased because there was nothing more
to rob. It was at least as great a disaster as the burning of Rome by the Gauls, or its plunder by Alaric.
No persons nor property were spared. After the sack
came famine and after the famine pestilence, which lasted
not for days or weeks but for months. It was impossible
to pass through any street of Rome which was not
crowded with dead or dying. The miserable inhabitants in
vain hoped for assistance. The army of the league under
the Duke of Urbino advanced southwards by slow marches,
and reached Isola Farnese on May 22. After long
consultations they determined not to relieve the city, and
at the beginning of June marched back again to Viterbo
The conditions granted to the Pope were extremely hard.
He agreed to pay 100,000 ducats at once, 50,000 in
twenty days, and 250,000 in two months. As a pledge
of fulfilment, he gave up the castles of St. Angelo, Ostia,
Civitavecchia, Civita Castellano, Parma, Piacenza, and
Modena. He promised to absolve the Colonna, to remain
for the present a prisoner in the Castle of San Angelo,
and then to repair to Naples or Gæta to await the
decision of the Emperor. Five of the noblest Romans,
including two Cardinals, were delivered up as hostages
and with difficulty escaped with their lives. In order to
pay these enormous sums Clement was reduced to the
humiliation of asking Benvenuto Cellini to melt even his
tiara, and what was perhaps still more bitter, to borrow
300,000 ducats from the Duke of Ferrara.

CHAPTER XIV

THE FALL OF FLORENCE

WE must now return to Florence, which will remain the centre of our narrative until we have traced the first subjection of Italy to its close. The news of the sack of Rome reached Florence on May 12. The enemies of the Medici, who were called at this time the Libertini, thought that the time had come for them to throw off the yoke. Niccolò, the son of Piero Capponi, a man of high position in the state, respected by all the citizens for his integrity and moderation, and for the services rendered to the state by his great ancestor, placed himself at their head. One of the most prominent citizens of Florence at this time was Filippo Strozzi, a man of great wealth and great authority. He had married Clarice de' Medici, the sister of Lorenzo, Duke of Urbino, and was therefore regarded as being in a certain sense a member of that house. Passerini, Cardinal of Cortona, had been appointed governor of Florence in 1524 by Pope Clement VII. The most determined of the partisans of the Medici now urged him to act with vigour in repressing the popular movement, but he showed an entire want of courage and resolution. He hovered between the different plans

proposed to him, and he was at length induced to consent
to the summoning of a *pratica* or an informal assembly of
citizens to consider the condition of the state. The *pratica*
discussed the reopening of the Great Council, the creation
of a *Balia*, or committee of twenty citizens, for the reform
of the constitution, and the setting up of a Council of
a hundred and twenty persons. It was understood that
Ippolito and Alessandro de' Medici should leave the city,
Alessandro the mulatto, and Ippolito, the son of Giuliano,
Duke of Nemours, then a youth of eighteen. Filippo
Strozzi was sent to the young princes, to tell them that
they must go, and deliver up the fortresses. His manner
was stern and severe, and his orders were enforced by the
violence of his wife, who poured the vials of her scorn
upon Ippolito and Alessandro, whom she regarded as
unworthy scions of her illustrious house. The Cardinal
agreed to do everything that Strozzi desired, provided the
lives of the young men were safe. Passerini and the two
Medici left the city on May 17, accompanied by Strozzi
and others representing the *Balia*. He had orders to follow
them to Pisa in order to secure the surrender of the
fortress of that city as well as the citadel of Leghorn.
But a Pisa they contrived to elude the guard of Strozzi
and escaped to Lucca in safety without having surrendered
the fortresses. This cast a great slur on the reputation
of Filippo Strozzi. He became an object of suspicion to
the popular government. He left Florence to take refuge
at Lyons, he abandoned politics and made peace with
the Pope.

After the departure of the Medici Florence was in the
greatest confusion, being torn asunder by opposing
factions. These were the moderate *Ottimati*, the supporters

of a tempered aristocracy, the *Arrabiati*, who were strong democrats, and the *parta Pallesca* which consisted of the open and secret partisans of the Medici. For the moment the Ottimati triumphed. They saved the town from disorder and confusion and set to work to reconstruct the government. The arms and ensigns of the Pope were pulled down and the ancient *giglio*, or lily of popular liberty, set up in their place. The *otto di Balia* were put an end to, and the Balia dissolved itself. On May 21 a great Council of the citizens was summoned in the hall of the Palazzo Vecchio, which was attended by 2,500 persons. Not only the hall itself but also the staircases were crowded. No such sight had been seen since the days of Savonarola. A constitution was formed which seemed likely to preserve the liberties of the state. A council called the Ten of Liberty and Peace, "Dieci di libertà e pace" was created; and the Council of Eighty was reinstituted. It was determined that the Standard Bearer should remain in office thirteen months and should be elected by the Great Council. Niccolò Capponi was appointed to the office. A *quarantia* or judicial board of forty was established in imitation of the similar institution at Venice.

The news of the capture of Rome was received with rejoicing in Germany but with different feelings in England and France, who were afraid of the exaggerated power of Charles. With these sentiments Henry and Francis signed a treaty at Westminster with the object of setting the Pope free. A French army under Odet de Foix, Lord of Lautrec, Marshal of France, crossed the Alps at the end of July, and in August, 1527, a league was formed between France, England, Venice, Florence, and Sforza of Milan. We now see the beginning of the policy which afterwards

induced Henry to divorce Catherine of Arragon in order
to free himself completely from Spain.   Charles might have
made whatever terms he pleased with the Pope.   He was
tempted at one time to have destroyed the temporal
power for ever, but he shrank from so strong a step.   It
is possible that to have established a Spanish dynasty of
Italian kings, with Rome for their capital, might have
anticipated the work of many years.   But the time was
not ripe for it and it is probable that it could not have
come to pass in any other epoch but our own.   On December
8, 1527, the Pope escaped from confinement and fled to
Orvieto. While he thanked Charles for being allowed to exist
as a monarch, his eyes naturally turned towards Francis.
Florence was not altogether at peace.   Capponi had many
enemies, and the memory of recent woes, and the revival of
the Great Council, induced the remains of the Piagnoni to
recall the memory of Savonarola.   The monks of St. Mark
aimed at a religious revival. This would have added strength
to the turbulent faction of the Arrabiati.   But Capponi ruled
with moderation and kept both the contending parties in
check.   The Piagnoni, however, succeeded in proclaiming
Christ the King of Florence.   At the same time the city made
preparations for the coming war.   The "Bande Nere",
the Black Bands which had once obeyed Giovanni de' Medici, were now reorganized by Orazio Baglioni.   On January
28, 1528, the war of the league against the Emperor was
solemnly proclaimed.   Lautrec determined to avoid the
territory of Rome, and marched, as so many previous
invaders had done, through the great central valley of
Italy to Naples.   Baglioni, to the misfortune of Florence,
led his Black Bands through the Campagna of Rome
and joined Lautrec at Lucera.   The Imperial troops

advanced southwards to oppose him, carrying with them
the corpse of the Constable Bourbon in a leaden
coffin. Lautrec began the siege of Naples on May 1,
while Clement began to approach Rome, moving from
Orvieto to Viterbo, from which place he despatched Cardinal Campeggi as legate to England, a memorable event
in the history of our country. Italy was in a state of
the deepest misery : from one end of the peninsula to the
other it was a battle-field for Spaniards, Germans, French
and Italians. All the different powers were tearing Clement
asunder. Henry VIII. was suing for a divorce. If the
Pope refused it he drove the king into the arms of
Luther, if he granted it he offended the Emperor. The
Emperor's fleet was severely defeated by Filippino Doria
off Capo d'Orso in the neighbourhood of Sorrento ;
Moncada and Cesare Fieramosca were killed; but this
victory proved the ruin of the French. Reinforcements
were despatched to the contending armies on either side.
Francis Bourbon, Lord of St. Pol, led a large host in the
pay of France and England, while Archduke Ferdinand
sent to the army of the Emperor ten thousand infantry
and six hundred horse under the command of Henry of
Brunswick. These armies engaged each other in the north
of Italy, but worse than all Andrea Doria, the great Genoese
admiral, following the instincts of a Condottiere, abandoned
the cause of the French, and sent orders to his nephew
Filippino to desist from the siege of Naples. The army
of Lautrec was destroyed by pestilence, of 25,000 infantry
there only remained 4,000; of 800 men-at-arms only 100
survived. Lautrec himself fell ill and died on August 16.
Bagliano had died of a wound at Capua the month before,
and was succeeded in the command of the Black Bands

by Ugo Pepoli. The Germans said that the French had never had good fortune in Naples, and that the blood of Conradine still cried aloud for vengeance.

In October Genoa threw off the French yoke, and elected as Doge Uberto Cattaneo. This change of fortune in favour of the Emperor induced the Pope to make peace with him, and on October 6, 1528, he was able to return to his desolated capital. It resembled the return of Honorius after the destruction of Rome by Alaric. Out of the 85,000 inhabitants which were numbered under Leo X. only 32,000 now remained. The Pope now began to contrive vengeance against his persecutors. He was specially enraged against Florence, which was still under the wise and moderate rule of Capponi. The arms of the Medici had been pulled down and trampled in the dust. His nephews had been insulted, and the charge of bastardy which had been brought against them was equally valid against himself. Clement knew that the most acceptable bait which could be offered to the Emperor was the reduction of Florence. Capponi entered into negotiations with Clement. But the party of the Ottimati was weak and that of the Arrabiati impetuous. The correspondence was discovered and Capponi was arrested and brought to trial. His acquittal was complete, even his enemies acknowledged the integrity of his mind, and the purity of his intentions. But he felt bound to retire from Florence and sought rest in a quiet villa where he could meditate on the approaching ruin of his country. The people thronged round him as he left the city, full of sympathy and reverence for his character. Francesco Carducci, a representative of the democrative party, was elected Gonfaloniere in his place.

On June 12, 1529, De' Leyva, the general of the Emperor in Milan, defeated the French under St. Pol in the battle of Landriano. The result of this was to make Charles V. master of Lombardy and peace became possible. The treaty of Barcelona signed on June 29, 1529, between the Emperor and the Pope provided that Ravenna and Cervia should be taken from the Venetians; Modena, Reggio, and Rubiera from the Duke of Ferrara and held by the Pope as Imperial fiefs; the Medici were to be restored to Florence, Alessandro de' Medici was to marry Margaret, the Emperor's natural daughter, Charles was to suppress the Reformation and come to be crowned at Rome. The Pope was to be restored to his estates, and Sforza to Milan if he should be proved to be innocent. Charles was to be invested with the kingdom of Naples. This was followed by the peace of Cambray between Charles and Francis, published on August 5 in the cathedral of that city. By this Francis gave up all his rights over Italy, and left Venice, Florence and Ferrara to the vengeance of the Emperor.

Filibert, Prince of Orange, the last of the house of Châlon, the principality after his death passing into the house of Nassau, was marked out as the destroyer of Florence. He collected forces and money in Rome, where the soldiers were eager for the plunder of Florence as they had already plundered Rome. The Emperor Charles V. landed at Genoa on August 12, preceded by two thousand Spanish infantry. He was now at the height of his power and appeared to the subject world as a second Charles the Great. Florence sent ambassadors to him, four in number after the manner of the republic: Niccolò Capponi, Tommaso Soderini, Matteo Strozzi,

16

and Raffaele Girolami. They obtained an audience by
the intervention of Andrea Doria. They begged the
Emperor to preserve the liberty of their city and not to
surrender them to the Medici, but he received them
coolly and sent them away unconsoled. Strozzi went to
Venice, Soderini to Lucca, Capponi died on the way
home, but he had time to send a last message to his fellow-
citizens warning them of the uselessness of resistance.
His advice was unheeded; desperate attempts were made
to raise money, sacrilegious hands were laid upon the
property of the church and the endowments of the guilds.
Meanwhile the Prince of Orange continued to advance.
Malatesta Baglioni came to terms with the Pope, and
delivered Perugia into his hands. The Florentines determined to make a last effort for peace by sending an
embassy to the Pope. They chose for the purpose Francesco Vettori, Andreolo Niccolini, Jacopo Guicciardini,
and Pierfrancesco Portinari. They did not know what
instructions to give them and decided to allow them a
free hand. The Pope made answer to them that when
he returned to his own home he would show to the
world that he did not desire to be tyrant of his country
but only to secure its welfare. Arezzo revolted from Florence at the approach of Filibert, and declared itself a
free republic. This blow only stimulated the citizens to
greater efforts. They employed the great sculptor Michelangelo Buonarotti to repair their fortifications, especially
on the height of San Miniato. The delicious villas and
gardens which generations of cultured merchants had made
for their delectation were destroyed, the women themselves aiding in the work. Michelangelo visited Capponi in
his last moment and heard from his lips the dying cry,

"To what a pass have we led our miserable country!" In the first days of October, 1529, the heads of the invading columns appeared in the Valdarno, wasting as they went. The army of the Prince of Orange numbered between thirty and forty thousand. The Florentines again sent an embassy, but Filibert demanded the restoration of the Medici, and the nomination of half of the Great Council by the Pope. They replied that they would rather see Florence in ashes than under the Medici. The prince advanced and began to bombard the new fortifications of Michelangelo on San Miniato from the height of Arcetri.

At this time the Pope was at Bologna awaiting the arrival of the Emperor. One gleam of hope for the doomed city now illumined the scene. The Emperor heard at Piacenza that John Zapolya had received the crown of Hungary from the hands of the Sultan, and that Soliman was marching on Vienna with 250,000 Turks. For a moment Clement moderated his terms and asked only for the adhesion of Florence to the league of Cambray and that the Pope should be allowed to nominate ten members of the Council of Eighty. These hopes, however, were soon dispelled by the repulse of the Ottoman army. The Emperor arrived at Bologna on November 15. Charles knelt before Clement as Barbarossa had knelt at Venice before Alexander III. He kissed the Pope's hand and foot and did him homage. Nearly all the Italian princes were collected together at Bologna as if to a congress. Venice made her submission; Sforza received Milan as an Imperial fief. The end of the conference was that on December 23 a so-called everlasting league was signed between the Pope, the Emperor the King of Hungary, Venice, Milan, Mantua, Savoy, and

Montferrat. When peace was restored the arms of an united Europe were to be turned against the Turks, the Reformation was to be suppressed, and the church reformed by a council. The peace which sealed the political death of Italy was solemnly proclaimed on New Year's day, 1530, in the church of St. Petronius. On February 24, the lucky day of Charles, the day of his birth and of the battle of Pavia, Charles V. was crowned by the Pope after the custom of the ancient rite. Two days earlier he had been crowned King of Italy, not with the iron crown of Monza, which was too small for him, but with the crown of the King of the Romans. Even after the humiliation of the papacy the Emperor did not disdain to hold the Pope's stirrup. Very few Germans were present, but the pomp which accompanied the solemn cavalcade through the streets of Bologna had never been surpassed, Alessandro de' Medici bore the standard of the church, Trissino held up the papal train, Charles III. of Savoy carried the Emperor's cap, who wore the crown on his head, Bonifacio of Montferrat held the golden sceptre, and Philip of Bavaria the golden ball. About a month later Charles returned to Germany, and in June at Augsburg received the famous confession which bears the name of that city, the manifesto of the Protestant faith. A week later the Pope returned to Rome.

Clement now turned all his energies to the reduction of Florence. The city fought boldly against tremendous odds, the last bulwark of Italian liberty. She had lost many of her greatest men, among them Capponi. But a new captain arose for her needs, strict even to severity, stern even to inhumanity, courageous even to imprudence, stubborn even to obstinacy. This was Francesco Ferrucci, the scion of an ancient family who had been brought up as a merchant. He had learnt the career of arms under the French in Italy and had been made prisoner by the Imperialists. His first exploit was the recovery of San Miniato al Tedesco from the Spaniards. Still the cause which Ferrucci supported was desperate. Prato and Pistoria were abandoned in order to save Empoli, Pisa, and Leghorn. On January 26, 1530, Malatesta Baglioni was made captain-general and the bâton of command was solemnly presented to him in the great square of the Signory. No one believed that he could prove a traitor. Ferrucci wrote from Empoli to congratulate the Ten on his appointment. It was only in the time of their need that the Florentines found out that he had the common vice of all Condottieri and of all those who fight for money and for their own advantage. Two days after the appointment of Bagliano an ambassador came from France to counsel submission. Abandoned by all the world they determined to put their trust in God, and Benedetto di Forano, after preaching in the great hall of the public palace, gave to the Gonfaloniere a standard on which was painted the figure of Christ their King. Ferrucci now signalized himself by a brilliant feat of arms. Volterra revolted and gave herself to the Pope, but Ferrucci marching from Empoli, recovered the city, conquering it street by street and house by house. Unfortunately in the absence of Ferrucci the more important town of Empoli was seized and paved the way for the capture of Florence.

The Prince of Orange had promised to reduce the town in two months, but the siege lingered and the Pope was at the end of his resources. He created new Cardinals to obtain money. However, pestilence and famine took possession of the beleaguered city, meat became very scarce, and horses, cats, and even mice were used for food. A sortie was made on May 5, thirty companies of citizens fought for four hours, but could not break the lines of the besieging forces. After this the troops were counted, and they found that they had under arms 3,000 young men between eighteen and forty years of age and 2,000 between forty and fifty. The rest of the army was composed of mercenary troops under the command of Malatesta. The council of Eighty determined to continue the struggle as long as they had a crust of bread. On the night of June 20 to 21 the Florentines made a second sortie. Stefano Colonna led the attack upon the German camp while Malatesta prevented the Prince of Orange from marching to the rescue. The attempt failed and Malatesta was suspected of treachery. The end was now at hand. Orders were sent to Ferrucci who was then at Volterra to go to Pisa, and from his place to attack the besieging army, while at the same time Malatesta and the Florentines would make a final sortie from the city. He reached Pisa on July 21, passing by way of Leghorn. He got together with great difficulty three thousand infantry and six hundred cavalry, with ten large muskets, and twenty cannon. When ordered to make his departure he exclaimed, "We are going to death." It is said that he conceived the bold idea of marching to Rome and forcing the Prince of Orange to raise the siege and follow him, but the Ten of Liberty adhered to their plan and he obeyed. Marching through Lucca he met Orange on August 12 at Gavinone in the territory of Pistoria. The two armies entered the village at the same moment. The struggle was long and fierce. The Imperialists began to give way, the Prince of Orange was killed, Ferrucci's soldiers raised shouts of victory, but the rearguard composed of Germans stayed the flight and changed the fortune of the battle. Ferrucci was taken prisoner and led before Maramaldo, who had succeeded Orange in the command. Maramaldo struck the hero with his hand and the soldiers despatched him. The promised sortie from Florence never took place, it is said by the treachery of Malatesta. The Florentines could number 8,000 infantry, 6,270 mercenaries and twenty pieces of artillery. The Signory and the magistrates determined on the enterprise, and with this view they received the communion in the Church of Our Lady of the Flower. But at the last moment Malatesta and Colonna refused to march.

When the news of Ferrucci's death arrived, there was nothing left but to submit. Malatesta had been already in treaty with the enemy, perhaps with the idea of preventing needless bloodshed, but also with the hope of getting back Perugia from the Pope. He was now master of the town, and the citizens laid down their arms. Four ambassadors, Lorenzo Strozzi, Pierfrancesco Portinari, Bardo Altoviti and Jacopo Morelli concluded terms with Ferrante Gonzaga on August 12. Florence was to pay 80,000 ducats and the whole dominion of Florence without exception was to be subject to such a form of government as the Emperor might ordain within four months, liberty of the city being preserved. Florence had lost in the siege 8,000 citizens and 14,000 foreign soldiers. She was utterly impoverished by her efforts; she had spent 1,200,000 ducats during the eleven months of the siege. On August 20 a balia of twelve citizens was elected to reorganize the constitution and the exiles returned to the town. Alessandro de' Medici became Duke of Florence on July 6, 1530 and reigned till January 6, 1531, when he was murdered by his cousin Lorenzino. Thus Florence fell three years after the sack of Rome. Our history ends with her as it began with her. During the two hundred and eighty years we have traversed she never played an unworthy part. She was always the home of culture and the asserter of liberty. If Rome has a superior claim to sovereignty as the widowed mistress of the world, the love and reverence of every Italian must turn with pious yearning towards the towers of Florence.

THE END

APPENDIX

Popes.

1409 A.D.—1530 A.D.

Alexander V (Filargi) June 26, 1409—May 3, 1410.

John XXII (Cossa) May 17, 1410—May 29, 1415.

Martin V (Colonna) November 11, 1415—February 21, 1421.

Clement VIII (Mugnos) 1424—July 26, 1429.

Eugenius IV (Condolmieri) March 3, 1431—February 23, 1447.

Felix V (Amadeus VIII, Duke of Savoy) November 5, 1439—April 7, 1449.

Nicholas V (of Sarzana) March 6, 1447—March 24, 1455.

Calixtus III (Borgia) April 8, 1455—August 8, 1458.

Pius II (Piccolomini) August 19, 1458—August 15, 1464.

Paul II (Barbi) August 30, 1464—July 28, 1471.

Sixtus IV (della Rovere) August 9, 1471—August 12, 1484.

Innocent VIII (Cibo) August 29, 1448—July 25, 1492.

Alexander VI (Lenzuoli-Borgia) August 11, 1492—August 18, 1503.

Pius III (Todeschini-Piccolomini) September 22, 1503—October 18, 1503.

Julius II (della Rovere) November 1, 1503—February 21, 1513.

Leo X (Medici) March 11, 1513—December 1, 1521.

Hadrian VI (Boyens) January 9, 1522—September 24, 1523.

Clement VII (Medici) November 19, 1523—September 25, 1534.

Doges of Venice.

1409—1530.

Michele Steno, 1400—1413.
Tommaso Mocenigo, 1414—1423.
Francesco Foscari, 1423—1457.
Pascale Malipiero, 1457—1462.
Cristoforo Moro, 1462—1471.
Niccolò Trono, 1471—1473.
Niccolò Marcello, 1473—1474.
Pietro Mocenigo, 1474—1476.
Andrea Vendramini, 1476—1478.
Giovanni Mocenigo, 1478—1485.
Marco Barbadigo, 1485—1486.
Agostino Barbadigo, 1486—1501.
Leonardo Loredano, 1501—1521.
Antonio Grimani, 1521—1523.
Andrea Gritti, 1523—1539.

Doges and Lords of Genoa.

1409—1530.

Genoa under French domination, October 25, 1396—September 4, 1409.

Under Theodore II., Marquis of Montferrat, September 6, 1409—March 20, 1413.

Giorgio Adorno, 1413—1415.

Barnabà di Goano, 1415.

Tommaso Campo-Fregoso, 1415—1421.

Under the Duke of Milan, 1421—1436.

Isnardo Guano seven days in 1436.

Tommaso Fregoso, 1436—1443.

Raffaele Adorno, 1443—1447.

Barnabà Adorno, 1447.

Giovanni Fregoso, 1447—1448.

Ludovico Fregoso, 1448—1450.

Pietro Campo-Fregoso, 1450—1458.

Under French domination, May 11, 1458—1460.

Prospero Adorno, March 12, 1460—July 8, 1460.

Spinetta Fregoso, July 8, 1460—July 14, 1460.

Ludovico Fregoso, 1460—1463.

Archbishop Paolo Campo-Fregoso, 1463—1464.

Under Duke of Milan, 1464—1476.

Giovanni Battista Fregoso, 1483—1487.

Dukes of Milan, Lords of Genoa, October 30, 1487—1499.

King of France, Lord of Genoa, 1499—1512.

Giovanni Fregoso, 1512—1513.

Ottaviano Fregoso, 1513—1515.

Francis I. of France, Lord of Genoa, 1515—1522.

Antonietto Adorno, 1522—1527.

Doges for two years established by Andrea Doria December 12, 1528.

Kings of Germany and Emperors 1409–1530.

Sigismund of Luxemburg
King of Bohemia, 1419—1437.
King of Hungary, 1387
King of Germany, 1419
Emperor May 13, 1433— December 9, 1437.

Elizabeth = Albert II of Hapsburg-Austria
King of Germany, March 11, 1438—October 29, 1439.

Albert II (of Hapsburg-Austria, grandson of Rudolph of Hapsburg called "the Lame" and "the Wise").

Rudolph "the Founder"

Frederick III

Albert III

Albert "the Wonder of the World"

Albert II (see above)
Duke of Austria
1404—1439
King of Hungary
1437
King of Bohemia
1438
King of Germany
1438
Married 1422 Elizabeth of Bohemia and Hungary

Ladislaus (posthumous)
Duke of Austria,
1440—1457
King of Bohemia,
1440
King of Hungary,
1453

Leopold III "the Pious"

William

Leopold "the Fool"

Ernest "the Iron"

Frederick III
Duke of Styria,
1424—1493
King of Germany,
1440
Emperor 1452

Maximilian I
Joint King of
Germany, 1486
King of Germany,
1493
Emperor (elect)
1508
Married Mary of
Burgundy

Philip the Fair
d. 1506.

Charles V
King of Germany,
1519—1536

Frederick I
King of Germany,
1531
Emperor
1556—1564

Kings of Arragon and Castile

Peter IV "the Ceremonious" 1336—1387.

Martin 1395—1410
King of Sicily 1409

Martin Count of
Montalbano
King of Sicily 1387—1409
Married Maria Queen
of Sicily

(illegitimate)
Frederick of Tarsia
Count of Lucca

Eleonora
Married John I
King of Castile

Henry III
King of Castile
1390—1406

John II
King of Castile
1406—1454

Henry IV 1454—1474

Alfonzo

Isabella 1474—1504
Married Ferdinand the
Catholic

John I, 1387—1395
Married Yolanthe
Duchess of Bar

Iolanthe
Married Louis II of
Anjou
Count of Provence
d. 1417

René of Anjou
King of Naples
Duke of Bar
Counter-King
of Aragon
1467—1470

Ferdinand the Great
1412—1416
King of Sicily 1412

John II 1458—1479
King of Arragon and
Sicily

Frederick III
"the Catholic"

Frederick
King of Naples
1496—1501

Ferrante III
Prince of Taranto

Alfonzo V 1416—1458
King of Naples 1442

(illegitimate)
Ferrante of Naples
1458—1494

Alfonzo II = Ippolita
Sforza
King of Naples
1494—1495

Ferrante II
King of Naples
1495—1496

Kings of Spain.

Ferdinand "the Catholic" King of Arragon, Sardinia and Sicily 1479, of Granada 1492, of Naples 1504, of Navarre 1512.

Regent of Castile 1507—Rex Catholicus 1495.

Married (1) September 25, 1469   Isabella Queen of Castile 1464—
                                               November 16, 1504.

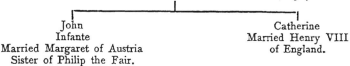

John	Catherine
Infante	Married Henry VIII
Married Margaret of Austria	of England.
Sister of Philip the Fair.	

(2) Germaine de Foix (Sister of Gaston de Foix).

Juana (la Loca, "the mad") Heiress and titular Queen with her husband 1504—1506; with her son 1516—1520

died April 13, 1555.

Married Philip I "the Fair" of Austria, King of Castile 1504—September 25, 1506.

Charles (Duke of Spain and of Germany) King of Spain, Naples, Sicily and Sardinia with his mother 1516—1520; alone 1520—January 16, 1556 (abdicated)

died September 21, 1558.

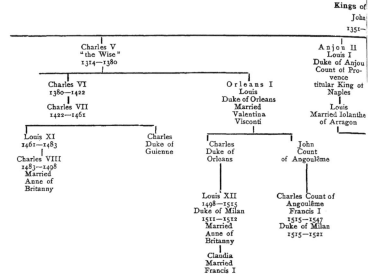

Kings of
John
1351—

Charles V
"the Wise"
1314—1380

Charles VI
1380—1422

Charles VII
1422—1461

Orleans I
Louis
Duke of Orleans
Married
Valentina
Visconti

Anjou II
Louis I
Duke of Anjou
Count of Pro-
vence
titular King of
Naples

Louis
Married Iolanthe
of Arragon

Louis XI
1461—1483

Charles VIII
1483—1498
Married
Anne of
Britanny

Charles
Duke of
Guienne

Charles
Duke of
Orleans

John
Count
of Angoulême

Louis XII
1498—1515
Duke of Milan
1511—1512
Married
Anne of
Britanny

Claudia
Married
Francis I

Charles Count of
Angoulême
Francis I
1515—1547
Duke of Milan
1515—1521

France

II

1364

John Duke of
Beira

Burgundy II
Philip "the Bold"

Maria
Married
Duke of Bar

Isabella
Married
Gian Galeazzo
Duke of Milan

Jean *Sans Peur*

Philip "the Good"

Charles
"the Bold"

Maria
Married Emperor
Maximilian

Louis III

René "the Good"
Duke of Bar
Duke of Lorraine
King of Naples
1435—1442
King of Arragon
1467—1470
Married
Isabella of
Lorraine

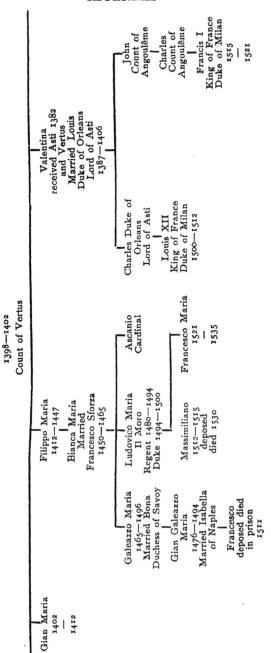

Dukes of Milan

Gian Galeazzo III Isabella of France
1398—1402
Count of Vertus

Gian Maria
1402
—
1412

Filippo Maria
1412—1447

Bianca Maria
Married
Francesco Sforza
1450—1465

Galeazzo Maria
1465—1496
Married Bona
Duchess of Savoy

Gian Galeazzo
Maria
1476—1494
Married Isabella
of Naples

Francesco
deposed died
in prison
1511

Ludovico Maria
Il Moro
Regent 1480—1494
Duke 1494—1500

Massimiliano
1512—1515
deposed
died 1530

Ascanio
Cardinal

Francesco Maria
1521
—
1535

Valentina
received Asti 1382
and Vertus
Married Louis
Duke of Orleans
Lord of Asti
1387—1406

Charles Duke of
Orleans
Lord of Asti

Louis XII
King of France
Duke of Milan
1500—1512

John
Count of
Angoulême

Charles
Count of
Angoulême

Francis I
King of France
Duke of Milan
1515
—
1521

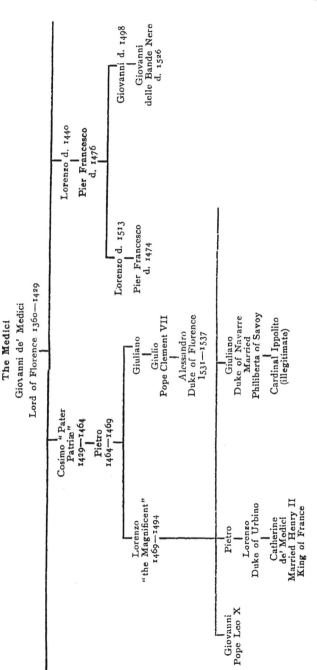

The Medici
Giovanni de' Medici
Lord of Florence 1360—1429

The family of della Rovere.

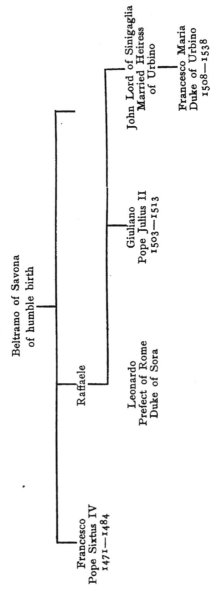

Beltramo of Savona
of humble birth

Raffaele

Francesco
Pope Sixtus IV
1471—1484

Leonardo
Prefect of Rome
Duke of Sora

Giuliano
Pope Julius II
1503—1513

John Lord of Sinigaglia
Married Heiress
of Urbino

Francesco Maria
Duke of Urbino
1508—1538

The Dukes of Savoy.

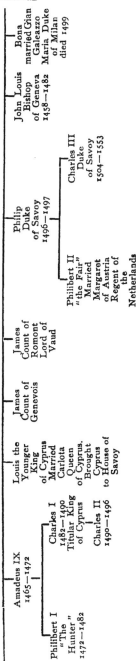

Amadeus VIII Count (1st Duke)
resigned
1391—1434
Bought Genevois 1401 Duke 1417
Inherited Piedmont 1418
Pope Felix V 1439—1449
resigned 1451

Louis the elder
1434—1465
Married Anne Princess of Cyprus

John Louis
Bishop
of Geneva
1458—1482

Bona
married Gian
Galeazzo
Maria Duke
of Milan
died 1499

Amadeus IX
1465—1472

James
Count of
Genevois

James
Count of
Romont
Lord of
Vaud

Philip
Duke
of Savoy
1496—1497

Philibert I
"The
Hunter"
1472—1482

Charles I
1482—1490
Titular King
of Cyprus

Charles II
1490—1496

Louis the
Younger
King
of Cyprus
Married
Carlota
Queen
of Cyprus.
Brought
Cyprus
to House of
Savoy

Philibert II
"the Fair"
Married
Margaret
of Austria
Regent of
the
Netherlands

Charles III
Duke
of Savoy
1504—1553

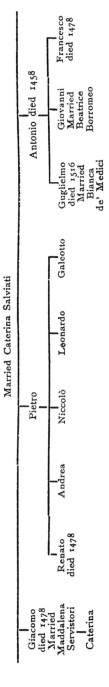

The Pazzi Family.

Andrea

born 1372—died 1445

Married Caterina Salviati

Giacomo
died 1478
Married
Maddalena
Servistori

Caterina

Renato
died 1478

Andrea

Pietro

Niccolò

Leonardo

Galeotto

Guglielmo
died 1516
Married
Bianca
de' Medici

Antonio died 1458

Giovanni
Married
Beatrice
Borromeo

Francesco
died 1478

The Family of Orsini.

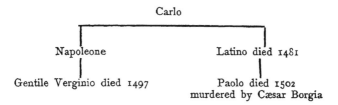

Carlo

Napoleone

Gentile Verginio died 1497

Latino died 1481

Paolo died 1502
murdered by Cæsar Borgia

The Family of Colonna.

Lorenzo Onofrio

Lorenzo — Antonio — Prospero Cardinal

Girolamo — Pompeo
rst soldier and then Cardinal

Giovanni
Cardinal May 5, 1480
died 1508

Prospero
died 1523

INDEX

INDEX

PRINTED IN HOLLAND.

1909905

Made in the USA